From Potsdam to the Cold War

AMERICA IN THE MODERN WORLD
STUDIES IN INTERNATIONAL HISTORY

Warren F. Kimball
Series Editor
Professor of History, Rutgers University

Volumes Published

Lawrence Spinelli, *Dry Diplomacy: The United States, Great Britain, and Prohibition* (1989). ISBN 0-8420-2298-8

Richard V. Salisbury, *Anti-Imperialism and International Competition in Central America, 1920–1929* (1989). ISBN 0-8420-2304-6

Gerald K. Haines, *The Americanization of Brazil: A Study of U.S. Cold War Diplomacy in the Third World, 1945–1954* (1989). ISBN 0-8420-2339-9

Harry Harding and Yuan Ming, eds., *Sino-American Relations, 1945–1955: A Joint Reassessment of a Critical Decade* (1989). ISBN 0-8420-2333-X

Lawrence S. Kaplan, Denise Artaud, and Mark R. Rubin, eds., *Dien Bien Phu and the Crisis of Franco-American Relations, 1954–1955* (1990). ISBN 0-8420-2341-0

Michael L. Krenn, *U.S. Policy toward Economic Nationalism in Latin America, 1917–1929* (1990). ISBN 0-8420-2346-1

Akira Iriye and Warren Cohen, eds., *American, Chinese, and Japanese Perspectives on Wartime Asia, 1931–1949* (1990). ISBN 0-8420-2347-X

Edward M. Bennett, *Franklin D. Roosevelt and the Search for Victory: American-Soviet Relations, 1939–1945* (1990). Cloth ISBN 0-8420-2364-X Paper 0-8420-2365-8

James L. Gormly, *From Potsdam to the Cold War: Big Three Diplomacy, 1945–1947* (1990). Cloth ISBN 0-8420-2334-8 Paper 0-8420-2335-6

From Potsdam to the

COLD WAR

Big Three Diplomacy
1945–1947

James L. Gormly

A Scholarly Resources Inc. Imprint
Wilmington, Delaware

The paper used in this publication meets the minimum requirements of the American National Standard for permanence of paper for printed library materials, Z39.48, 1984.

Portions of this volume were originally published as *De Yalta à Potsdam* by Arthur L. Funk. Copyright 1982 by Editions COMPLEXE, Brussels.

Scholarly Resources Inc.
104 Greenhill Avenue
Wilmington, Delaware 19805-1897

Library of Congress Cataloging-in-Publication Data

Gormly, James L., 1946–
    From Potsdam to the Cold War : Big Three
diplomacy, 1945–1947 / James L. Gormly.
        p. cm. — (America in the modern world)
    Includes bibliographical references (p.) and index.
    ISBN 0–8420–2334–8 (cloth). — ISBN 0–8420–2335–6 (pbk.)
    1. World politics—1945– 2. Potsdam Conference (1945)
3. Cold War. I. Title. II. Series: America in the modern
world (unnumbered)
    D445.G57 1990
    940.53'14—dc20
                                                        90–8662
                                                        CIP

About the Author

JAMES L. GORMLY was educated at the University of Arizona and the University of Connecticut, from which he received a Ph.D. in history. The author of numerous articles on U.S. foreign relations, in 1987 he completed *The Collapse of the Grand Alliance, 1945–1948*. He is currently a professor of history at Washington and Jefferson College in Washington, Pennsylvania.

Contents

Acknowledgments

This work would not have been possible without the suggestion and efforts of Dr. Arthur L. Funk, professor emeritus at the University of Florida. After Russell D. Buhite brought out *Decisions at Yalta* in 1986, it seemed logical to Dr. Funk that a volume dealing with the final summit conference of World War II, the Potsdam Conference, would be useful. The nucleus for such a study already existed in his own *De Yalta à Potsdam* (Brussels, 1982). After conferring with Richard Hopper of Scholarly Resources, it was agreed that an English version of Dr. Funk's chapters on the background of Potsdam and the conference itself could serve as a starting point for a more extended study of the meeting and its consequences.

Unfortunately, due to previous commitments, Dr. Funk was unable to take an active role in researching and writing the chapters that were to follow the section on the summit and deal with the meetings of the foreign ministers and the Paris Peace Conference. It was at this point that I was asked if I would be willing to complete the project, using my colleague's text as a point of departure and developing new materials to cover the final settlement of the Second World War, the postwar quest for stability. I am most grateful to him and Richard Hopper for the invitation. While Professor Funk and I have consulted regularly and while I have woven his material into the overall text and have greatly benefited from his suggestions and observations, I must take full responsibility for the form, content, interpretations, and conclusions of this work.

In writing the chapters on the London, Moscow, Paris, and New York meetings of the Big Three foreign ministers and the drafting of the peace treaties, I have had the support of several individuals and institutions and would like to announce my unending thanks. The editorial staff of Scholarly Resources, especially Richard Hopper and the project editor, John Paschetto, have provided aid and support along the way, from correcting my errors to accepting my reasons for missing deadlines. I would also like to thank the University of Texas—Pan American and Washington and Jefferson College for supporting my work on this volume. But I particularly would like to thank my most serious and demanding critic, commentator, and proofreader, my wife, Sharon.

Introduction

In the last months of 1989, major political changes swept across Eastern Europe. President George Bush referred to blowing breezes of democracy as the Communist regimes of Poland, Czechoslovakia, Hungary, East Germany, Bulgaria, and Romania showed signs of relinquishing political power to emerging new parties and leaders. The Iron Curtain that separated Western democratic states from Eastern Communist ones was being drawn back. The Berlin Wall, a stark symbol of the Cold War and of the divisions between the East and the West, was opened and even partially dismantled. Unlike the past, when Russian troops intervened to stop such events, the government under President Mikhail Gorbachev announced not only that the soldiers would stay in their barracks but also that Moscow supported the changes. Within the Soviet Union, President Gorbachev, *Time*'s "Man of the Decade," continued his own sweeping reforms: *perestroika* and *glasnost*.[1]

As December began the East German Communist regime collapsed, a new Czechoslovak government announced its openness to "radical changes," and Presidents Bush and Gorbachev met at Malta. Following the weekend summit (December 2–4, 1989), Gorbachev pronounced an end to the Cold War. Bush was less dramatic, but he was optimistic that the two superpowers could work toward establishing "a lasting peace and transform the East-West relationship into one of enduring cooperation." A *New York Times* public opinion poll taken that month found that only 13 percent of those asked still held unfavorable attitudes toward the Soviet Union. Americans, the *Times* pointed out, had not felt as friendly toward the Russians since 1945. With the rejection of communism throughout most of Eastern Europe, improving Soviet-American relations, and Gorbachev's reforms, to many it was obvious that the "cold war international system," which had maintained peace and stability by balancing two armed blocs, was losing its relevancy. The world seemed to be entering a new era, the nature of which was still unclear.[2]

As world leaders begin to contemplate the structure of a new "post-postwar" order, the needs of the participants have been reversed. When the Cold War system was constructed over forty years ago, it was most urgently needed by the United States and Great Britain. In 1944 and 1945, it appeared that the popularity and power of communism were growing rapidly and benefiting from the lack of an international arrangement that could impose limits on the ideology's expansion. In 1946 and 1947, to halt the extension of communism and Soviet influence, the United States developed the containment policy. As the 1990s begin, the post-World War II political, social, and economic structures of the Soviet Union and Eastern Europe appear to have failed. Unless internal and international changes are forthcoming, traditional communism and the Eastern bloc may cease to exist. From the Soviet perspective the need to build a new, stable international order must seem most pressing and vital. With or without a sense of urgency, as the leaders meet to shape the world system for the 1990s and the twenty-first century, they will face problems similar to those that puzzled their counterparts at the end of World War II.

When combat ceased in Europe, the three major powers—the United States, the Soviet Union, and the United Kingdom—agreed to meet in Berlin to discuss postwar issues and begin the transition from a wartime international system to one based on peace. In contrast to their earlier conferences, they only briefly considered the military strategies for defeating Japan, spending most of their time examining the situation in Europe. Stable peace was the common goal, but there was no guide or formula for achieving it.

In weighing alternatives, British, American, and Soviet leaders drew upon their limited knowledge of international relations, their recent histories, and their perceptions of each other. They believed that a "bad" peace, like that created at Paris following the First World War, probably would lead to international instability and eventual war.

A "good" peace and a stable system, on the other hand, like that devised at Vienna following the Napoleonic Wars, would contribute to a durable settlement and therefore provide prosperity and national growth. The structuring of peace and the shaping of international relations were regarded as parts of the "great game" of politics played by the most powerful governments. Then, as now, the leaders of the dominant nations were eager to enter the game, each confident of his abilities and sure that his views reflected the best possible solution.[3]

Thinking of the world's nations much like billiard balls careening through space and time, colliding and interacting with one another, diplomats and scholars believe that, to provide stability and peace, governments must create international structures that reduce or prevent confrontations and limit the damage done when they occur.[4] Focusing on the nation and its leaders, the goal is to establish rules for a game that would avoid total war and the subsequent destruction of both the global system and the state. Within this framework, attention often is devoted to concepts such as power politics, spheres of influence, international laws, and world organizations.

It is assumed that nations will promote harmony while at the same time protecting and asserting their own interests. Frequently, difficulties emerge when various interests do not align and when states have conflicting definitions of peace or no common rules of international behavior and law. During World War II the Big Three successfully established a system that permitted adjustments to each government's aims and ideology and allowed a large degree of cooperation and understanding. It was a multipolar arrangement that balanced the goals of the three major players with the overarching need to defeat the Axis powers—Germany, Japan, and Italy. Lesser nations participated within the system but generally took diplomatic and military directions from one or more of the Big Three. In large part the system worked because the major powers recognized that the primary goal was to conquer Adolf Hitler and because they accepted vague and even contradictory views about postwar issues. But, as the fighting in Europe rushed to an end, the relationship appeared more fragile and less useful. It was becoming difficult to maintain harmony as the points of friction increased. By the time of the Yalta Conference, in February 1945, it was clear that a new set of rules was necessary. Various international systems were possible, the viability of each depending on how well the powers would be able to cooperate and limit their individual interests in pursuit of the greater good. Among the most likely approaches were a cooperative multinational system, a spheres-of-influence system, and a competitive bipolar system.[5]

The Multinational System

Depending on the number of countries involved, several versions of a multinational approach were possible. At one end of the spectrum was a collective security system in which nearly all nations agreed to conform to established rules of international behavior and law and to punish those who violated the rules. In the 1930s such a system, the League of Nations, had failed. But its failure did not mean that the option could not work. The League's demise was commonly traced to two sources: the unwillingness of the United States to join the world organization and the League's inability to impose meaningful sanctions on countries violating the status quo and endangering the peace. Many observers believed that a new world organization, better organized, with American and Soviet participation, could provide an effective system of collective security.

At the other extreme were the Big Three working through a variety of international organizations to ensure global stability. Lip service would be given to smaller nations and agencies, but the success of the system would rest on the cooperation of the major powers. It would be much like the wartime arrangement already in place. The image of the three powers supervising the world flowed easily into that of the second possible international system: spheres of influence.

The Spheres-of-Influence System

Spheres of influence differed from a multinational, Big Three approach in that there would be less emphasis on big-power harmony and the roles of smaller nations and international organizations. Within its sphere, each major power, with either the consent or the acquiescence of the others, would assume the sole responsibility for maintaining stability. The amount of exclusivity within the sphere would depend upon the rules established or accepted by the players. The arrangement could provide a means to remove, or at least reduce, the friction that commonly exists among major nations. It would maintain peace as long as the rules were accepted by all parties.

Closely connected to the concept of spheres of influence was that of the balance of power. Within this system, there exists an almost automatic understanding that the players are no longer harmoniously working together, that a degree of rivalry has emerged. As the rivalry intensifies, stability is increasingly the product of balancing power to ensure that one nation is not stronger than the others. Peace depends more on an equilibrium in military, economic, political, and social forces than on collective agreements and cooperation. Many historians consider the lack of a major war between 1815 and 1914 as the result of such a balance among the European states. The Great War occurred when the arrangement and the rules that governed it broke down.

The Bipolar System

As the emphasis on balancing power increases and the trust between the players decreases, a third international system becomes probable, a competitive and hostile bipolar arrangement. When the major powers cannot agree on a structure or violate the existing rules, stability must rest on deterrence and the understanding that mutual destruction is possible. As American, British, and Russian armies converged on central Europe in 1945, some observers believed that in the postwar period there would be only two superpowers, the United States and the Soviet Union. British officials already were beginning to lament that the Russians and the Americans tended to ignore their interests and treat them as a second-class power. At the same time, many in the West were becoming suspicious of Moscow's intentions and goodwill. In May 1945, 38 percent of Americans questioned Russian friendship, according to one poll.[6]

In 1945 none of the leaders of the Big Three had had any formal training in international relations, but all could claim various firsthand experiences. As they met and discussed war and postwar issues at Yalta and in their subsequent conferences, they understood that it was necessary to consider what form of system would govern the postwar world. They had no clear guide, but they all agreed that big-power cooperation was essential and that one of the first steps would be to draft peace treaties for the defeated Axis nations. They knew that nearly every war eventually had led to peace treaties and that the structure, content, and spirit of the documents had played an important role in establishing a good or bad international system.

When James F. Byrnes agreed to become President Harry S. Truman's secretary of state in April 1945, he said that he was accepting the job out of a desire "to take part in the making of peace."[7] This book will examine the efforts to forge a stable and durable peace[8] by looking at summit[8] diplomacy—the meetings among policymakers of the United States, Great Britain, and the Soviet Union to deal with the political, economic, territorial, and social problems raised by the defeat of Nazi Germany and Imperial Japan and their attempt to draft treaties for Hitler's European allies: Italy, Bulgaria, Romania, Hungary, and Finland. Although they realized that they had differences of opinion about postwar issues, the Big Three believed that compromise and collaboration were possible. By working together to write the peace treaties, they hoped that they would be establishing a firm foundation for future cooperation; for the subsequent drafting of the Austrian, German, and Japanese treaties; and for a workable international system.

The quest for stability began for the Truman administration at the Potsdam Conference, in July 1945, and proceeded through the Paris Peace Conference and many meetings of the Council of Foreign Ministers. By the beginning of 1947 the treaties for Italy, Romania, Bulgaria, Hungary, and Finland were finished, but the concurrent search for harmony had failed. In their discussions and efforts to draft the documents, the Big Three had germinated the seeds of the Cold War and a new world system based not on their cooperation, as projected at Potsdam, but on a balance of power between the Soviet Union and the United States. By the time the treaties were ratified in early 1947, President Truman and his advisers had determined that collaboration with the Russians was nearly out of the question and that Washington needed to implement a policy in Europe to ensure that the power of the Soviet Union did not expand any farther—the policy of containment. The Cold War had begun.

Notes

1. *Time* 135 (January 1, 1990); *New York Times*, December 4, 1989.

2. *New York Times*, December 3, 1989; ibid., November 26, 1989; ibid., December 10, 1989; ibid., November 12, 1989; "To the Stalin Mausoleum," by "Z," *Daedalus* 119 (Winter 1990): 295–344; Joseph S. Nye, Jr., "Arms Control after the Cold War," *Foreign Affairs* 68 (Winter 1989–90): 44–64.

3. For a historical overview see Paul Kennedy, *The Rise and Fall of the Great Powers: Economic Change and Military Conflict from 1500 to 2000* (New York, 1987); Gordon A. Craig and Alexander L. George, *Force and Statecraft: Diplomatic Problems of Our Time* (New York, 1983); and Charles S. Maier, "The Two Postwar Eras and the Conditions for Stability in Twentieth Century Western Europe," *American Historical Review* 86 (April 1981): 327–52.

4. Studies on the nature of international affairs and politics seem almost without end. Most of these studies (frequently referred to as the realist school) emphasize the role of nations and war as the most important factors in shaping international relations and systems. Recently other scholars have suggested alternative approaches that reduce the importance of the nation and instead focus on wider networks of human and societal affairs. Some, known as pluralists, stress large-scale movements and attempt to discover a pattern for the development of world systems. Others, the structuralists, examine the basic social and economic structures, seeking the foundations of political trends that in turn dominate international affairs. For examinations of the variety of approaches to international studies see Kenneth W. Thompson, *Understanding World Politics* (Notre Dame, 1975); Michael Banks, "Where We Are Now," *Review of International Studies* 11 (1985): 220–37; J. E. Dougherty and R. L. Pfalatzgraff, Jr., *Contending Theories of International Relations: A Comparative Survey* (New York, 1981); Hans J. Morgenthau, *Politics among Nations: The Struggle for Power and Peace*, 5th rev. ed. (New York, 1985); and J. W. Burton, *World Society* (New York, 1972).

5. John Lewis Gaddis, *The Long Peace: Inquiries into the History of the Cold War* (New York, 1987), 215–45; idem, "The Evolution of U.S. Policy Goals toward the USSR in the Postwar Era," in *Gorbachev's*

Russia and American Foreign Policy, ed. Seweryn Bialer and Michael Mandelbaum (Boulder, 1988), 303–46.

6. Robert Dallek, *The American Style of Foreign Policy: Cultural Politics and Foreign Affairs* (New York, 1983), 158–59.

7. James F. Byrnes, *Speaking Frankly* (New York, 1947), 49.

8. Summit is used in this book to refer not only to meetings between heads of state but also to high-level meetings between secretaries of state or foreign ministers.

I

The Road to Potsdam

By April 1945 the war in Europe was nearly at an end. Soviet forces were fighting street to street within Berlin, American troops were pushing eastward to the Elbe River, and British and American troops were sweeping into the Po Valley of northern Italy hoping to capture the city of Trieste before the arrival of Yugoslav forces. In the Pacific theater, U.S. forces were moving closer to Japan's home islands, storming the Japanese fortifications on Okinawa. Within months the most destructive war in history was over, leaving vast areas of the world in ruins. The total damage was estimated at more than $2,000 billion, and over 50 million people were dead, including nearly 25 million civilians. The Soviet Union suffered the greatest physical and human losses. Between 20 and 25 million Russians lost their lives in the Great Patriotic War, as the Soviets called their participation in the Second World War. Poland, too, was devastated, losing about 5.8 million, almost 15 percent of its population, and suffering terribly under German and Soviet invasions. In central Europe the German Reich lay prostrate with nearly 4.5 million people dead or missing, and much of its industrial capacity destroyed. Farther west the damage was less severe, but, nevertheless, the figures were staggering. In Asia the damage and fatality figures were less accurate but equally appalling: Over 3 million Chinese and 2.3 million Japanese were dead. Damage was estimated in the billions.

In comparison the United States had lost roughly 330,000 soldiers, and, except for Hawaii, the Pacific possessions, and part of the Aleutian Islands, U.S. territory had been untouched by war. Jubilant that the fighting was over, most Americans looked to the future with optimism.[1] National

industrial output had doubled, and it was clear that the
United States was the world's foremost economic and
military power. What was unclear in the spring of 1945 was
the role it would play in postwar world politics.

The war not only engulfed the world in a bitter and costly
conflict but also altered the existing patterns of
international relations. The prewar pattern that had rested
on a balance of power between the nations of central and
Western Europe had been destroyed by the defeat of
Germany and Italy. The war to prevent Germany and Italy
from dominating Europe had created a new alignment and,
ironically, propelled the United States and the Soviet Union
into positions of power from which they might dominate not
only Europe but the world as well. Both nations had the
capacity to establish large spheres of influence and to expect
obedience from smaller and weaker states. In the 1920s and
1930s both countries had been on the periphery of
international relations, but in the 1940s, as leaders of the
Grand Alliance, each vowed to play a central role in
postwar politics.[2]

President Franklin D. Roosevelt made it clear to Winston
Churchill and Joseph Stalin that there was "literally no
question, political or military," in which the United States
was not interested. In the minds of most Americans, there
was no doubt that their country had won the war in Europe
and the Pacific and, with its atomic monopoly and its virtue,
should be recognized as the world's leader. The Soviets were
equally proud of their war record and equally blunt about
informing the West that they expected to be respected as a
major force in the postwar world. As one Soviet official put
it: "In 1856 we were a defeated state. In 1919 we were not
asked to be present. . . . Now we are a victorious Power. It
may be that matters should be arranged somewhat
differently now." Clearly, the world of 1945 was not that of
1939, and it was evident that a new international system
would have to be structured, one that incorporated the Soviet
Union and the United States.[3]

To those considering postwar international relations in
the spring of 1945, three possible systems seemed most
likely: a world organization, big-power unity and
cooperation, or a new balance of power. Observers
recognized that the form would depend on the willingness
and ability of the United States, the Soviet Union, and Great

Britain to cooperate and even share global responsibility with a world organization.

Many American liberals preferred a true world government as an international system and hoped that the Big Three would pass leadership to a world organization. They applauded the economic and trade agreements made at Bretton Woods in July 1944 and the formation of the United Nations Organization as moves in the right direction. The editors of the *New Republic* called upon liberals and "one worlders" to support the emerging United Nations while working to reduce world hostility.[4]

Only a few, however, truly wanted a world government. The majority, if they favored a world organization, preferred one led by the major powers. Describing themselves as "realists," they approved President Roosevelt's idea of big-power "policemen" providing security for the world under the umbrella of the United Nations. Writer and commentator Herbert Agar observed that "Russia, the United States, and the British Empire will be the great world powers when the war ends, whether they want to or not. Power exists where it exists, and nowhere else. Power cannot be bequeathed . . . power cannot be stowed away in a bank or left idle." Calling the Big Three "elephants," he held that the United Nations possessed power only to the extent that the elephants collaborated. He concluded that the world organization would be powerless if the elephants disagreed.[5]

Agar's emphasis on the cooperation of the Big Three suggested the second possible postwar system: Big Three cooperation without consideration of a world organization. The United Nations would exist but only as window dressing, an international gathering with little power or importance. Instead, peace and stability would depend on the ability of the Big Three, perhaps joined by France and China, to cooperate and respect one another's interests. Ernest Bevin, who became British foreign minister in July 1945, considered the world organization a powerless "international talkshop" that should never replace Britain as the means to protect national interests. Stalin and Harry S. Truman agreed with Bevin's sentiments. Both stressed the need for continued good relations among the Great Powers. The United Nations, Stalin commented, would work only if the powers acted "in a spirit of unity and collaboration." Truman, who became president when

Roosevelt died in April 1945, stated that "unless there is complete understanding between [the] Great Powers, there will be no peace." *Time* noted that for the world's "little nations" there appeared to be two choices: fit themselves either "into an overall pattern agreed upon and supported by the Big Three, or into the sphere of an individual Great Power."[6]

Time's latter alternative reflected the third possible postwar option. If the Big Three failed to cooperate, a system of hostile, opposing blocs would emerge. Stability and security would depend on a political, economic, and military balance of power. By mid-1944, Churchill and several Foreign Office officials, distrustful of Soviet intentions, visualized British and Soviet spheres of influence colliding in the Balkans and eastern Mediterranean. Seeking to protect British influence in the region, especially in Greece, Churchill offered a sharing of power. In the negotiations that followed, the Soviet Union received 99 percent of influence in Romania and, in return, allowed Britain an equal degree of influence in Greece. Differing amounts of influence were established in Bulgaria, Yugoslavia, and Hungary. Publicly, American officials rejected spheres of influence. Privately, however, they accepted their existence and even acknowledged an American version. Truman fully expected the United States to maintain its dominant position in Latin America and the Pacific, but, like most Americans, he defined U.S. influence as a beneficial and constructive force.[7] When the war in Europe ended on May 8, 1945, it seemed that an international system reflecting the second and third options was most likely to emerge. Nearly everyone agreed that the exact form of the system would largely depend on the goals and actions of the leaders of the Big Three—Stalin, Churchill, and Truman.

Joseph Stalin

Of the three leaders, Marshal Joseph Stalin had held power the longest and ruled most completely. His reputation for craftiness, toughness, and even cruelty was well deserved. He had survived brutal power struggles within the Soviet Union in the 1920s, and he had triumphed over his opponents in the 1930s, thereby eliminating his opposition. Never far from his primary considerations was the protection of his own position and the totalitarian system upon which his power rested. Adolf Hitler and the war had threatened both. Drawing upon his own experiences and that of the Communist party, Stalin knew the dangers and the possibilities created by war. He had seen the czar's armies collapse in 1917 and had experienced firsthand the sufferings and fears of the civil war that had followed. He had been witness to the indignity of a Russia emasculated, its western frontiers stripped away by neighboring Finland, Poland, and Romania.

In the east, Russia had been incapable of stopping the expansion of the small island empire of Japan. For Stalin the strength and loyalty of the Red Army underlined everything he hoped to achieve: the continued dominance of the Communist party, preservation of Russian independence, reestablishment of the Soviet Union as a Great Power, protection of its borders, and recovery of its lost territories.[8]

Despite their recognition that Stalin led an ideologically based regime, observers in the State Department and the Foreign Office saw him as a realist, with Soviet policy based less on Communist ideology than on the realities of power and territory. Soviet expert Charles E. Bohlen considered Stalin "100 percent practical." Comparing him with Hitler, the Foreign Office noted that, although both directed expansive dictatorships, Stalin was not a gambler and did not have Hitler's sense of mission. "As long as Stalin lasted," Churchill commented following the Yalta Conference, British-Soviet "friendship could be maintained. . . . Poor Neville Chamberlain believed he could trust Hitler. He was wrong. But I don't think I'm wrong about Stalin."[9]

Experiencing diplomatic isolation after the revolution and knowing that the Soviet Union had been admitted to the League of Nations only out of fear of Germany, Stalin even before World War II was determined to play any diplomatic role necessary to protect his rule and his country. Finding little willingness on the part of France and Britain to stand firm against the Nazis, he hastened in August 1939 to associate the Soviet Union with Fascist Germany. He hoped that his nonaggression pact with Hitler would keep his country out of the war, at least temporarily. In June 1941, as

German troops occupied large sections of Soviet territory, Stalin moved to ally himself with the capitalist West, helping to create the Grand Alliance. For the next four years, his relations with the Allies ranged from trusting to suspicious, from cooperative to obstructive, but always stressed the need for unity.

For four years the Russians fought largely on their own against Germany and its allies, frequently demanding a second front in Western Europe. While the lack of one before June 1944 produced some acrimony between the Soviet Union and the Allies, Stalin continued to assure them of his cooperation. He acknowledged the importance of materials delivered under Lend-Lease and stated that he had no intention to "Bolshevize" other countries or to intervene in their internal affairs. He pointed out that he had even dissolved the Comintern. No dyed-in-the-wool Marxist, he was prepared to suppress Communist ideology and even to seek a postwar loan from the United States. Anxious to maintain Roosevelt's assistance, Stalin promised support for the United Nations and the ideals of the Atlantic Charter, provided Soviet freedom of action was preserved and Soviet interests respected. As the war in Europe approached its end, there appeared to be no change in his policy.

Among Stalin's highest objectives was his desire to preserve the Grand Alliance, especially to maintain a rapport with the United States. Equally important was British and American recognition of the Soviet Union as a major power with legitimate geopolitical-territorial needs. Kremlin spokesmen repeatedly asserted that world peace depended upon Big Three unity and secure Soviet borders. By the end of 1944, Estonia, Latvia, and Lithuania already had been incorporated in the Soviet Union. In addition, Stalin had gained control over strategic parts of Finland and eastern Poland. Looking beyond his frontiers, he informed his colleagues that Soviet national security rested on friendly governments in bordering states, especially Poland and Romania. He wrote Churchill that it was essential that the Polish government cooperate with Moscow and that "only people who . . . demonstrated by deeds and actions their friendly attitude toward the Soviet Union" should be allowed to rule.[10]

Stalin could not be expected to view a government as friendly if its members had been associated with pro-Fascist regimes that either had been allied with Hitler or had let Nazi forces into their country. While liberated East European governments did not have to be Communist-led or dominated, local Communists needed to play an important part in them. The Russian dictator and his commissar for foreign affairs, Vyacheslav M. Molotov, were suspicious as well of many popular anti-Fascist but non-Communist leaders and groups. As V-E Day neared, it was questionable at best whether Stalin and the Politburo would really accept a government in a neighboring region without a Communist majority in control to ensure a friendly attitude toward the Soviet Union.[11]

Beyond Eastern Europe lay what Stalin and nearly every Russian accepted as their nation's greatest threat: Germany. For Soviet security, three policies were followed. First, to remove the possibility of a dangerous German military buildup, the Soviet Union approved of dismemberment plans already discussed by Churchill and Roosevelt. Second, to keep Germany weak and to aid the reconstruction of his country, Stalin favored dismantling German factories and shipping them to the Soviet Union as part of a total reparations package. Finally, Stalin accepted the placing of the Ruhr and the Rhineland, the heart of Germany's industrial base, under international control. In taking these positions the Soviets generally paralleled France, Britain, and the United States. Therefore, as Stalin took his leave of Churchill and Roosevelt at the Yalta Conference, he could be pleased with the apparent unity of views on the postwar treatment of Germany.

The meeting at Yalta, officially known as the Crimean Conference, took place between February 4 and 11, 1945, in rehabilitated czarist palaces along the Black Sea. In the course of a single week, the Allied leaders not only discussed wartime strategy and goals but also tossed back and forth their views on issues certain to be faced at the war's end, with each head of state jockeying for an advantageous position in postwar diplomacy. They agreed to divide Germany into occupational zones. France, although not invited to Yalta, would not only be granted a zone but given a seat on the Allied Control Council as well. If Britain and the United States were pleased about the inclusion of

France in controlling Germany, Stalin no doubt was
relieved that the Americans accepted his suggestion
concerning reparations. He established a working figure of
$20 billion, one half of which would go to the Soviets.

Agreements on Eastern Europe were more difficult to
reach, especially concerning the structure of the newly
formed Polish government and the future borders of the
nation. The three leaders reaffirmed that the Curzon Line
would serve as the basis for settling the border between the
Soviet Union and Poland,[12] making it almost certain that the
former would retain the Polish territory gained in the 1939
pact with Hitler. Although willing to accept Soviet
expansion at the expense of Poland, both Churchill and
Roosevelt wanted to see a broadening of the pro-Soviet, de
facto "Lublin" government of Poland. To differing degrees,
Britain and the United States wanted the government at
Lublin reconstituted to include political factions friendlier to
the West. After much, sometimes heated, debate the leaders
agreed to appoint a three-power committee to explore the
enlarging of the Lublin government in order to create a
provisional government of national unity. It was not the best
solution, Roosevelt admitted, but it was the best that could be
obtained.

As for the rest of Eastern Europe, Roosevelt and
Churchill sought means to prevent the Soviet zone of
military occupation from turning into a region of Soviet
political domination. Both recognized that the Soviets could
do almost anything they wanted in Eastern Europe, while
the occupational system permitted exclusive Anglo-
American control of Italy. Churchill already had concluded
his "percentage agreements" with Stalin to protect British
influence in Greece, and there were some in the Foreign
Office who recommended writing off Eastern Europe as the
price of future Soviet cooperation. Roosevelt, too, was
inclined to sacrifice parts of the region for Stalin's
continued collaboration. Still, the president arrived at Yalta
with the Declaration on Liberated Europe, a general and
vaguely worded statement that kept open the possibility of
trilateral action in the political affairs of Eastern Europe.
After some adjustment to meet criticisms made by the
Soviets, the declaration pronounced that the provisional
governments in liberated areas would be "broadly
representative of all democratic elements . . . pledged to

establish responsible governments through free election."[13] Roosevelt hoped that the promise to create democratic governments might provide the United States and Britain an opportunity to shape the composition of East European regimes.

More to Roosevelt's liking were the discussions on the formation of the United Nations. Prior to the meeting at Yalta, a conference at Dumbarton Oaks had drawn up a draft charter for the United Nations, but the delegates had not been able to resolve questions relating to membership, voting, and seats in the General Assembly. By secretly agreeing to the Soviet Union's having three seats, Roosevelt obtained Stalin's approval for a conference at San Francisco to finalize the UN Charter.

In both the military and the political spheres the delegates to Yalta had reason to register satisfaction over what they believed had been accomplished. Each leader had gained some advantages, and each had made concessions. Regarding Poland, for example, Roosevelt and Churchill gave away nothing that Stalin did not have already. In exchange, they received some fine-sounding declarations on democracy and elections that would convey to the British and American public the impression that the Kremlin did not intend to Sovietize and impose dictatorships in Eastern Europe. Also, they obtained approval of the American formula for voting at the United Nations and the elevation of France to major-power status. In addition to an agreement on Poland that protected their nation, the Russians gained a working figure for German reparations and important territory in Asia. In a secret agreement, Roosevelt ceded to the Soviets the Kuril Islands, lower Sakhalin, and concessions in Manchuria. In return, the president received Stalin's promise to declare war on Japan within three months of Hitler's defeat. Combined with Chinese forces, Russian troops on the Asian mainland easily would ensure the surrender of nearly two million Japanese soldiers.[14]

Winston Churchill

Of the three leaders, Winston Churchill was most disappointed with the Yalta Conference. He believed he had compromised too often, as on the issues of Poland and Germany. He had gained a degree of equality for France and had prevented Germany from being dismembered, but it was clear that Britain's influence was declining. Roosevelt and Stalin had controlled the meeting from the beginning; Churchill was not even told about their Asian agreement.

The prime minister had his finest hour when he mustered England's defenses against the Luftwaffe during the desperate months of 1940. At that time, England stood alone against Germany, but, by the end of the following year, it had acquired two allies, the United States and the Soviet Union. Both represented massive potential and would eventually reach the rank of superpower, dwarfing the British Empire by their political and economic strength.

Churchill accepted his new allies with gratitude, for with their entry into the war he knew that England was saved. But he had to tread a precarious diplomatic path because he feared that the Soviets might negotiate a separate peace or that the Americans might turn all of their attention to the Pacific war. The prime minister had long been an opponent of communism and saw the Soviet Union as his nineteenth-century forebears had seen czarist Russia: a colossus whose arms could stretch toward the Balkans, the eastern Mediterranean and the Suez Canal, Afghanistan and India, threatening areas of vital British interest. Yet, for the sake of victory, Churchill believed he had no choice; he gratefully embraced his potential rival and signed a mutual assistance pact in 1942.

However important Churchill judged his understanding with the Soviet Union, he gave utmost priority to his relations with the United States. Even before Pearl Harbor, Roosevelt and Churchill had met in Newfoundland and had promulgated the Atlantic Charter. Affirmed later by the Soviets, the charter called for seeking no territorial expansion, opposition to territorial change that did not conform to the desires of the people concerned, recognition of the right of citizens to select their own form of government, and free access to the world's economic resources—the Open Door policy. These concepts reflected an American vision of postwar capitalism, democracy, and free trade, along with a current opposition to Fascist expansionism. While they signed the Atlantic Charter, later incorporated in the UN Declaration, neither the Soviets nor the British fully believed in its ideals. Churchill never expected to apply all of the charter to the empire or to parts of the Italian colonies. Likewise, Stalin placed the needs of the Soviet Union before the principles of the charter. Both saw nothing wrong with supporting such fine-sounding, harmonious phrases in order to encourage American support, at least until Germany and Italy were defeated.

In his effort to remain on good terms with the United States, Churchill took inordinate pains to keep Roosevelt informed of his actions and interests. Their correspondence, sometimes involving two or three exchanges in a single day, was massive. Consistently, the prime minister tried to persuade the Americans that British interests could be identified with U.S. interests. But, as the war progressed, as American troops and supplies poured into Europe and North Africa, Churchill found himself forced more and more to defer to American attitudes and policies.

To safeguard Britain's postwar position, Churchill and the Foreign Office intended to make it the leader of Western Europe, supported by the empire and a strong France. Therefore, the prime minister became the champion of France's rearmament and ranking as a major power. He worked to see the French assume substantial postwar responsibilities, a seat on the European Advisory Commission, a role in organizing the United Nations, occupation of Germany, and participation in Big Three discussions. It was not an easy task, especially since neither Roosevelt nor Stalin was especially keen on elevating France and Charles de Gaulle to major-power status. But Churchill could be, and frequently was, persuasive.[15]

Even with all his great rhetorical powers, Churchill faced the spring of 1945 with apprehension. Britain and its people were exhausted from five years of war, and the economy was nearly bankrupt. The war to stop Germany from dominating Europe was finishing, with the prospect of the Soviet Union's taking Germany's place. Americans might help protect Europe and British interests against Russian expansion, but Washington was increasingly critical of British policies in Italy and Greece and questioned the need for Anglo-American unity.

Nonetheless, within the Foreign Office there was no lack of
optimism that the United States could be moved in the right
direction.   Bernard Gage, closely watching the United
States, thought that the Americans eventually would
recognize their lack of international experience and be
forced to ask for British help in demonstrating "the proper
application of their power." With the death of Roosevelt and
Truman's becoming president, the British were even more
convinced that their help would be necessary. Truman was,
at best, "a bungling if well-meaning amateur" at
international affairs.   Britain would defend itself with
determination and intelligence. A popular inside verse
spelled out the view: "In Washington Lord Halifax / Once
whispered to Lord Keynes / 'It's true *they* have the money
bags / but *we* have all the brains.' "[16]

Harry S. Truman

The death of Roosevelt brought a new player to the scene, a
man who represented the most powerful and important
nation seeking to shape the postwar world. The chief
executive, Harry S. Truman, sixty years of age, had become
associated with Roosevelt during the 1944 campaign when
he had been selected to run as vice president. A Democratic
senator since 1934 and a staunch supporter of Roosevelt's
New Deal, Truman had distinguished himself during the
war years as a chairman of the Special Committee
Investigating National Defense. This committee had looked
into all aspects of war activity and, through its vigor,
efficiency, and thoroughness, had obtained widespread
positive publicity.
    Truman was, however, in 1945 largely unknown to the
American public and the world. His crisp, midwestern
twang gave his speeches none of the sonorous importance
associated with Roosevelt. Where Roosevelt was long-
winded and given to using anecdotes, Truman was brief
and to the point. Where Roosevelt appeared ambiguous and
procrastinating, Truman seemed clear and decisive.
Secretary of War Henry L. Stimson wrote that "it was a
wonderful relief to . . . see the promptness and snappiness
with which Truman took up each matter and decided it."[17]

The new president was infatuated with history and especially with the great figures who made it. He loved to cite historic men he admired, particularly the honest and austere such as Cincinnatus, Cato the Younger, and George Washington. He once wrote a friend: "I read anything I could get my hands on about men who made history. The simplest conclusion I reached was that the lazy men caused all the troubles and those that worked hard had the job of rectifying their mistakes." Truman prided himself on his decisiveness and had a plaque on his desk that read, "The Buck Stops Here."[18] As president, he was determined to be one of the hard workers. He had read history, and now he would shape it.

Despite his extensive reading and years in government, Truman had no practical experience in diplomacy or as a world leader, nor had Roosevelt worked to prepare him for international dealings. He wanted to continue Roosevelt's policies, but he had no clear idea of exactly what they were. As vice president, Truman was left in the dark about American foreign and military affairs. Roosevelt had not briefed him on Yalta, and he was ignorant of the construction of the atomic bomb. He might have been familiar with domestic issues and politics, but in the international arena he was a novice, a point not lost on other world leaders. General de Gaulle, who soon confronted the new president regarding French interests, noted sardonically:

> As for the complex problems of the Old World, they in no way intimidated Harry Truman who regarded them from a position which simplified everything: For a nation to be happy, it need only institute democracy like that of the New World; to put an end to the antagonisms which opposed neighboring countries, for instance France and Germany, all that was necessary was to establish a federation of rivals, as the states of North America had done among themselves . . . the free world could do nothing better, and nothing else, than adopt the "leadership" of Washington.

Inexperienced Truman was, but, as de Gaulle and others soon discovered, the new president was determined to ensure that the United States received "influence and concrete benefits" equal to its postwar position. More than Roosevelt, he relied on the State Department and other "in-the-know" officials for direction and advice on foreign policy.[19]

Those seeking to inform and educate Truman on foreign policy and national security generally identified two paths in protecting and achieving U.S. interests: the application of American strength unilaterally or, perhaps, bilaterally; and international cooperation, especially among the Big Three. Those advocating the first path believed that there was scarcely a chance of working with the Soviet Union. They emphasized that there could be little collaboration between a democracy and a totalitarian nation, particularly one that rejected capitalism and Western-style civil liberties. The best means, they argued, to have American interests respected was to face the Soviets with blunt language and a show of power. Especially critical of the Soviets were Admiral William D. Leahy and Ambassador to the Soviet Union W. Averell Harriman. Leahy had objected to Roosevelt's cooperative diplomacy at Yalta, while Harriman equated the Russian advance into central Europe with a barbarian invasion. Almost immediately they met with the new president to persuade him to assume a tougher position with Stalin. They argued that the Soviet Union had violated the letter and spirit of the recently concluded Yalta agreements on Eastern Europe. The provisional Polish government was unacceptable, as was the recent Soviet-installed government of Romania.[20]

Advisers in favor of the second approach viewed Moscow's foreign policies as driven by realistic needs and concerns and not by ideological or totalitarian goals. Individuals such as Secretary of Commerce Henry A. Wallace, former Ambassador to the Soviet Union Joseph E. Davies, and presidential adviser Harry Hopkins argued that, if Washington showed that it trusted Moscow and considered its needs, the Soviets would work to ease tensions among the Big Three and conduct their foreign policy along internationally acceptable lines. In May and June 1945, Wallace asked Truman to promote postwar trade with the Russians and to reconsider the anti-Soviet recommendations he was receiving from the State Department. Wallace and other Democratic liberals wanted Truman to follow what they believed to be former President Roosevelt's policies and attitudes toward the Kremlin.[21]

Truman, the Soviets, and Eastern Europe

Both Poland and Romania lay within the Soviet Union's inner circle of interest. The Soviets believed that both countries needed to look to Moscow for leadership. The two nations presented a similar problem for Soviet security: Their peoples had a long history of being anti-Russian and, if left alone, no doubt would look to the West. While the government in Poland had been shaped to meet Soviet requirements, the government in Romania remained independent of, if not hostile toward, Soviet interests. On February 27, Andrey Vyshinsky, Molotov's deputy, arrived in Bucharest to engineer a change of government. Local Communists and the Soviets had grown tired of the provisional government and the increasingly friendly relations between the leaders of the traditionally anti-Soviet parties and British and American representatives. Vyshinsky demanded that King Michael name Dr. Petru Groza, a non-Communist but pro-Soviet politician, as prime minister. On March 6 the king succumbed to Vyshinsky's pressure and Groza became prime minister.

When American and British representatives protested the direct involvement of the Soviet Union in Romanian internal affairs, Vyshinsky pointed out that the Soviets had not protested British intervention in Greece. "Why don't you support us," he asked, "instead of trying to thwart us?" Confronted with a fait accompli and aware of the double standard they were applying, both the United States and Britain were unwilling to protest too strongly.[22]

Dreadful reports also were coming out of Poland: released Allied prisoners of war were treated harshly, dissident Poles were being imprisoned and deported, and the Soviets were denying Western observers entrance to the country. Furthermore, there was disagreement about the meaning of the Yalta decision on the broadening of the Lublin government. Molotov insisted that the agreement simply meant expanding the existing government and not, as the British and Americans held, creating a new one. Molotov also wanted the Lublin government to be allowed to send representatives to San Francisco for the UN conference.

Truman's advisers were virtually unanimous in advocating a strong stand on reconstructing the Polish

government. This view was reiterated by Churchill and his
foreign minister, Anthony Eden, who said that the United
States had nothing to lose in facing up to the Soviets.
Truman replied that he was not afraid of the Russians and
that he meant to be firm but fair. There was a direct
connection between an acceptable government in Poland
and Senate support for the United Nations, he informed
Eden, and he meant "to tell Molotov just that in words of one
syllable."[23]

When Molotov arrived in Washington en route to the San
Francisco Conference to organize the United Nations, he
met with a determined Truman. The president wanted
Molotov to understand that he was not going to allow
American interests to be ignored and that he expected the
Soviet Union to behave itself, even in Eastern Europe.
Molotov and Truman conferred twice, at an informal
meeting on April 22 and a formal one the following day. The
Soviet minister seemed unaffected by the laconic Truman
and most concerned about getting the president's
commitment to endorse the Yalta agreements on the Far
East. Having shown his willingness to uphold the accords
that clearly were in the Soviet Union's interests, Truman
fully supposed that Molotov would match his desires
regarding Eastern Europe. But, when the foreign minister,
in their formal meeting, showed no sign of fulfilling these
expectations and even justified the cosmetic changes in the
Lublin government, the president responded with fiery
rhetoric. Bluntly he told Molotov that the Kremlin needed to
live up to its agreements. When Molotov replied that he had
"never been talked to like that in my life," Truman coolly
stated, "Carry out your agreements and you won't get talked
to like that." Leahy, Harriman, and the powerful
Republican Senator Arthur H. Vandenberg were pleased,
and the American press became more critical of Soviet
policies.[24]

Truman's attempt at forceful diplomacy did not produce
the desired results. Molotov was not impressed or
intimidated by the new president. At San Francisco he
quickly became the focal point of contention by linking UN
membership of Argentina to that of Poland. Argentina had
been pro-Nazi during the war, argued the commissar,
while the Poles had fought Hitler from the first day of the
war. It was not correct to invite the former to participate in

the United Nations Organization and not the latter. Secretary of State Edward R. Stettinius, Jr., countered that the United States was not opposed to Poland, only to its present government. Meanwhile, Argentina had altered its policy and had declared war on Germany. Still smoldering from his confrontation with Truman, Molotov was not inclined to make compromises, even when Stettinius hinted that American aid might be withheld.

Nor did Stalin seem impressed with Truman's tougher tones, responding to American and British complaints about the Lublin government by asking for freedom of action in Eastern Europe. He wired Churchill and Truman that he did not know whether the Greek and Belgian governments were democratic or not, and did not care. Appreciating that these countries were vital to the security of Great Britain, he added, he did not insist on being consulted over their internal matters. Why could the Western allies not have the same consideration for Russia? "You are asking too much," he said. "To put it plainly, you want me to renounce the interests of the security of the Soviet Union."[25]

Tensions reached a critical level when, on May 4, it was revealed that the sixteen Polish underground leaders who had been missing since late March were in Moscow and about to be tried. The Western powers, not to mention the Western press, demanded an explanation from the Soviets. Silence was their only reply. That silence was dramatized when Molotov suddenly flew home, leaving his deputy, Andrey Gromyko, to carry on as the Soviet representative. Conservatives and hard-liners boasted that Molotov's behavior at San Francisco and the trial of the sixteen Poles showed the Soviets' true colors: uncooperative and repressive. Such observers applauded the new tough stance of the United States toward the Soviet Union.[26]

Liberals were concerned that the understanding with the Soviet Union, upon which world stability rested, was fading. They argued that postwar security depended on friendly relations with the Soviets and that it was counterproductive to push them into a corner. The *Nation* editorialized that "bad poker was being played with Russia" and that the administration might "have underestimated the strength of Russia's hand, and that Russia may get tired and decide to pull out of the game." Respected columnist I. F. Stone expressed a similar view: "I do not wish to be alarmist, and I put this down in the utmost sobriety: it is beginning to seem as if the main business of the United Nations Conference . . . is not to write a charter for a stable peace but to condition the American people psychologically for war with the Soviet Union."[27] Suddenly, Truman, too, was concerned. His toughness had not brought the desired results. Not even the sudden halt in Lend-Lease materials had made the Soviets more cooperative. Consequently, the president shifted gears, reversed his approach, and blamed everyone but himself.[28]

Meeting in mid-May with Joseph Davies, Truman condemned the press, claiming that "these damn sheets [were] stirring things up," and he blamed the State Department and his advisers for bad information and recommendations. Davies replied that no one could outdo the Russians in toughness: they responded to it in kind. He suggested that Truman develop a personal relationship with Stalin and send a special envoy to talk to the Soviet leader. Davies's counsel hit a responsive note. Truman, like many Americans, believed that Stalin was a sensible politician who wanted to work with the United States but whose freedom of action was limited by Molotov, the military, and the Politburo.

On May 19, Truman reversed his previous policy. He asked his personal envoy, Harry Hopkins, to travel to Moscow to convince Stalin that the United States was not "ganging up" with the British against the Soviet Union. The president had a high regard for Hopkins's ability: he had been at Yalta, he knew Stalin and Molotov, and he had been a close friend to Roosevelt. Better than anything else, his mission would signify a return to the more cooperative, Roosevelt policy. To Hopkins, Truman gave wide discretion: "I told Harry he could use diplomatic language, or he could use a baseball bat if he thought that was proper approach to Mr. Stalin."[29]

He also told Hopkins to inform the Soviet leader that the United States would uphold its agreements, and that he expected the Soviets to do likewise. But Truman was a realist as well. Writing in his diary about the mission, he noted:

> He said he'd go, said he understood my position and that he'd make it clear to Uncle Joe Stalin that I knew what I wanted— and that I intended to get it—peace for the world for at least 90 years. That Poland, Rumania, Bulgaria, Czechoslovakia,

Austria, Yugoslavia, Latvia, Lithuania, Estonia et al. made no difference to U.S. interests only so far as World Peace is concerned. That Poland should have a "free election" at least as free as . . . Tom Pendergast, Joe Martin, or Taft would allow in their respective bailiwicks . . . and Uncle Joe should make some sort of gesture—whether he means it or not to keep it before our public that he intends to keep his word. Any smart political boss will do that.[30]

Hopkins remained in Moscow until June 7 and met with Stalin six times. In his initial meeting, on May 26, he explained to Stalin and Molotov that it was most important they shore up the deteriorating structure of American-Soviet relations. In addition to the Polish imbroglio, Hopkins stated other points that needed attention: the date and place of a summit meeting, the inauguration of the Allied Control Council for Germany, and Soviet entry into the Pacific war.

Stalin replied by accepting Berlin and July 15 as the site and date, respectively, for the summit. He said that the Soviet Union was ready to begin participating in the Allied Control Council for Germany and that Marshal Georgy K. Zhukov had been named the Soviet representative. He also informed Hopkins that he was not going to push for a dismemberment of Germany, although he would keep an open mind on the subject if the others wished to consider it. Regarding the Pacific war, he assured Hopkins that the Soviet Union would attack Japanese forces in August.[31] During the conversations, Stalin affirmed that he would support the unification of China under Chiang Kai-shek and would undertake to negotiate with him over rights in Manchuria.

Having responded favorably to U.S. concerns, Stalin announced that there were still other issues to be resolved: Argentina's admission to the United Nations, the American proposal that France be made a member of the Reparations Commission, the political future of Poland, the termination of Lend-Lease, and the division of the German navy and merchant marine.

Except for the Polish issue, Hopkins was able to provide answers that Stalin deemed acceptable. In reviewing the Argentine matter the envoy implied that it was merely a teapot tempest created by Molotov to draw attention away from the Lublin government. Stalin dismissed the issue, stating that "the Argentine question belonged to the past."

Hopkins also told Stalin that the United States would not press for French membership on the Reparations Commission. Regarding Lend-Lease, he said that the cancellation had been a mistake and was now being rectified. Stalin appreciated this explanation, pointing out that it was the abrupt way in which the termination had occurred that concerned him. He wondered if Washington was trying to exert economic pressure against the Soviet Union. Hopkins assured him this was not the case. Finally, on the matter of shipping, the president's representative concurred with a three-way distribution of captured German vessels.

The major discussion, however, was on Poland. Stalin insisted that the Soviet Union needed a friendly government there. Although he did not believe the London government-in-exile qualified as friendly, Stalin said he was willing to accept Stanislaw Mikolajczyk, who was associated with the London Poles. He also suggested that the Lublin government of eighteen to twenty ministers would be willing to accept four from other democratic groups but that it might be wise to ask some of the Polish leaders to come to Moscow first for discussions. In turn, Hopkins promised that the United States would not press for exiles in London to be included in the Lublin government and would support the Soviet proposal. By agreeing to Stalin's position, Hopkins had ended the stalemate on Poland.

On his last day in Moscow, Hopkins was able to bring about another breakthrough. At San Francisco the Soviets had been taking a position on the Security Council voting procedure that would give the permanent members a veto over all submitted proposals. In Washington, Secretary of State Stettinius wondered if Hopkins, by personally intervening with Stalin, might persuade the Russian delegation to accept the veto only on substantive matters, leaving procedural items to a mere majority vote. Hopkins brought this question to Stalin's attention. After some discussion with Molotov, the Soviet leader overruled his foreign minister and approved the American formula. Thus the gloom that had descended on San Francisco was lifted, the last barrier to the adoption of the UN Charter was broken, and in due course the organization of the United Nations was able to begin its functions. Hopkins's mission had moved the Big Three away from an international system based on opposing blocs and balance of power and toward one based on big-power cooperation. Truman confided in his diary that "I'm not afraid of Russia. . . . They've always been our friends and I can't see any reason why they shouldn't always be."[32]

If American-Soviet relations were improved, Hopkins's mission brought resentment in London. Churchill had not been consulted on the approach to Stalin and, if asked, would have opposed it. The prime minister had applauded Truman's tough tone and hoped to establish an Anglo-American partnership against the Soviets. Therefore, Hopkins's talks with the Soviet leader represented a defeat for Churchill. Clearly, the United States was avoiding an Anglo-American bloc.

Knowing that the overture toward the Soviet Union would not be taken well in London, Truman sent Davies to meet with Churchill as Hopkins met with Stalin. In briefing Davies, Truman told him, "I was having as much difficulty with Prime Minister Churchill as I was having with Stalin—that it was my opinion that each of them was THE PAW OF THE CAT to pull the chestnuts out of the fire and if there was going to be any cat's paw I was going to be the paw and not the cat."[33]

Davies was not the best envoy to send. Since he was an acknowledged friend of the Russians, his mission might not raise Soviet suspicions, but it was not likely to soothe Churchill. He and the prime minister did not see eye to eye on a variety of issues, especially how to deal with the Soviets. Rather than informative, the meetings were argumentative. Despite Davies's efforts, Churchill was not convinced that the primary reason for Hopkins's trip was to prevent the appearance of Anglo-American "ganging up" on the Soviets. While the prime minister accepted a Big Three conference for mid-July, he did not like the idea of a private Truman-Stalin summit beforehand. After Davies had left for Washington on May 31, Churchill wired Truman that he would not participate in a "meeting which was a continuation of a conference between yourself and Marshal Stalin." He concluded, "We should meet simultaneously and on equal grounds." Faced by a determined Churchill, Truman agreed. The Big Three would meet on July 15, 1945, in the capital of their former enemy.[34]

James F. Byrnes

As Truman prepared for his first face-to-face meeting with
Stalin and Churchill, he had reason to be confident. In
addition to the U.S. economic strength at the negotiating
table, he could count upon the presence of an able negotiator
in his new secretary of state, James F. Byrnes, and the
power of a new weapon, the atomic bomb. For the poker-
playing president, the combination of himself, Byrnes, the
atomic bomb, national economic strength, and America's
moral position constituted a royal flush.

Admiral Leahy, Senator Vandenberg, and other
advocates of taking a hard line with the Soviets were not
pleased with Byrnes's appointment. Like Hopkins, he was
regarded as part of the Roosevelt team and seemed another
indication that Truman was moving in the wrong direction,
toward a more cooperative policy with the Soviet Union. The
president had selected Byrnes partly for the Roosevelt
connection but not out of any desire to better relations with
the Soviets. The former senator was chosen because he was
known as an effective negotiator and as having influence in
Congress. Truman was looking for an individual who had
clout and could "do some persuading . . . of the Senate,"[35] as
Byrnes had done in selling the Yalta agreements to
Congress. The president wanted a secretary of state who
could negotiate treaties with the Soviets and then have them
approved by the Senate.

Truman had approached Byrnes within hours of
Roosevelt's death. Meeting a few days later, the new
president discussed a variety of domestic and foreign policy
issues and finally asked Byrnes to replace Secretary of State
Stettinius. Frequently called Assistant President, Byrnes
became one of the most powerful men in Washington. Born
in 1879 in Charleston, South Carolina, of humble origins,
Byrnes left school at fourteen and largely educated himself,
eventually learning law while working as a court recorder.
In 1930 he won election to the Senate and soon became one of
Roosevelt's strongest and most capable supporters. For his
loyalty, Byrnes was appointed to the Supreme Court in 1941.
He was on the bench only briefly. In October 1942 he left the
Court to become director of war mobilization, wielding
tremendous power. In April 1945, citing poor health, he

resigned. His retirement was short-lived, for on July 3 he officially became secretary of state.[36]

Despite being with Roosevelt at Yalta, Byrnes had had little real experience in international affairs. State Department officials saw in him, as in Truman, a bias against "striped-pants" diplomats. He nevertheless had the trust of the president, who respected his opinions and gave him free access to the White House. What Byrnes lacked in experience, he made up for in personal attributes and his global view of American interests. High on his list of assets was a reputation for being a smooth negotiator. One colleague noted that Byrnes managed to settle cases "so that everyone looked good, didn't look as though they had been weakened by it." British Ambassador to the United States Lord Halifax informed the Foreign Office that the new secretary of state fulfilled Truman's desire that his officials be "good American horse traders" capable of winning benefits equal to their country's power.[37]

As Byrnes and Truman readied themselves for their first summit meeting, they both were confident in their ability to promote American interests and views on how peace and stability should be obtained. To support their diplomacy, they counted on their skill at negotiating with Stalin, the postwar economic power of the United States, and the atomic bomb.

The bomb was the joker in Truman's hand: It could be an extremely powerful card but was not easily played. Truman had discovered the existence of the atomic bomb project on April 25. He quickly created an organization, the Interim Committee, to consider the military and diplomatic issues involved in developing and using the weapon. Four major questions confronted the committee: Should the weapon be employed against Japan and when? Should the Japanese government be warned? Should the Soviets be notified of the bomb before its use? And should information and control of the device be shared with the Soviet Union and other nations? In part to provide more time for considering answers to these questions, Truman pushed the date for the summit meeting back to mid-July, by which time the first full test of the atomic bomb would be over.

Based on Byrnes's proposal, the Interim Committee approved using the atomic bomb on Japan as soon as possible and without warning. The committee also seconded

Byrnes's belief that a target with maximum psychological value should be selected, one that combined civilian and military resources. Aware that Stalin probably knew about the bomb—the Manhattan Project—through spies, a majority of the committee believed that Truman should inform the Soviets of the project and the decision to use the new weapon. Byrnes thought otherwise. Seeing increased diplomatic tension between the United States and the Soviet Union, he foresaw the bomb's playing a diplomatic as well as military role. American possession of the weapon might make the Soviets more willing to respect U.S. views in Europe and, perhaps, remove the Soviets from Asia totally. In private, Byrnes hoped that it would force Japan to surrender before the Soviets could enter the Pacific war.[38]

However, before the bomb could be used, before Japan would surrender, Truman and Byrnes were to meet with Churchill and Stalin at Potsdam. Truman had mixed feelings about the trip. On the one hand, as he wrote his mother, it was a bother: "I am getting ready to go see Stalin and Churchill . . . and it is a chore. I have to take my tuxedo, tails . . . high hat, top hat, and hard hat . . . I have a briefcase all filled up with information on past conferences and suggestions on what I'm to do and say. Wish I didn't have to go but I do and it can't be stopped now." On the other hand, since he was forced to go, Truman thought that he could easily promote American interests. "We didn't have to go to the Russians for anything," he commented, "and the Russians very definitely had to come to us for many things."[39]

The president was convinced that the Soviets required American financial support to rebuild their economy. Only the United States had the resources, and the Soviets knew it. Truman meant to meet with Stalin at Potsdam, establish a good working relationship, and thus begin the process of making peace in Europe while ending the war with Japan. Truman and his delegation were confident of their ability to negotiate with both the Soviets and the British. The United States had the cards, and its representatives, the ability to play them.

Notes

1. Thomas G. Paterson, *On Every Front: The Making of the Cold War* (New York, 1979), 1–19.

2. E. F. Penrose, *The Revolution in International Relations: A Study in the Changing Nature and Balance of Power* (London, 1965), 179–212.

3. James L. Gormly, *The Collapse of the Grand Alliance, 1945–1948* (Baton Rouge, 1987), 26–32.

4. *New Republic*, 113 (September 24, 1945): 366–67.

5. Herbert Agar, "Our Last Great Chance," *Survey Graphic* 34 (May 1945): 153–57.

6. *Time* 45 (May 8, 1945): 23–25; Victor Rothwell, *Britain and the Cold War, 1941–1947* (London, 1982), 1–25; Deborah Welch Larson, *Origins of Containment: A Psychological Explanation* (Princeton, 1985), 141–42.

7. Paterson, *On Every Front*, 33–53.

8. On Joseph Stalin and the roots of his foreign policy see Adam B. Ulam, *Expansion and Coexistence: The History of Soviet Foreign Policy, 1917–1967* (New York, 1968); and William Taubman, *Stalin's American Policy: From Entente to Detente to Cold War* (New York, 1982), 3–72.

9. Gormly, *Collapse of the Grand Alliance*, 13–15, 106.

10. Ministry of Foreign Affairs of the USSR, *Correspondence between the Chairman of the Council of Ministers of the U.S.S.R. and the Presidents of the U.S.A. and the Prime Ministers of Great Britain during the Great Patriotic War of 1941–1945* (New York, 1965), 1:346–48.

11. Lynn Ethridge Davis, *The Cold War Begins: Soviet-American Conflict over Eastern Europe* (Princeton, 1974), 89–171. On the Soviet Union's foreign policy see Ulam, *Expansion and Coexistence*; Vojtech Mastny, *Russia's Road to the Cold War: Diplomacy, Warfare, and the Politics of Communism, 1941–1945* (New York, 1979); William O. McCagg, Jr., *Stalin Embattled, 1943–1948* (Detroit, 1981); and Taubman, *Stalin's American Policy*. For interpretations by Soviet writers see B. Ponomaryov, A. Gromyko, and V. Khvostov, eds., *History of Soviet Foreign Policy* (Moscow, 1974); V. Berezhkov, *History in the Making* (Moscow, 1980); and Vilnis Sipols, *The Road to Great Victory* (Moscow, 1985).

12. Named after Lord George Curzon, the Curzon Line was proposed in 1919 by the Allied Supreme Council as the border between the Soviet Union and the new nation of Poland. Both the Soviets and the Poles disliked the arbitrary line and sought through force of arms to change it. The Treaty of Riga, which ended hostilities between Poland and the Soviet Union in 1921, established the border between the two nations 150 miles to the east of the Curzon Line (Russell D. Buhite, *Decisions at Yalta: An Appraisal of Summit Diplomacy* [Wilmington, DE, 1986], 39–41).

13. U.S. Department of State, *Papers Relating to the Foreign Relations of the United States: Diplomatic Papers, The Conferences at Malta and Yalta, 1945* (Washington, DC, 1955), 977–78.

14. For the verbatim record of the Yalta Conference see *FRUS: Malta and Yalta, 1945.* For detailed examinations of the Yalta Conference see Buhite, *Decisions at Yalta*; and Diane S. Clemens, *Yalta* (New York, 1970).

15. For an analysis of Winston Churchill's foreign policy see Kenneth Thompson, *Winston Churchill's World View: Statesmanship and Power* (Baton Rouge, 1983); Elisabeth Baker, *Churchill and Eden at War* (London, 1978); and Warren F. Kimball, ed., *Churchill and Roosevelt: The Complete Correspondence*, vol. 3, *Alliance Declining* (Princeton, 1984). For British policy in general see Sir Llewellyn Woodward, *British Foreign Policy in the Second World War*, 3 vols. (London, 1970–71).

16. Gormly, *Collapse of the Grand Alliance*, 17–19 (emphasis in original).

17. Robert J. Donovan, *Conflict and Crisis: The Presidency of Harry S. Truman, 1945–1948* (New York, 1977), 20.

18. *Off the Record: The Private Papers of Harry S. Truman*, ed. Robert H. Ferrell (New York, 1980), 294, 355–56.

19. *The Complete War Memoirs of Charles de Gaulle* (New York, 1967), 906; Larson, *Origins of Containment*, 129–40.

20. Larson, *Origins of Containment*, 143–57; Lloyd C. Gardner, *Architects of Illusion: Men and Ideas in American Foreign Policy, 1941–1949* (Chicago, 1970), 55–72.

21. Richard J. Walton, *Henry Wallace, Harry Truman, and the Cold War* (New York, 1976), 34–55; Larson, *Origins of Containment*, 175–78.

22. Paul D. Quinlan, *Clash over Romania: British and American Policies toward Romania, 1938–1945* (Los Angeles, 1977), 118–26; Gormly, *Collapse of the Grand Alliance*, 39–44.

23. Harry S. Truman, *Memoirs*, vol. 1, *Year of Decisions* (Garden City, NY, 1955), 71–76; Larson, *Origins of Containment*, 155–57.

24. Larson, *Origins of Containment*, 157–59.

25. *Correspondence between the Chairman and the Presidents and the Prime Ministers* 2:208–9; Louis Liebovich, *The Press and the Origins of the Cold War, 1944–1947* (New York, 1988), 56–63.

26. Liebovich, *Origins of the Cold War*, 56–63.

27. "Shall America Help Russia Rebuild?" *Nation* 160 (May 26, 1945): 588–89; I. F. Stone, "Trieste and San Francisco," ibid., 589–90. See also Frederick L. Shuman, "Might and Right at San Francisco," *Nation* 160 (April 28, 1945): 479–81; J. Alverez Del Vayo, "America and the Coalition," ibid. (April 21, 1945): 430–31.

28. I. F. Stone, "Truman and the State Department," *Nation* 160 (June 9, 1945): 637–38; Larson, *Origins of Containment*, 157–78.

29. Larson, *Origins of Containment*, 174–80; *Private Papers of Harry S. Truman*, 31.

30. Larson, *Origins of Containment*, 177–78.

31. The Soviets remained vague about the exact date of their entry into the Pacific war until the day they declared war on Japan. At

Potsdam, during Joseph Stalin's meeting with Harry S. Truman, the Soviet leader stated that his government would declare war on Japan "by the middle of August." As in his earlier discussions with W. Averell Harriman, Stalin repeated that the actual date depended on agreements with the Chinese. Following the exchange at Potsdam, Truman wrote in his diary that the Soviets would be at war with Japan on "August 15th."

On August 6 the United States dropped the first atomic bomb on Hiroshima. Two days later, August 8, even though negotiations with the Chinese were still in progress, Vyacheslav Molotov told Harriman that "the Soviet Union would consider itself at war with Japan on August 9." By this time, a second atomic bomb was being readied for use against Nagasaki. On August 8 the Soviet Union declared war against Japan and invaded Manchuria. See Robert E. Sherwood, *Roosevelt and Hopkins: An Intimate History* (New York, 1948), 902–4; W. Averell Harriman and Elie Abel, *Special Envoy to Churchill and Stalin, 1941–1946* (New York, 1975), 493–97; *FRUS: Diplomatic Papers, The Conference at Berlin (The Potsdam Conference), 1945,* 2 vols. (Washington, DC, 1960), 2:1585; and *Private Papers of Harry S. Truman,* 53.

32. Sherwood, *Roosevelt,* 887–916.

33. *Private Papers of Harry S. Truman* 31–32.

34. Robin Edmonds, *Setting the Mould: The United States and Britain, 1945–1950* (New York, 1986), 51–52.

35. Lord Halifax to Sir Anthony Eden, August 20, 1945, document A4.410.4.5, microfilm roll 2, Lord Halifax Papers, Churchill College Library, Cambridge University.

36. Robert L. Messer, *The End of an Alliance: James F. Byrnes, Roosevelt, Truman, and the Origins of the Cold War* (Chapel Hill, NC, 1982), 1–93.

37. Ibid., 77–85; Gormly, *Collapse of the Grand Alliance,* 3–5.

38. Edmonds, *Setting the Mould,* 52–54; Hugh Thomas, *Armed Truce: The Beginning of the Cold War, 1945–1946* (New York, 1987), 433–39; Gregg Herken, *The Winning Weapon: The Atomic Bomb in the Cold War, 1945–1950* (New York, 1980), 12–19.

39. Margaret Truman, *Harry S. Truman* (New York, 1973), 264–65; Larson, *Origins of Containment,* 187–89.

II

The Potsdam Conference, July 17–August 2, 1945

By the beginning of June 1945, the Big Three had agreed to meet in July at Potsdam, a war-torn suburb of Berlin. Their meeting was made easier by Harry Hopkins, who, as special envoy for Truman, had discussed the United Nations and Polish problems with Stalin, and seemingly had found solutions. Thus, as Truman, Stalin, and Churchill prepared for their meeting, some of the major issues that had posed threats to big-power harmony were nearly resolved by Hopkins's mission to Moscow.

With the question of the UN voting procedure settled, the formation of the world organization appeared assured. Steps to solve the more serious problem of the Polish government at Lublin were under way. Stanislaw Mikolajczyk and other non-Lublin Poles had agreed to participate in a government led by those already in power and had flown to Moscow to negotiate their actual positions. By the time Truman arrived in Berlin a modified Polish government had been announced, with fourteen Lublin and six non-Lublin Poles. Optimistic that the new government would soon hold "unfettered" elections, the United States and Great Britain had renewed diplomatic relations with Poland on July 5. The issue of the country's postwar borders, especially the western border, was the only question regarding Poland that remained high on the agenda for the Potsdam meeting.[1]

Another issue that had not faded from importance concerned southeastern Europe. Truman and Churchill, having found an acceptable way to modify the Polish government, hoped to discover a means to limit further Soviet influence in Eastern Europe, ensure the region's economic integration into the West European system, and promote popular, representative government in southeastern Europe. Truman intended to use the Declaration on Liberated Europe, which had been agreed upon at Yalta, and nonrecognition as his primary weapons to encourage the Soviets to loosen their hold over Romania, Bulgaria, and Hungary. The British were divided on how best to reduce Soviet influence. Sir Orme Sargent, deputy undersecretary of state, recommended writing off southeastern Europe and putting British efforts toward building influence in the eastern Mediterranean and Western Europe. Others, led by British officials stationed in Moscow, believed that, by taking a tough position on the unrepresentative governments in the region and by supporting U.S. efforts, there was "some hope of bringing the Russians around to a more cooperative frame of mind." Churchill preferred to steer a middle course intended to protect British interests in the Mediterranean while protesting, but not too strongly, Soviet influence in southeastern Europe. In the back of the prime minister's mind was the possibility of de facto Soviet and British spheres of influence, much along the lines of the percentage agreements he had struck with Stalin in October 1944.[2]

By far the most pressing question was that of Germany. With its surrender and occupation, the Big Three could no longer put off determining a policy for the most important state in central Europe. Anxious to keep as much of Germany in Western hands as possible, Churchill had pleaded with Truman not to withdraw American forces to the prearranged lines of demarcation. The prime minister believed that, by withdrawing, the West would lose a good bargaining position. His arguments had little effect, and, beginning on June 21, American forces moved westward, leaving more German territory to be occupied by the Soviets. Truman, wanting to maintain the good relations that Hopkins had generated with Moscow, strongly believed in honorably fulfilling agreements. The president played by the rules and expected Stalin and Churchill to do likewise.

Although the United States withdrew its troops, Washington was undecided in its policy toward Germany.

Truman refused to support Secretary of the Treasury Henry Morgenthau's plan, which called for turning Germany into pastureland. Rather than have Morgenthau as an adviser at Potsdam, he had accepted the secretary's resignation the day before leaving for the conference. Replacing Morgenthau's suggestion was a still-imprecise plan to consider Germany as a whole and allow the reestablishment of its industrial base, making the country economically viable.

Since American policy now supported German industrialization, reparations needed careful reconsideration, especially concerning the type and amount. Realizing that the Soviets were already dismantling factories in their zone, Truman and his advisers could not accede to the $20-billion figure mentioned at the Yalta Conference. Furthermore, Truman was unwilling to permit German industrial production to be siphoned off by the Soviet Union while American money was poured into Germany to avoid malnutrition and unrest. The United States would not repeat the experience that followed World War I and subsidize Germany's economy while the Germans paid reparations to others, especially the Soviets. To present and defend the American position, the president had named businessman Edwin W. Pauley as his representative on the Reparations Commission that was meeting in Moscow. He regarded Pauley as "a tough bargainer, someone who could be as tough as Molotov." Despite Pauley's firmness, by early July the Reparations Commission had been unable to agree on policies and had decided to refer the whole matter to the Big Three meeting in Potsdam.[3]

Another possible problem area that Truman recognized was the war with Japan. Still envisaging long and bloody fighting in East Asia, Truman sought confirmation and specific details about the Soviet Union's entry into the war. Stalin had renounced his nonaggression pact with Japan and, since V-E Day, had moved divisions and equipment to the Manchurian border. In telling Hopkins that his offensive would begin in August, the Soviet leader also had made it clear that when Japan surrendered he expected more than the territorial and railroad concessions promised at Yalta. He stated that he was thinking in terms of zones of occupation and representation on the Allied Control

Council. Upon leaving for Potsdam, Truman placed a high priority on reaffirming that the Red Army's offensive would begin on schedule, although he did not want to see the Soviets directly involved in the occupation and control of Japan.[4]

Churchill, much as he wished to play a dominating role in world affairs, reluctantly faced the realization that Britain's resources could not support a position of global preeminence. In the weeks before he traveled to Potsdam, the prime minister was moody and despondent. When he later wrote his memoirs, he gave the last volume the ambiguous title *Triumph and Tragedy*. The triumph of V-E Day had given way, he feared, to the tragedy of a postwar settlement that was not of Britain's making. As the conference approached, he also brooded over the coming elections in England. The meeting was to begin on July 17, and he planned to return to England around the 25th for the election results made public on the 26th. He could not be sure whether he or Clement Attlee, leader of the opposition Labour party, would be the next prime minister. While vacationing in southern France, Churchill confided to his physician, Lord Charles Moran: "I'm very depressed. . . . Nothing will be decided at the conference at Potsdam. I shall keep in the background at the conference."[5]

Churchill, Truman, and Stalin

Both President Truman and Prime Minister Churchill arrived in Berlin on July 15, 1945; Stalin was delayed— according to some reports he had suffered a mild heart attack—and did not arrive until the following day. Suspicious of any American efforts to discuss matters with the Soviets without British input, Churchill made a point of visiting Truman before the Soviet leader arrived. The prime minister believed that the "United States stood on the scene of victory, master of world fortunes, but without a true and coherent design."[6] This was his first face-to-face meeting with Roosevelt's successor, and he was convinced that it was vital to impress upon the new president the need for continued Anglo-American collaboration, so that Britain could provide direction for American policies.

Outwardly they got along well, although privately each was slightly critical of the other. Churchill was impressed with Truman's "gay, precise, sparkling manner and obvious power of decision." Truman too was impressed: "I had an instant liking for this man who had done so much for his own country and for the Allied cause. There was something very open and genuine in the way he greeted me." But the president was less touched by the prime minister's efforts to win over the United States to British policies. "He gave me a lot of hooey about how great my country is and how he loved Roosevelt and how he intended to love me. . . . I am sure we can get along if he doesn't try to give me too much soft soap." Nonetheless, both men believed the initial meeting had been productive.[7]

The two Western leaders were housed within walking distance of each other. They had insisted that, although the conference was to be held in the Russian zone, each delegation would have completely separate and independent quarters. The official meetings were to be held at Potsdam, in the Cecilienhof, a palace belonging to the former crown prince, and the accommodations were located in Babelsberg, heart of the prewar German film colony, some twelve miles southeast of Berlin. The Americans were at 2 Kaiserstrasse, in a large mansion surrounded by groves and gardens, and looking out on a small lake. The British were a few yards away, at 23 Ringstrasse. The Russians were housed farther along the road toward Potsdam.[8]

Many of the key British and Soviet officials were the same as at Yalta. Churchill, Foreign Minister Anthony Eden, and Undersecretary of State Sir Alexander Cadogan headed the British delegation. Attlee, head of the Labour party, and Ernest Bevin had joined the British group as observers. For the Soviets it was the usual trio: Stalin, Vyacheslav Molotov, and Andrey Vyshinsky. Of the three, Molotov was considered the most anti-Western and the most obstructive. The American team had changed since Yalta, most notably in having a new president and secretary of state. Yet the U.S. supporting cast was much the same as at previous conferences, led by Admiral William Leahy, Ambassador W. Averell Harriman, and Russian expert and adviser Charles E. Bohlen.

On the morning of July 17, hours before the first official meeting of the conference, Stalin made an informal call on

Truman. Rising from his desk, the president was surprised to discover that he was taller than Stalin. Truman assured the Soviet leader that he had come to be his friend. Their exchanges were polite, even good-humored. The American liked the succinct directness of the Russian, which stood in such contrast to Churchill's verbosity and "soft soap." Admitting that he was no diplomat, the president proudly stated, "I won't beat around the bush but say yes or no to questions after hearing all the arguments." At Truman's insistence the Soviet leader stayed for lunch.

During their meeting, Stalin discussed Soviet intentions, concerns, and possible additions to the agenda. He told the president that he would try to consider American views in dealing with all issues and that the Soviets would fulfill their Yalta pledge to declare war on Japan in early August. But before Truman could relax, Stalin added that a declaration of war depended on first reaching agreements with the Chinese. The Soviet generalissimo (who just recently had promoted himself from marshal) went on to explain that the Chinese wanted to haggle over every point and that arrangements on Outer Mongolia, railroads in Manchuria, and the status of Port Arthur and Dairen had not been finalized. However, he assured Truman that Dairen would be a free port, open to trade from all nations. The president was pleased with Stalin's commitments to negotiate with the Chinese and to open the port of Dairen. He bragged to Secretary of War Henry Stimson that he had just "clinched the Open Door in Manchuria." The Potsdam Conference had not yet started, and Truman had accomplished a major goal. "There were many reasons for my going to Potsdam," he later wrote, "but the most urgent, to my mind, was to get from Stalin a personal reaffirmation of Russia's entry into the war against Japan, a matter which our military chiefs were most anxious to clinch. This I was able to get from Stalin in the very first days of the conference. . . . This was the only secret agreement made at Potsdam."[9]

However, Truman was not pleased to learn that Stalin wanted the United States to recognize the Soviet Union as deserving a key role in deciding postwar affairs even in areas not usually considered Russian concerns. Specifically, the Soviet leader was interested in removing General Francisco Franco as ruler of Spain, dividing Italy's

African colonies among the three powers, and directing political affairs in the Near East and in other areas of North Africa. Truman considered Stalin's interests "dynamite," but he was not too worried. The United States had no intention of allowing the Soviets to establish a diplomatic or political foothold in the Mediterranean region. Believing that above all Stalin respected military power, Truman reflected on the diplomatic possibilities of the atomic bomb. "I have some dynamite too, which I'm not exploding now," he wrote in private.[10]

Prior to his meeting with Stalin, the president had learned information that would loom large over the Potsdam deliberations. At Alamogordo, in the desert of New Mexico, the first detonation of an atomic bomb had just occurred. On July 16, Stimson had delivered a cryptic telegram: "Operated on this morning. Diagnosis not yet complete but results seem satisfactory and already exceed expectations."[11] However, as observers of the atomic detonation soon discovered, to "exceed expectations" did not do justice to the results. A few days later, Lieutenant General Leslie R. Groves, head of the Manhattan Project, reported:

> The test was successful beyond the most optimistic expectations of anyone . . . I estimate the energy generated to be in excess of the equivalent of 15,000 to 20,000 tons of TNT; and this is a conservative estimate. There were tremendous blast effects. For a brief period there was a lighting effect within a radius of 20 miles equal to several suns in midday; a huge ball of fire was formed which lasted for several seconds. This ball mushroomed and rose to a height of over ten thousand feet before it dimmed. . . .
>
> One-half mile from the explosion there was a massive steel test cylinder weighing 220 tons. The base of the cylinder was solidly encased in concrete. Surrounding the cylinder was a strong steel tower 70 feet high, firmly anchored to concrete foundations. . . . The blast tore the tower from its foundations, twisted it, ripped it apart and left it flat on the ground. The effects on the tower indicate that, at that distance, unshielded permanent steel and masonry buildings would have been destroyed. . . .
>
> The cloud traveled to a great height first in the form of a ball, then mushroomed, then changed into a long trailing chimney-shaped column and finally was sent in several directions by the variable winds at the different elevations.
>
> The effect could well be called unprecedented, magnificent, beautiful, stupendous and terrifying. No man-made phenomenon

of such tremendous force had ever occurred before. The lighting
effects beggared description. The whole country was lighted by a
searing light with the intensity many times that of the midday
sun. It was golden, purple, violet, gray and blue. Thirty seconds
after the explosion came first, the air blast pressing hard against
the people and things, to be followed almost immediately by the
strong, sustained, awesome roar which warned of doomsday and
made us feel that we puny things were blasphemous to dare
tamper with the forces heretofore reserved to The Almighty. Words
are inadequate tools for the job of acquainting those not present
with the physical, mental and psychological effects. It had to be
witnessed to be realized.[12]

Armed with such information from General Groves,
Truman informed Churchill of the test. The prime minister
quickly agreed that the atomic bomb should be used as soon
as possible against Japan and that it might end the war
before the Soviets became involved. The Western leaders also
agreed that they should not give Stalin details about the new
weapon.[13]

The Conference Begins

At 5:00 P.M. on July 17 the Big Three and their advisers sat
down around a large circular table in the
Cecilienhof.[14] Stalin asked Truman to preside, and he
accepted, noting that directing discussions was as tough as
leading the Senate. The first order of business was to
establish an agenda. Having conferred with his advisory
team at length during the Atlantic crossing, Truman
presented four items for consideration: 1) establishment of a
council of foreign ministers, 2) principles to guide the Allied
Control Council for Germany, 3) implementation of the
Declaration on Liberated Europe, and 4) membership of
Italy in the United Nations. Anxious to be businesslike,
Truman neglected to make any gracious introductory
comments. Rather belatedly he delivered a eulogy on his
predecessor, President Roosevelt.

Stalin then listed the issues the Soviets wished to
discuss: 1) division of the German navy and merchant
marine, 2) German and Italian reparations, 3)
trusteeships, 4) relations with Axis satellites, 5) the Franco
regime in Spain, 6) Tangier, 7) Syria and Lebanon, and 8)

Poland. Churchill had no set agenda except for Poland and in general seemed disturbed at the rapidity with which the Americans and Soviets were proceeding. He would not be brief, launching into a lengthy oration that seemed pointless. Undersecretary of State Cadogan worried that Churchill's actions were hurting British interests. He "butts in on every occasion and talks the most irrelevant rubbish," wrote the undersecretary, "and risks giving away our case at every point." The prime minister finally ended his speech by suggesting that the foreign ministers draw up a recommended final agenda for the next day. Agreeing to let the ministers tackle the unpleasant job of constructing an agenda, Stalin wondered what the heads of state should do for the rest of the meeting.[15]

Truman wanted to get things done, to start making decisions, as he put it in his memoirs:

> I said I did not want just to discuss. I wanted to decide.
> Churchill asked if I wanted something in the bag each day.
> He was right as he could be. I was there to get something accomplished, and if we could not do that, I meant to go back home. I proposed that we meet at four o'clock instead of five in order to get more done during the time we would be meeting. The others agreed to this.

Stalin, being of a similar mind, asked that they continue by considering the first point on the American agenda, the formation of the Council of Foreign Ministers.[16]

Truman, James Byrnes, and the State Department favored the formation of the Council of Foreign Ministers to avoid a "slow and unwieldy" peace conference of the Versailles type, with its "heated atmosphere of rival claims." Composed only of the foreign ministers of the five permanent members of the United Nations Security Council (Great Britain, the Soviet Union, the United States, France, and China), the Council of Foreign Ministers would provide the means of writing the peace treaties and finding territorial settlements. American planners believed that the limit of five members would forestall efforts by Britain and the Soviet Union to include countries "closely identified with their respective foreign policies." It also would "tend to reduce the possibilities of unilateral action by either the Soviets or the British and serve as a useful means through which the United States could work for the liquidation of spheres of influence."[17]

The American proposal for the council clearly demonstrated that the United States favored an international system based on big-power cooperation and leadership. As visualized by Byrnes and the State Department, the rest of the United Nations would be involved in the peace process only as ratifiers of decisions made by the Big Three. The inclusion of France and China in the formula would give the United States two almost always dependable votes.

Stalin and Churchill liked the American plan in general but questioned the membership and roles of France and China. Churchill saw no reason to include China, while Stalin was uneasy about including either nation. The British wanted to expand France's diplomatic role; the Soviets sought to limit it. After some discussion the question was referred to the foreign ministers, who agreed that China should not debate European matters but were less certain about France. Finally the ministers recommended that meetings on the peace treaties should include those countries that had signed armistices with the Axis powers concerned and their satellites. This formula permitted France to discuss the German treaty but not that of Italy, Romania, Bulgaria, or Finland. Voting on the treaties, however, would be reserved for those nations that had signed surrender documents.[18] Whether France, China, or other nations would be involved in additional questions before the Council of Foreign Ministers was set forth in a purposely imprecise formula: "Other members will be invited to participate when matters directly concerning them are under discussion." Upon Byrnes's suggestion, it was agreed that the Council of Foreign Ministers would meet in September in London and begin drafting peace treaties for Italy and the satellite nations.[19]

Over the next two weeks the negotiations at Potsdam continued as the Big Three dealt with the transition from wartime policies, with their obvious constraints, to postwar policies, whose constraints were not yet clear. The work took place at various interconnected levels and cut across a wide range of war and postwar issues and perceptions. The off-stage diplomacy associated with private meetings between and among the heads of state probably did the most to shape the tone and thoughts of the leaders. During these negotiations, Stalin appeared to play the best cards, persuading Truman and Churchill, and later Attlee, to see him as a reasonable man with reasonable goals, a man who could be trusted.

If harmony and goodwill were the apparent products of the private meetings among the heads of state, the opposite was the case when the foreign ministers gathered. Indeed, it was largely because most of the battles were fought at the ministers' level that the on-stage sessions of the three leaders went as smoothly as they did. At the center of the ministers' frequently heated and acrimonious morning debates was Stone Bottom or Iron Bottom, as Molotov was called. The commissar often refused to budge on issues, making the United States and Britain accept the Soviet view.

Vyacheslav Molotov

Born in 1890, Vyacheslav Molotov was the son of either a shopkeeper or a member of the upper middle class. In any case, he renounced his middle-class origins in secondary school and became a Bolshevik. In good revolutionary fashion, he was arrested for political activity in 1909 and shunted off to northeastern Russia for two years. Once back in Saint Petersburg, he cofounded *Pravda* in 1912, and by 1920 he was the secretary of the Communist party's Central Committee. Five years later, based on Stalin's recommendation, he became a full member of the Politburo. In 1939, in the face of growing German threats, he became the head of the People's Commissariat of Foreign Affairs and immediately began negotiations with the Germans to keep the Soviet Union out of the war and gain territory at Poland's expense. By 1945 many Kremlin watchers believed that Molotov, Stalin's close friend, was the second most powerful man in the Soviet Union and would likely be the country's next leader. Some even thought that Molotov determined foreign policy by limiting Stalin's and the Politburo's information.

Molotov was certainly one of the toughest minded and most patient statesmen of the period. His disciplined diplomatic style was characterized by his always being well prepared and informed. His tone was frequently pontifical and argumentative. An intelligent, hard bargainer, Molotov could argue that black was white for hours and then reverse his position in a second without blinking an eye. His negotiating ability earned him his nicknames and a general distaste among Western diplomats. One American official wrote: "God made Vyshinsky to be a fundamentally decent human being. As for Molotov . . . God made Molotov to be Molotov." When confronted with strong opposition, he would either refuse to discuss the issue or counterattack with another topic. When he was angered, his face twitched.[20]

While the formation of the Council of Foreign Ministers generated little debate, other items on the final agenda, approved on July 19, were sure to raise problems. It included 1) a policy for the political control of Germany, 2) Poland, 3) disposition of the German fleet and merchant marine, 4) Spain, 5) the Declaration on Liberated Europe, 6) Yugoslavia, and 7) Romania. Even as the agenda was being approved, the heads of state had reached a near agreement on the first item.

Germany

On July 18, Truman had opened discussion of the German question by presenting the most recent U.S. position. The president viewed Germany as a political and economic whole divided into four temporary occupation zones. In matters affecting the entire country, authority would be exercised by the Allied Control Council, whose decisions had to be unanimous.[21] The American position also affirmed that, while there should be no central German government for the time being, some German economic agencies should be established under the Allied Control Council to administer industry, finance, transport, communications, and foreign trade on a national basis. Because the proposal provided each of the occupying powers a veto over policies with which it disagreed, Truman's plan was accepted with little argument.[22]

The proposal, which became the guiding directive for the zonal commanders, ordered that, within each zone, supreme authority be exercised by the commander in chief. The commanders were to ensure that everything pertaining to the Nazi regime be extirpated. Nazi laws were to be abolished, and the educational and legal systems restructured, to eliminate any taint of Nazi influence and ideology. Local German governments, elected by non-Nazi, democratic parties, were to be established in each zone and members of the Nazi party excluded from important positions, if not tried and punished.

Germany was to be deprived of all capability for making war. The Allied Control Council was to supervise "the complete disarmament and demilitarization of Germany and the elimination or control of all German industry that could be used for military purposes."[23] At the same time, the country was to be encouraged to become a peace-loving, responsible member of the community of nations, guaranteeing freedom of speech and religion. So far as practicable, there was to be uniform treatment of the entire German population.

Having accepted the political guidelines for Germany, the Soviets restated their wish to discuss economic issues, including the division of the German fleet and merchant marine, but they agreed to wait until another day. The issue was easily resolved during the next plenary session. All German vessels were to be distributed among the three powers with the exception of submarines, most of which would be sunk. Merchant ships would be distributed after the war against Japan. Economic policies, however, were less easy to determine and produced serious strain on the harmony of the three powers.[24]

At the core of the German economic problem were reparations and the country's eastern border. The Russians, having been overrun and plundered since 1941, wanted as much in repayment as they could get. The British and the Americans, while agreeing that the Soviet Union deserved reparations, could not accept the denuding of western Germany, for it meant Anglo-American subsidies would be needed to keep the defeated people from starvation. The basic question was: Could these contrary views be squared with the negotiations at Yalta, where the United States (but not the British) had taken as a basis of discussion $20 billion in reparations, one half of which would go to the Soviet Union?

As discussions continued the basic issue became very complicated. If a monetary figure was to be used, would it be necessary to value in dollars the goods and equipment designated as reparations? How much had the Soviets already taken? There were reports not only in Germany but also from Romania that they were dismantling factories and shipping them east. At one point, Secretary Byrnes bluntly asked Molotov: "Is it true that Soviet authorities have taken large quantities of equipment and materials out of their zone? We've even heard that household equipment, such as plumbing, silver, furniture, etc., had also been removed."

Negotiating at the Potsdam Conference, July–August 1945. Seated at the table, clockwise starting with third from left: Joseph Stalin (sitting back, looking at ceiling), two Soviet interpreters, Admiral William D. Leahy, James F. Byrnes, Harry S. Truman, Charles E. Bohlen, Joseph E. Davies, Sir Alexander Cadogan, Sir Anthony Eden, Winston Churchill, a British interpreter, Clement Attlee, Andrey Vyshinsky, and Vyacheslav M. Molotov. Fedor Gusev is standing to the left of Admiral Leahy. (Robert M. Cooper Library, Clemson University)

Unashamed, Molotov replied, "Yes, this is the case," and he offered to knock off $300 million for incidental removals. This cavalier suggestion oversimplified the question. How could one itemize and evaluate such varied material? The ministers could not agree on how to define reparations. Should "war booty," "trophies of war," or identifiable goods taken from the Nazis for which restitution would be made be considered reparations? Clearly, reaching agreement on economic issues was not going to be easy.[25]

Another complication of the reparations question was Poland's frontier with Germany. After some argument, Stalin agreed that Germany should be defined by its 1937 boundaries. This left unclear the exact eastern boundary of the Soviet occupation zone. Did it include the area east of the Oder River, formerly part of Germany but now administered by the Poles and considered part of the new Poland? Would the factories and goods in that area be part of the Soviet Union's reparations, or should they go to Poland? If the Soviets turned the factories over to the Poles, should the material still be counted as Soviet reparations?

Even more tangled were the problems involving German exports and imports. Suppose, in the American and British zones, coal or food had to be imported to maintain a minimum standard of living. How could the goods be paid for if reparations had a higher priority? The Soviets were willing to place imports and reparations on an equal basis, but the British and Americans insisted that the former had greater significance. Byrnes put it curtly: "There will be no reparations until imports in the American zone are paid for. There can be no discussion of this matter. We do not intend, as we did after the last war, to provide money for the payment of reparations."[26]

Recognizing the complexity of German economic issues, the Big Three postponed such questions until they had heard from the foreign ministers and the previously created Reparations Commission. For days the commission and a subcommittee on economic matters struggled to solve the economic puzzle. British and American spokesmen argued that their position on imports did not show a "greater sympathy for the German people than for the Soviet people." The Soviets were not convinced and accused Britain and the United States of changing the Yalta agreement on reparations.[27]

Concluding on July 22 that the discussions were producing only ill feelings and seemingly at an impasse, Byrnes decided upon a completely new approach. The next day he sought out Molotov for a private conference and dumped his novel plan into the startled commissar's lap. Byrnes "wondered whether it would not be better to give

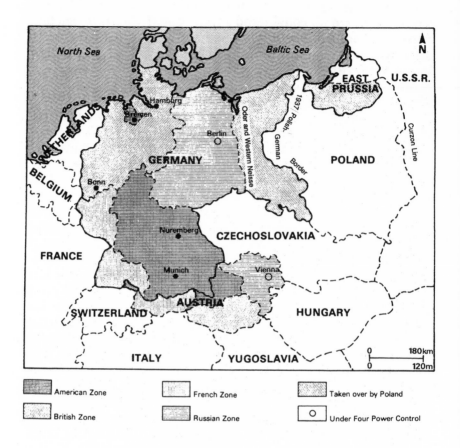

Map 1. Occupation zones of Germany. (*Historical Maps on File*)

consideration to the possibility of each country taking
reparations from its own zone. For example, according to
their estimates, about 50% of the existing wealth of
Germany was in the Soviet zone and that, therefore, the
Soviet Union could receive its share of reparations from its
own zone."[28]

Dumbfounded by the new proposition, Molotov consulted
Stalin. When he next saw Byrnes, he complained that the
Western powers were seeking to reverse Yalta by not
acceding to the $20-billion figure. Byrnes retorted that the
United States had not committed itself to that amount but
had accepted it only as a "basis for discussion." And that, he
went on, is exactly what Edwin Pauley, on the Reparations
Commission at Moscow, had done. Pauley "had been in
Moscow for thirty-five days and discussed it; then he had
come to Berlin and . . . continued to discuss it." As a result
of these negotiations and as previously explained to Molotov,
the United States "had decided . . . that the figure was not
practical." Molotov was not persuaded. He disliked
percentages and wanted a precise amount. Shifting his
argument away from Byrnes's solution, Molotov included
reparations from the Ruhr. He announced that the Soviets
"would be prepared to reduce their reparation figure even to
eight and a half or eight billion, but they must insist on a
fixed amount, say two billion, from the Ruhr."[29]

The secretary of state and Eden would give Molotov no
satisfaction. This is where the matter rested when, on
July 25, Churchill and his foreign minister flew back to
England for the election results. The argumentation would
resume when the new team, Attlee and Bevin, returned to
Berlin.

Eastern Europe

On the first day of the conference, President Truman had
said he wished to discuss the status of formerly occupied
countries, and he read an American memorandum
asserting that the Yalta Declaration on Liberated Europe
had been violated. He called for reorganization of the
Romanian and Bulgarian governments along democratic
lines, and asked for consultation on how to hold "free and
unfettered" elections in Greece, Romania, and Bulgaria.

Stalin was angered by Truman's position; at a dinner with Churchill on July 18, he told the prime minister that "he had been hurt by the American demand for a change in Government in Rumania and Bulgaria. He was not meddling in Greek affairs, and it was unjust of them" to want to make changes in an area of Soviet interest.[30]

The U.S. stand should not have been a surprise to Stalin. The issue of British and American recognition of Romania and Bulgaria had been discussed during Hopkins's visit to Moscow. In addition, Truman publicly had protested the lack of free expression in the Balkans. Even though Stalin had declared that the Romanian and Bulgarian governments were as democratic as the Italian, the United States had not seen fit to agree. Nevertheless, it seemed clear that the Soviets meant to use Italy as a precedent for their policies toward southeastern Europe.

Stalin referred to Italy again on July 24, when the three powers examined the question of recognizing Germany's former satellites. The United States proposed that Italy be invited to join the United Nations,[31] and the British quickly seconded the motion. Stalin immediately objected, not so much because he opposed the proposition but because he considered an artificial distinction was being made between Italy and the other satellites—Romania, Bulgaria, Hungary, and Finland. He could not believe that Italy was any more "democratic" than the Balkan countries, and he could not understand why they should be denied equal diplomatic recognition. Stalin had changed the nature of the proposal from providing Italy with a seat in the United Nations to recognizing the governments of Romania and Bulgaria.

There ensued what Truman characterized as the bitterest debate of the conference. From the viewpoint of the Western leaders the proposition was simple: One could not recognize a regime that was neither responsible nor democratic, and that would not permit freedom of action or speech within its borders. At first the discussion fell between Stalin and Truman, who was supported by Churchill. The president defended the Anglo-American decision not to recognize Romania and Bulgaria until there was a change of governments. When the American and Soviet leaders finally reached an impasse, Churchill added to the obstruction by vehemently insisting that Italy met all democratic criteria, whereas the Soviet-occupied states did not. In ringing terms he praised the growth of democracy in Italy. There was no political censorship; the Italian press even attacked him frequently. With the war in Europe over, the Italians were getting ready to stage democratic elections. The opposite was true in Romania and Bulgaria. There was little news coming from either of the nations, and the British missions in both countries, Churchill bluntly informed Stalin, were placed in conditions of isolation resembling internment.

Stalin immediately questioned the validity of Churchill's statement, and the prime minister responded that his information came from the British mission. "Fiction!" replied Stalin. Churchill was unaffected by the heated exclamation. "Of course, you are free to call our statement fiction," he told Stalin, "but I have full confidence in our political representatives."[32] The face-off between Churchill and Stalin continued for several more moments, each protesting events in the other's sphere of influence. Finally, Byrnes and Truman stepped in to end the fruitless confrontation. The president suggested that their meeting was not the place to discuss problems of the political missions. Byrnes, in turn, offered a modification of the proposal that he believed would be acceptable to both Churchill and Stalin. He suggested that the words "responsible government" be replaced by "recognized government." Stalin thought it was a move in the right direction and wanted to add an amendment that the Western governments would "examine the question of establishing diplomatic relations" with Romania, Bulgaria, Hungary, and Finland in the near future.

Churchill opposed Stalin's addition, saying it suggested that diplomatic recognition was imminent, whereas Britain had no intention of quickly recognizing either Romania or Bulgaria unless they altered their governments and policies. Churchill then explained what bothered him: The Council of Foreign Ministers, in attempting to draw up the peace treaties, would be conferring with governments that Great Britain and the United States did not recognize. Therefore, it would be impossible to prepare the treaties.

"What makes you think so?" snapped Stalin.

"It follows logically," replied the prime minister.

"No, it does not," declared Stalin.

Neither could convince the other, for the discussion had become a conflict of power in which their niceties of phraseology were shown up as embarrassing shams. "We say," Churchill continued, "that we shall conclude peace treaties with Governments to which we accord recognition, but we have no intention of recognizing these Governments. I find this almost absurd."[33]

By this time, Truman was exasperated and wanted to shunt the whole question to the foreign ministers, but the prime minister persisted with another suggestion—that the Council of Foreign Ministers prepare the peace treaties not *with* the satellite countries but *for* them. This semantic alteration was accepted, and the revised formula enabled the proceedings to continue. The fact that Churchill rather than Truman had carried the brunt of the exchange with Stalin suggests that the president had by now become bored with meaningless oratorical displays in a game where the Soviets held all the trump cards.

Truman nevertheless retained the hope of freeing Europe from the nationalistic restraints that had impeded the flow of goods throughout the Continent. He might not have suspected that advocating the Open Door principle could be construed by proponents of a socialist-controlled economy as capitalist imperialism. In any case he presented to the conference an American plan that looked toward free navigation on the Rhine and Danube rivers. Stalin evinced absolutely no interest in this proposal and countered by calling for a revision of the Montreux Convention, which limited access of non-Turkish warships to the Black Sea, so that the Soviet Union and Turkey together could exercise control over the Dardanelles. A rambling discussion on these matters went nowhere, and the session was soon adjourned.[34]

Poland

First introduced as an agenda item during the plenary session of July 18, Poland was an issue that both Churchill and Stalin wanted to discuss, but for very different reasons. By this time all three powers had recognized the new provisional government. Stalin accordingly argued that no vestiges of the London government-in-exile should remain.

All of its assets, plus the Polish army that had maintained allegiance to the London group, should be returned to Poland. The prime minister said he had no quarrel with Stalin's request, but he took the opportunity to launch into a long oration on the bravery and sufferings of the Poles and on Britain's role in supporting them. Truman became restless during Churchill's wandering speech, which added little to the debate. Finally, the president was able to put in an appeal for elections as soon as possible in Poland. Stalin proposed that the issue be referred to the foreign ministers, and the other leaders agreed.[35]

On July 21, having received more detailed information about the power of the atomic bomb, Truman entered the debates with greater self-assurance. Secretary of War Stimson noted that "the President was tremendously pepped up by it and spoke to me of it again and again when I saw him. He said it gave him an entirely new feeling of confidence." Truman's new spirit did not go unobserved; Churchill believed that the president was "a changed man" who "told the Russians just where they got off and generally bossed the whole meeting."[36]

The session began with reports from the foreign ministers. The three leaders then turned once more to the Polish question. Churchill and Truman were indignant that no one really knew what was happening in Poland and urged that journalists be permitted to file reports without censorship. Stalin was not enthusiastic. The most significant problem remaining, now that the United States and Britain had recognized the provisional government, concerned Poland's western boundary. Since the Soviet Union occupied all of eastern Germany, there was little Churchill and Truman could do other than protest. The president complained that there were now five occupation zones because the Soviets had turned over the area extending along the Oder and western Neisse to the Poles. This was in violation of the Yalta agreement. The president did not see how economic controls or reparations could operate if Germany was thus broken up.

The prime minister came to Truman's support. He had a special concern for Poland not only because England had signed a treaty of alliance with it in 1939 or because thousands of Polish troops had fought loyally with the British, but also because the freedom or bondage of Poland was a signal to all the other countries in Eastern Europe. Churchill entered the debate like a wounded lion, yet he was no longer his old self. As Lord Moran, his physician, put it: "The P.M.'s health has so far deteriorated that he has no energy left to seize his opportunities . . . he is not mastering his brief. He is too tired to prepare anything; he just deals with things as they come up." Churchill also may have been reluctant to decide anything until the election results were known. Furthermore, as Moran pointed out, he wanted to heal rather than exacerbate the fissures in the Grand Alliance.

Churchill spoke strongly against giving the Poles control over an area in which some eight million Germans lived. Stalin insisted that the Germans had all fled and that the Poles were needed to fill the vacuum. They debated at considerable length in a heated atmosphere but reached no conclusion. The next day, July 22, they went at it again, each repeating his argument and disputing the other's figures.[37]

By this time, Truman was becoming irritated at the interminable rhetoric of Churchill and the gruff responses of Stalin. Practical and efficient, the president could see that no headway was being made and that in any case Poland was a lost cause. He preferred to leave the whole question to the peace conference, but meanwhile he drew the other leaders' attention to a clause in the Yalta communiqué stating that the opinion of the provisional Polish government "should be sought in due course" regarding additional territory Poland might obtain. Stalin, Truman, and Churchill agreed to invite the new provisional government to Potsdam.

On July 24 the Polish delegation arrived in Berlin, headed by Prime Minister Boleslaw Bierut and including Mikolajczyk and Foreign Minister Wincenty Rzymowksi. They consistently held to the position that the Oder and western Neisse rivers should be the frontier, and they vehemently argued their case before the foreign ministers, Churchill, and Truman, in turn. Churchill used the occasion to practice his own flamboyant oratory, whereas Truman accorded the delegation only twenty minutes and told them he did not like "the arbitrary manner" in which the boundary question was being handled. He informed them that the issue would eventually be settled at a peace conference.[38]

When the Big Three met the following morning to continue discussing the Polish question prior to Churchill's return to England, the prime minister's ill-concealed bitterness set the tone of his conversation with Stalin.

Churchill: The Poles are driving the Germans out of the Russian zone. That should not be done without considering its effect on the food supply and reparations. We are getting into a position where the Poles have food and coal, and we have the mass of [the] population thrown at us.

Stalin: We must appreciate the position of the Poles. The Poles are taking revenge for centuries of injuries.

Churchill: If the conference ends in ten days without agreement on the present state of affairs in Poland, and with the Poles practically admitted as the fifth occupation power, and no arrangement for the spreading of food over the whole of Germany, it will mark the breakdown of the conference. I suppose we will have to fall back on the proposal of the Secretary of State, and each of us fall back on our own zones. . . . We must recognize that we have made no progress so far on this point.

Stalin: Coal and metal from the Ruhr is more important than the food supply.

Churchill: Coal will have to be paid for by food. We could not agree that Russia could dispose of everything in her zone and still claim supplies from our zone.

Stalin: Supplies will have to be drawn from the whole of Germany.

Churchill: Why not food?

Stalin: That should be discussed. . . . Germany has always had to import foodstuff.

Churchill: How will she pay reparations?

Stalin: There is much fat in Germany.

Churchill: I am not going to consent to an arrangement which will lead to starvation in the Ruhr, when the Poles have all the feeding grounds. . . .

Stalin: The Poles are selling their own coal, not the coal from the former German territories. I am not accustomed to complaining. We have lost five million men in this war. We are short of coal and

many other things. If I describe our situation and our needs, I
might make the Prime Minister weep.

Churchill: We will sell coal from the Ruhr for food.

Stalin: This question must be discussed, or thought over.

Churchill: We were only exchanging views. I am finished.

Stalin: What a pity.[39]

And so ended the discussion, with no fruitful conclusion.

That afternoon Churchill and Eden left for the results of
the election. Neither would return. Defeated by a large
majority, the Conservative party could no longer support
Churchill as prime minister. He could now express only his
own opinions and, as a spokesman for the political
opposition, those of his party. But he had not given up trying
to mold the postwar world into conformity with his views.[40]

During the interruption from June 26 to 28, as the
British change of government took place, Secretary of State
Byrnes devoted his energies to exploring ways to break
through the impasse that threatened to end the conference.
When the British delegation returned to Berlin, headed by
Prime Minister Attlee and Foreign Minister Bevin, Byrnes
was ready with a new approach to the whole problem.

Clement Attlee and Ernest Bevin

The replacement of Churchill and Eden by the Labour team
came as a shock to the American and Soviet delegations.
Both had expected the Conservative party and Churchill to
win easily. The Russians were astonished by the election
results. Would there be a change in British policy? Could the
new leaders effectively negotiate? There was considerable
concern about Prime Minister Attlee's ability to fill
Churchill's shoes. Head of the Labour party since 1935, he
was short and slight, modest and realistic—not at all like
Churchill. Many considered him mousy. Churchill once
quipped that Attlee was "a sheep in sheep's clothing." While
he did not have the ebullience or the experience of
Churchill, he nevertheless possessed a businesslike
approach that accorded quite well with Truman's
personality. Both men liked to be concise, solve problems

quickly, and leave foreign affairs to specialists, that is, the foreign ministers.

A longtime member of Churchill's war cabinet, Attlee was fully informed of British interests and foreign policy and was on record as not totally agreeing with them. He believed that Britain was overextended and needed to reduce its commitments, especially in the Middle East. More than Churchill and Eden, Attlee placed trust in the eventual ability of the United Nations to resolve international difficulties and to examine issues from the Soviets' perspective. He had informed Churchill of his views while

The Big Three at Potsdam. Seated, left to right: Clement Attlee, Harry S. Truman, and Joseph Stalin. Standing, left to right: Admiral William D. Leahy, Ernest Bevin, James F. Byrnes, and Vyacheslav M. Molotov. (Robert M. Cooper Library, Clemson University)

at Potsdam, telling the prime minister that, if they were to oppose the Soviets, it should be "done with the requirements of a world organization for peace, and not with the needs of the defence of the British Empire." Neither Churchill, Eden, nor the British military thought highly of Attlee's global view. First Sea Lord Admiral Andrew Cunningham commented: "Attlee has apparently written what appears to be a damn silly letter to the P.M. saying we ought not oppose a great country like Russia having bases anywhere she wants them. What an ass." Fortunately for Cunningham and the rest of the British delegation, Attlee's choice for foreign minister, Ernest Bevin, thought more along their lines. Perhaps even more fortunately for the continuity of British policy at Potsdam, Attlee generally deferred to his foreign minister. Undersecretary Cadogan, with some pleasure, noted that Bevin took "the lead over Attlee, who recedes into the background by his very insignificance."[41]

Round of face, squat of build, and a seasoned labor leader, Bevin had built up during his career a considerable reputation for tough bargaining and a short temper. Born in 1881 in rural western England, the youngest of five children, he was left an orphan at age six. He finished his formal schooling at eleven and became a laborer. In 1911, as Byrnes was entering the House of Representatives, Bevin became a full-time labor organizer; he eventually helped to form the Transport and General Workers' Union, which became a central component of the Labour party.

His selection as secretary of state for foreign affairs surprised most observers, who expected him to be named chancellor of the exchequer. Considering Bevin the best man in the Labour party, Eden was pleased with the choice. If the Soviets had any illusions that Bevin, with his socialist background, would be sympathetic to their needs and demands, they were mistaken. The new foreign minister possessed a long-standing antipathy to communism, dating back to his days as a labor organizer. While his earthy manner contrasted markedly with the urbanity of Eden, he was not outdone by his predecessor in defense of British overseas interests or in opposition to Russian expansionism. Being briefed on British policy, he murmured, "My God, my God, what a mess. My God"; too many baubles had been thrown to the Soviet government. Determined to resist any further reduction of his country's interests, Bevin, much more than Attlee, served as the British spokesman.[42]

The Conference Resumes

On the evening of July 28 the plenary sessions were resumed, but the new British team did not alter the basic lines of disagreement. Molotov read a list of fifteen issues still to be resolved. Ignoring his foreign minister, Stalin demanded to know why the Soviet government had not been informed about the Potsdam Proclamation, an Anglo-American declaration issued on July 26 and calling upon Japan to surrender or face destruction.[43] After a brief exchange in which Stalin informed the other delegations of a new peace feeler from Japan, attention was turned to some of the topics on Molotov's list. Some progress was made in discussions regarding the entry of Italy into the United Nations and the reparations it would pay. The Americans and the British flatly refused to allow the Soviets to claim any industries or goods as reparations except those that could not be used in peaceful pursuits. Truman said that he had no intention of allowing goods and money provided by the United States for the Italians to be used as reparations. "We don't object to reparations, but we are not going to send the money to pay them."[44]

Following the July 28 session, there was another lull of several days. Stalin was indisposed. Whether he was really ill or simply needed time to consider the implications of the Anglo-American declaration on Japan and to assess the new British delegation cannot be known, but the two-day suspension of plenary meetings gave Byrnes the opportunity to horse-trade in an effort to save the conference.

On July 29, Byrnes and Truman labored with Molotov to find common ground on the Polish and German issues. The Americans indicated they might reconsider the reparations question if the Poles would accept the Oder and eastern Neisse rivers as a frontier. Molotov was sure the boundary was not possible but asked if the Soviet Union might receive a specific amount, $2 billion, in reparations from the Ruhr. While the Americans conceded that the Soviet Union could get 50 percent of all reparations as promised at Yalta and 25 percent of the equipment found in the Ruhr, they shied away from commitments to amounts in hard currency.[45]

To the Soviets, reparations were more important than boundaries, and Stalin might have sold out the Poles if they had not so vociferously protested when, in spite of his "illness," he consulted with them during the evening of July 29. At the same time, the Americans and British were reconsidering their positions. The following day, Byrnes was ready with a series of proposals. He announced that the United States was willing to accept the western Neisse as Poland's western border. This concession was part of a package that included reparations and criteria for admission to the United Nations. Byrnes recommended that each occupying power take reparations from its own zone and that the Soviet Union be permitted additional reparations from the western zones. The third part of the proposal was to allow the forthcoming Council of Foreign Ministers to give the drafting of the Italian peace treaty first priority so that Italy could be invited to join the United Nations.

It was now up to the Soviets to modify their demands. When Molotov clung to the old ones, Byrnes told him to consult Stalin, coldly informing the Soviet foreign minister that the United States "would agree to all three or none and that the President and I would leave for the United States the next day."[46]

The absence of a plenary session the following day provided Truman with a chance to enter his observations in his diary:

> I am wondering what would happen to Russia and Central Europe if Joe [Stalin] suddenly passed out. . . . I also wonder if there is a man with the necessary strength and following to step into Stalin's shoes. . . . I've seen no one at this Conference in the Russian line-up who can do the job. Molotov is not able to do it. He lacks sincerity. Vishinsky same thing and [Ivan M.] Maisky [deputy commissar of foreign affairs] is short on honesty. We shall see. Uncle Joe's pretty tough mentally and physically but there is an end to every man and we can't help but speculate.
>
> We are at an impasse on Poland and its western boundary and on reparations. Russia and Poland have agreed on the Oder and West Neisse to the Czechoslovakian border. Just a unilateral arrangement without so much as a by your leave. I don't like it. Roosevelt let Maisky mention twenty billion as reparations—half for Russia and half for everybody else. Experts say no such figure is available.
>
> I've made it plain the United States of America does not intend to pay reparations this time. I want the German war industry machine completely dismantled and as far as U.S. is concerned the other allies can divide it up on any basis they

choose. Food and other necessities we send into the restored countries and Germany must be first lien on exports before reparations. If Russians strip the country and carry off population of course there'll be no reparations.

I have offered a waterway program and a suggestion for free intercourse between Central European nations which will help keep future peace. Our only hope from the European War is restored prosperity to Europe and future trade with them. It is a sick situation at best.

On the same day, Truman wrote to his mother that "you never saw such pig-headed people as are the Russians."[47]

When the delegations met on July 31, Byrnes reintroduced the American proposals, hoping they would be accepted intact. He clarified the American position on the percentage of reparations to come from the western zones. Having set it at 20 percent of the total, he announced that only 7.5 percent would be a free grant to the Soviet Union. To receive the remaining 12.5 percent the Soviets would have to provide coal and food to the western zones. Stalin did not like the proposal and argued for a simple figure of $10 billion for total Soviet reparations, but neither the British nor the Americans would agree to a dollar amount. Seeing Attlee and Truman willing to move, Stalin turned to negotiating the percentages to be received from the western zones. The outcome was that 25 percent of all industrial equipment in the three western zones not needed for Germany's peacetime economy would be transferred to the Soviet Union. Ten percent of that amount would be free; the rest would have to be exchanged for coal and food from the Soviet zone.

The second and third parts of Byrnes's package received approval after little debate. Bevin had strong reservations about accepting the western Neisse as Poland's administrative border but agreed after emphasizing that the border would not be finalized until the peace conference.[48] Italy was given first priority in the drafting of its peace treaty, and following Italy's the treaties for Bulgaria, Romania, Hungary, and Finland would be considered.[49]

Having broken their deadlock on reparations and the Polish frontier, the delegates directed their attention to the items that were assigned to special committees or, being relatively uncontroversial in nature, had a low priority. In rapid succession, agreements were reached. First was to establish the general economic principle that Germany should be considered as a single economic unit. Second, they agreed that German nationals living in Poland, Czechoslovakia, and Hungary should be expelled from those countries. It was a quick and callous decision that affected an estimated fifteen million Germans and may have resulted in the deaths of nearly two million of the displaced.[50]

The leaders next divided up Germany's shipping, agreeing that the navy and merchant marine should be split equally among the three powers. Seeing that the hour was late, the conferees assigned Truman's project on the internationalization of inland waterways to the Council of Foreign Ministers. After a few more observations the delegates agreed that they should be able to conclude their deliberations within the next two days.

August 1 was an extremely busy day, as the delegates wound up their affairs at Potsdam. The foreign ministers worked all morning preparing final drafts of the agreements reached. During the afternoon session, Stalin abruptly stated that the Soviets claimed nothing in the western zones, but he added that everything east of the military demarcation line "should go to us." Clarifying Stalin's remarks, Truman and Attlee accepted that German assets in Finland, Hungary, Romania, Bulgaria, and eastern Austria would go to Russia, but not those in Czechoslovakia, Yugoslavia, and Greece. This candid division of the spoils gave open recognition to the reality of power politics, establishing shadowy outlines of spheres of influence.

In a relaxed mood the three leaders marched through a host of minor issues, agreeing to some and deferring many to the Council of Foreign Ministers. Unspecified Nazis would be brought to trial (Stalin had wanted to name them), France could join the Reparations Commission, and no reparations would be demanded from Austria. They agreed that their armed forces would be withdrawn from Iran, and Stalin promised that the Soviet chairmen of the Allied Control Councils in Soviet-occupied countries, especially in Romania and Bulgaria, would give the American and British representatives more say in deliberations. A few hours later the Big Three met again to approve more corrections, more modifications, and the wording of the communiqué.[51]

Truman asked if any secret agreements had been made and was assured that there were none.[52] In reality, he was aware of three related secrets: the approaching Soviet entry into the Pacific war, a Japanese peace effort being made through the Soviets, and the decision to drop atomic bombs on one or more targeted Japanese cities. The first two "secrets" were known to all three delegations; the last, only to the Americans and the British. The public knew of none.

Ending the War with Japan

Months earlier, Stalin had promised to enter the war against Japan, as he reaffirmed on July 18 to Truman. The middle of August was projected as a date, but the official communiqué only stated that the three chiefs of staff had met "on military matters of common interest." At the time that Stalin had promised to join the war against Japan, he had informed Truman of receiving an overture from the Japanese regarding peace. It was something the United States already knew, having intercepted the diplomatic message from Tokyo to Moscow. Truman made light of it, saying that the Japanese were untrustworthy and that he knew of similar information from the Allied powers and Sweden. It was agreed that the Soviets would send a "general and unspecific answer." Neither Truman nor Stalin seemed interested in following up any possibility that Japan wished to surrender.[53]

The other secret, which might have shaped Truman's response to any Japanese motion toward peace, involved the exact nature of the new, powerful weapon to be used against Japan. As the Potsdam meeting began, Truman received confirmation that the atomic bomb had been tested successfully and would be ready as early as August 1. He immediately authorized its use as soon as possible and informed Churchill that it could be dropped at almost any time. The two Western leaders had agreed not to tell Stalin the specifics of the bomb before it was employed. Some within the American and British delegations, including Churchill, hoped that dropping the bomb early in August would end the war before the Soviet Union became involved.

Churchill told Eden that "it is quite clear that the United States do not at the present time desire Russian participation in the war against Japan."[54]

Churchill's assessment was only partially correct. Several high-ranking advisers, including Secretary of State Byrnes, hoped that the atomic bomb would end the war before a Soviet invasion of Manchuria and Korea, and that it even would make the Soviets more manageable in Eastern Europe. But there were other equally powerful officials, including Secretary of War Stimson, who believed that information about the bomb should be shared with the Soviets. Truman selected a path between the two views; he decided to tell Stalin only that a previously unknown weapon was available. Truman later wrote: "On July 24, I casually mentioned to Stalin that we had a new weapon of an unusual destructive force. The Russian Premier showed no special interest. All he said was he was glad to hear it and hoped we would make 'good use of it against the Japanese.' "[55]

Stalin's lack of reaction and follow-up questions was probably due to his already knowing about the atomic bomb. The Soviets had spies within the Manhattan Project and may have known about the test in New Mexico almost as soon as Truman. According to Marshal Georgy Zhukov, that evening Stalin told him and Molotov: "They simply want to raise the price. We've got to work on [I. V.] Kurchatov [the director of atomic research in the Soviet Union] and hurry things up."[56]

Truman and Churchill's knowledge of the "secrets" prompted the July 26 release of the Potsdam Proclamation. The writing of the proclamation was begun earlier by Stimson and State Department officials. By July 24 it was complete enough for the president to show it to Churchill. The prime minister made a few minor changes and signed it. The document was then forwarded to Chiang Kai-shek for his approval. Stalin was not informed until two days later, once the proclamation had been sent to Japan and was about to be made available to the press.

Without specifically mentioning the atomic bomb or the Soviet pledge to enter the conflict, the proclamation warned Japan that unprecedented, enormous forces were about to be unleashed if it did not surrender unconditionally. The document established terms, the most important of which were the following:

> There must be eliminated for all time the authority and influence of those who have deceived and misled the people of Japan into embarking on world conquest. . . .
>
> The Japanese military forces, after being completely disarmed, shall be permitted to return to their homes with the opportunity to lead peaceful and productive lives. . . . stern justice shall be meted out to all war criminals, including those who have visited cruelties upon our prisoners.
>
> The occupying forces of the Allies shall be withdrawn from Japan as soon as these objectives have been accomplished and there has been established in accordance with the freely expressed will of the Japanese people a peacefully inclined and responsible government. We call upon the Government of Japan to proclaim now the unconditional surrender of all Japanese armed forces, and to provide proper and adequate assurances of their good faith in such action. The alternative for Japan is prompt and utter destruction.[57]

When the heads of state met on July 28, two days after the release of the proclamation and one day after Attlee and Bevin had arrived to assume command of the British delegation, Stalin suddenly was interested in discussing Japan. After complaining that he had not been informed of the proclamation, he said that the Japanese government wanted to know if the British and Americans would be willing to meet with former Prime Minister Prince Fumimaro Konoe to negotiate a surrender on less rigid terms than those mentioned in the proclamation. Stalin suggested that a negative reply be sent to Japan; Truman and Attlee agreed. Pierson Dixon, of the British delegation, noticed that Stalin seemed suddenly frightened by the knowledge "that all the victories which he had gained over months and years through guile and military strength could be washed away in hours by the Anglo-American nuclear weapon."[58]

An official and public response to the proclamation came on July 30. Prime Minister Baron Kantaro Suzuki publicly announced: "The Japanese Government has found nothing important or interesting in the Allied declaration, and anticipated no action than to ignore it completely."[59] Thus ended all communication between the parties; the West concluded that the Japanese were not prepared to surrender. Truman confirmed his decision to use the atomic bomb during the first week in August.

Truman was at sea, returning home from Potsdam, when the *Enola Gay* dropped an atomic bomb over Hiroshima, at 9:15 A.M. on August 6. Hiroshima was Japan's eighth largest city, with a population of nearly 250,000. Almost 100,000 were killed or terribly maimed by the awful detonation, and another 100,000 would be crippled or finally die from the effects of radiation.

In Washington, Stimson authorized a presidential declaration already prepared for release: "It was to spare the Japanese people from utter destruction that the ultimatum of July 26 was issued at Potsdam. Their leaders promptly rejected that ultimatum. If they do not now accept our terms, they may expect a rain of ruin from the air, the like of which has never been seen on this earth."[60]

Suzuki and Foreign Minister Shigenori Tojo, having obtained confirmation that what had destroyed Hiroshima was an atomic bomb, intensified their efforts to seek a negotiated peace by way of Moscow. But the Soviets would no longer consider playing the role of intermediary. Molotov not only refused to accept the Japanese plea but also informed the ambassador on August 8 that the Soviet Union was declaring war on Japan. Within hours, Soviet troops poured across the border into Japanese-held Manchuria.

The following day, as a high-level Japanese government council was being convoked, the second atomic bomb, Fat Man, fell on Nagasaki, killing nearly sixty thousand people and inflicting enormous damage, although not as great as that which devastated Hiroshima. The United States had one atomic bomb left, which was yet to be assembled and whose earliest use probably would have been around August 18. But the Japanese government had no way of knowing when, how many, or which additional cities might be attacked. Prime Minister Suzuki and the emperor supported surrender, while the military opposed it. Finally, during the small hours of the morning on August 10, Emperor Hirohito personally instructed a stunned cabinet that Japan must "support the insupportable" and sue for peace. A message was then sent through Switzerland informing the United States that Japan accepted the Potsdam Proclamation, provided nothing prejudiced the emperor's prerogatives.

How much authority to leave to the emperor was a matter of serious debate among American officials. A number of Truman's advisers saw wisdom in letting the emperor retain some power, but hard-liners believed that it would be a mistake to soften the doctrine of unconditional surrender. After much discussion, Truman finally decided to assure the Japanese that the ultimate form of government would be established by the freely expressed will of their people. It was a statement that left the position of the emperor ambiguous. But, with Soviet forces rapidly advancing through Manchuria and southern Sakhalin Island, and with the possibility of a third atomic bomb's being exploded, Emperor Hirohito accepted the American ultimatum. On August 15 his voice was broadcast throughout the empire, announcing the official surrender. Fighting gradually ceased over the vast area still held by Japan, and on September 2, aboard the USS *Missouri* in Tokyo Bay, Japanese representatives signed the documents of surrender, ending the Second World War.[61]

By September 2, American, British, and Soviet officials were evaluating the results of the Potsdam Conference in preparation for the first meeting of the Council of Foreign Ministers. The heads of state and their delegations had conferred for sixteen days, and, despite underlying tensions, their meetings had been more open and relaxed than those at Yalta and Tehran. The Big Three all believed that the summit had been a success.

The Soviets had a short list of important diplomatic accomplishments. They accepted the understandings about German policy, especially reparations, and were pleased that Poland's western border was established at the Oder and western Neisse. The Soviet Union had received the city of Königsberg and a sizable part of East Prussia. The governments it sponsored in Poland, Romania, Bulgaria, and Hungary were still in control, although the Americans and the British had not agreed to recognize those regimes. *Izvestia* concluded that the conference had "strengthened the ties between the three governments and widened the limits of their cooperation and understanding."[62]

Despite Churchill's bitter words that after he left there was no one to oppose the ambitions of Stalin in the West and in the Mediterranean, the British delegation believed it, too, had accomplished some worthwhile results. Bevin had proved to be as hard-nosed as Churchill, conducting British policy in a businesslike manner and providing "confidence to all around" him. The British noted that the Soviets, while receiving a larger percentage of reparations from the western zones with Byrnes's approval, had given up claims to German assets in the West and efforts to participate in controlling the Ruhr. If Stalin had protected his interests in Eastern Europe, the British thought that they had protected theirs in the Mediterranean. Churchill had championed Franco and resisted Soviet efforts to expand their influence into Tangier, Libya, Turkey, Syria, Suez, Iran, Trieste, and Greece; Bevin had not given away any British positions and had made it clear that he and his government would not be ignored. Dixon concluded that, while the British might have been able to extract "concessions from the Russians over eastern Germany and the Satellites," it probably would have meant making "concessions in Western Germany and the Middle East." To his question, "Was it worth having democracy in Eastern Europe if it meant having the Russians in the Mediterranean?" for most within the British delegation the answer would have been, No.[63]

For the Americans the most important issues had been resolved: Soviet entry into the Japanese war and support for the Open Door in China, a means of establishing peace treaties with Germany and its European allies (the Council of Foreign Ministers), and a general understanding about political and economic policies for Germany. The United States also had upheld its dislike for the East European regimes and its demand that more representative governments be created. As the delegation returned home, however, its attention was focused more on Japan and the atomic bomb than on the results of the Potsdam meeting.

Truman learned of the bombing of Hiroshima a few minutes before noon on board the cruiser *Augusta* as he and his delegation sailed back to the United States. Upon reading the telegram, the president exclaimed that "this is the greatest thing in history." He might have overestimated the place of the bombing in history, but he did not miss the fact that the world had entered a new era. Secretary Stimson was more circumspect, writing in his diary: "Great events have happened. The world is changed and it is time for sober thought."

Stimson worried that nuclear power might add to the world's problems rather than help solve them. He was especially concerned about the connection between the bomb and Soviet-American relations. The difficulty was that "satisfactory relations" with the Soviet Union were "virtually dominated by the problem of the atomic bomb." He believed that the way to establish cooperation and to lighten the burden of atomic responsibility lay in a three-power "covenant"-style agreement that the Russians would not develop atomic weapons and the United States would share the peaceful applications of nuclear energy with the world. The alternative to such an agreement, he believed, would be an arms race "of a rather desperate character" that would prevent any hope of world stability.

Much to Stimson's disappointment and dismay, he found his view unpopular among policymakers. The majority seemed to agree with Byrnes that U.S. control of atomic information and bombs constituted an effective diplomatic tool. After meeting and talking to the secretary of state, Stimson lamented in his diary that he "found Byrnes was very much against any attempt to cooperate with Russia . . . and he looks to have the presence of the bomb in his pocket so to speak as a great weapon."[64] Any chance for an international system built upon cooperation and understanding, especially among the Big Three, was being replaced by old-fashioned politics and a balance of power. It was a matter of debate whether Byrnes's post-Hiroshima approach would fulfill the world's desire for stability and security.

Notes

1. Davis, *Cold War Begins*, 202–54.

2. Ibid., 282–87; Raymond Smith, "A Climate of Opinion: British Officials and the Development of British-Soviet Policy, 1945–7," *International Affairs* 64 (1988): 633; Foreign Office Correspondence, memorandum, June 11, 1945, F.O. 371, U4283/445/70, Public Record Office, Kew, England (hereafter cited as F.O. 371, followed by the document number); minute, July 9, 1946, F.O. 371, N9419/140/38, PRO.

3. Truman, *Memoirs* 1:302–4, 308, 327; John Gimbel, *The American Occupation of Germany, 1945–1949* (Stanford, 1968), 1–70.

4. Truman, *Memoirs* 1:314–15.

5. Lord Charles Moran, *Churchill: Taken from the Diaries of Lord Moran: The Struggles for Survival, 1940–1945* (Boston, 1966), 276.

6. Fraser J. Harbutt, *The Iron Curtain: Churchill, America, and the Origins of the Cold War* (New York, 1987), 110.

7. Winston S. Churchill, *The Second World War*, vol. 6, *Triumph and Tragedy* (Boston, 1953), 620; Truman, *Memoirs* 2:302–4, 327; *Private Papers of Harry S. Truman*, 50–52; Harbutt, *Iron Curtain*, 111–15.

8. Charles L. Mee, Jr., *Meeting at Potsdam* (New York, 1975), 29–31.

9. Truman, *Memoirs* 1:411; *Private Papers of Harry S. Truman*, 53; *FRUS: Berlin, 1945* 2:43–47, 1582–87.

10. *FRUS: Berlin, 1945* 2:1582–87; Herken, *Winning Weapon*, 345.

11. *FRUS: Berlin, 1945* 2:1360.

12. Ibid., 1362–66.

13. *Private Papers of Harry S. Truman*, 53–54; Lisle A. Rose, *After Yalta: America and the Origins of the Cold War* (New York, 1973), 78–79.

14. The verbatim texts of the conference are found in volume 2 of *FRUS: Berlin, 1945*; the Soviet version of the plenary sessions is found (in English) in *Tehran, Yalta and Potsdam Conferences* (Moscow, 1969). For studies of the Potsdam Conference see Herbert Feis, *Between War and Peace: The Potsdam Conference* (Princeton, 1960); John Wheeler Bennett and Anthony Nicholls, *The Semblance of Peace* (New York, 1972); and Sipols, *Road to Great Victory*.

15. *FRUS: Berlin, 1945* 2:52–63; *The Diaries of Sir Alexander Cadogan, 1938–1945*, ed. David Dilks (London, 1971), 765. Pierson Dixon, a member of the British delegation, called the sessions "acrimonious from the moment that the formal discussions began" (Pierson Dixon, *Double Diploma: The Life of Sir Pierson Dixon, Don and Diplomat* [London, 1968], 154).

16. Truman, *Memoirs* 1:349.

17. *FRUS: Berlin, 1945* 1:263, 285–86.

18. Legally, this provision excluded France from voting on any of the treaties, although ultimately it was accepted that France should be considered as having signed the Italian surrender instrument and allowed to vote on provisions of the peace treaties and the final treaty.

19. *FRUS: Berlin, 1945* 2:66–70; Rose, *After Yalta*, 46–48; Patricia D. Ward, *The Threat of Peace: James F. Byrnes and the Council of Foreign Ministers, 1945–46* (Kent, OH, 1979), 12–16.

20. *Life* 21 (September 19, 1946): 10; John C. Campbell, "Negotiating with the Soviets," *Foreign Affairs* 24 (January 1956): 305–19; State Department briefing paper, "Molotov," September 1, 1945, Department of State, RG 59, 740.00119 (Council), National Archives, Washington, DC (hereafter cited as DS, followed by file name or decimal file number).

21. Although France was allocated an occupation zone and a seat on the Allied Control Council, no French delegates attended the Potsdam meetings. This created an unusual situation in which France would be expected to accept the decisions made at Potsdam without having signed the final communiqué. Later, France announced that it had reservations

regarding certain of the decisions and argued that it was not bound by all of them.

22. *FRUS: Berlin, 1945* 2:78; Keith Eubank, *The Summit Conferences, 1919–1960* (Norman, OK, 1966), 116.

23. *FRUS: Berlin, 1945* 2:775.

24. Ibid., 775–78.

25. Ibid., 296–98; Robert A. Pollard, *Economic Security and the Origins of the Cold War, 1945–1950* (New York, 1985), 88–89.

26. *FRUS: Berlin, 1945* 2:277–79.

27. Ibid., 852.

28. Ibid., 275.

29. Byrnes, *Speaking Frankly*, 84; *FRUS: Berlin, 1945* 2:297.

30. *FRUS: Berlin, 1945* 2:53–54, 643–44; Davis, *Cold War Begins*, 288–90; Churchill, *Second World War* 6:636.

31. Italy already had been recognized by the three powers.

32. *Tehran, Yalta and Potsdam*, 248. The American version of the dialogue uses the words "fairy tales" in place of the word "fiction" in the Soviet version (*FRUS: Berlin, 1945* 2:362).

33. Truman, *Memoirs* 1:384; *Tehran, Yalta and Potsdam*, 248–51; *FRUS: Berlin, 1945* 2:359–64.

34. Truman, *Memoirs* 1:385–87; *FRUS: Berlin, 1945* 2:362–64; Davis, *Cold War Begins*, 290–93.

35. *FRUS: Berlin, 1945* 2:91–94.

36. Ibid., 225, 1361.

37. Ibid., 205–21, 247–52, 261–64; Churchill, *Second World War* 6:654–68; Moran, *Churchill*, 300; Truman, *Memoirs* 1:340.

38. *FRUS: Berlin, 1945* 2:251–52, 356–57; Truman, *Memoirs* 1:373; Churchill, *Second World War* 6:659–61.

39. *FRUS: Berlin, 1945* 2:389–90.

40. Churchill, *Second World War* 6:674; Harbutt, *Iron Curtain*, 78–81, 155–83, 280–85.

41. Raymond Smith and John Zametica, "The Cold Warrior: Clement Attlee Reconsidered, 1945–7," *International Affairs* 61 (1985): 237–42; Smith, "Climate of Opinion," 631–33; Mee, *Meeting at Potsdam*, 36–37. See also Kenneth Harris, *Attlee* (London, 1982).

42. Smith, "Climate of Opinion," 631–33; Gormly, *Collapse of the Grand Alliance*, 23–25; Rothwell, *Britain and the Cold War*, 222–25.

43. Truman believed that it was unnecessary to inform the Soviets, because they were not at war with Japan; but, in a gesture of good faith, he notified the Soviet delegation by letter on July 26 after the proclamation had been sent to Japan and prior to its being released to the press on the morning of July 27. In reply the Soviets wrote a request to postpone issuing the statement for two or three days, but the response came too late to prevent the delivery to either Japan or the press (*FRUS: Berlin, 1945* 2:449–50; Truman, *Memoirs* 1:387).

44. Dixon, *Double Diploma*, 168–69; *FRUS: Berlin, 1945* 2:466–70.

45. *FRUS: Berlin, 1945* 2:472–76; Byrnes, *Speaking Frankly*, 85.

46. Mastny, *Road to the Cold War*, 299; Byrnes, *Speaking Frankly*, 85; *FRUS: Berlin, 1945* 2:480–83.

47. *Private Papers of Harry S. Truman*, 58; Truman, *Memoirs* 1:402.

48. The Soviet historian Vilnis Sipols points out that, because the Potsdam Conference provided for the German population to be evicted from the territories granted the Poles, the decisions were in effect final (Sipols, *Road to Great Victory*, 297). The boundaries became final by treaties between East and West Germany in 1950 and 1970.

49. *FRUS: Berlin, 1945* 2:528–38.

50. For a thorough study of this too little known episode see Alfred M. de Zayas, *Nemesis at Potsdam: The Anglo-Americans and the Expulsion of the Germans* (London, 1977).

51. *FRUS: Berlin, 1945* 2:511–40.

52. Truman, *Memoirs* 1:409.

53. *FRUS: Berlin, 1945* 2:43–46, 1582–90.

54. Churchill, *Second World War* 6:639; Herken, *Winning Weapon*, 17–22. On the issue of the Truman administration's reasons for dropping the atomic bomb see J. Samuel Walker, "The Decision to Use the Bomb: A Historiographical Update," *Diplomatic History* 14 (1990): 97–114.

55. Truman, *Memoirs* 1:416; Churchill, *Second World War* 6:639; Herken, *Winning Weapon*, 17–20.

56. Georgy K. Zhukov, *The Memoirs of Marshal Zhukov* (New York, 1971), 674–75. In his description of this incident the Soviet historian Vilnis Sipols does not provide any further information about Soviet nuclear work. He adds that "the first attempt of the U.S. President to resort to atomic blackmail failed. Then he decided to make a public demonstration of the atomic bomb, for the benefit, above all, of the Soviet Union" (*Road to Great Victory*, 294). The dropping of the atomic bomb on Hiroshima on August 6 probably advanced the date of the Soviet declaration of war and invasion of Manchuria to August 8. Stalin, in his earlier conversations with Truman, had stated that the Soviets would enter the war in the middle of the month, perhaps between August 12 and 25 (Herken, *Winning Weapon*, 21).

57. *FRUS: Berlin, 1945* 2:1474–76.

58. Dixon, *Double Diploma*, 168–69; *FRUS: Berlin, 1945* 2:467.

59. The Japanese word translated as "ignore" for President Truman is closer in meaning to "no comment"; the inaccurate translation therefore may be partly responsible for the conclusion drawn by the Allies. See Robert J. C. Butow, *Japan's Decision to Surrender* (Stanford, 1954), 145.

60. Barton J. Bernstein, "The Perils and Politics of Surrender: Ending the War with Japan and Avoiding the Third Atomic Bomb," *Pacific Historical Review* 48 (1977): 1–27.

61. Bernstein, "Politics of Surrender," 2–23; Butow, *Japan's Decision*, 189–227. For details on the events relating to Japan's decision to surrender see also Herbert Feis, *The Atomic Bomb and the End of World War II* (Princeton, 1966); Edwin P. Hoyt, *Closing the Circle* (New York, 1982); and Leon V. Sigal, *Fighting to a Finish: The Politics of War Termination in the United States and Japan* (Ithaca, 1988).

62. William H. McNeil, *America, Britain, and Russia: Their Cooperation and Conflict, 1941–1946* (New York, 1953), 628–29; Taubman, *Stalin's American Policy*, 111–12.

63. Dixon, *Double Diploma*, 176–77; Eubank, *Summit Conferences*, 132–34; McNeil, *America, Britain, and Russia*, 628–29; Alan Bullock, *Ernest Bevin: Foreign Secretary, 1945–1951* (New York, 1983), 25–30.

64. Herken, *Winning Weapon*, 22–27.

III

The Decline of the Grand Alliance, September– December 1945

A large part of the success of the Potsdam Conference was purchased by deferral: the explosive issues of the peace treaties with Romania, Bulgaria, and Italy were referred to the newly created Council of Foreign Ministers. The council was an affirmation that the postwar settlement would be primarily a product of cooperation among the Big Three. With the addition of France and China, it resembled Franklin D. Roosevelt's concept of the Five Policemen more than the United Nations, which was to assemble in six months. The Soviet press stated that the collaboration of the war years could continue only if the governments were inspired by the spirit of Yalta.

The spirit of Yalta and, to a lesser extent, Potsdam, however, was a result of the war. The war was over. Gone were the immediate diplomatic needs mandated by the cooperation necessary to defeat the Axis powers. The international situation was fluid, yet all realized the fluidity would not last long. Already, new priorities and policies were being formulated, reflecting new perspectives and goals. As one British official said, it was the time to stake claims and establish positions, before the world situation hardened.[1]

Over the weeks and months following Potsdam the foreign ministers met to test their new policies and perceptions. As they debated and negotiated with one another, their wartime collaboration dissipated into distrust and rancor. Eventually, the peace treaties with Germany's

allies would be written, but the postwar settlement to
emerge would be vastly different from that symbolized by
Yalta and the Five Policemen. The London Conference of
the Council of Foreign Ministers was the beginning of the
process that would mold postwar international relations
and the world.

As hosts of the meeting, the British began preparing the
draft agenda in mid-August 1945. It included issues
referred to the council at the Potsdam Conference and
questions the Foreign Office thought one or more of the
conferees would want to discuss. Of the fourteen original
draft topics, British officials speculated that three Potsdam
referrals (the peace treaties for Italy, Romania, and
Bulgaria) and two expected questions (Romanian internal
affairs and Japan) would generate the most debate. Each of
the five reflected strong national interests and concerns.
Each represented areas where such interests and concerns
overlapped and impinged upon one another.

The controversy over Romania and Bulgaria arose from
the unwillingness of Britain and the United States to give
the Soviet Union a free hand in the Balkans, which, they
feared, would shut out Western influence. The Americans
and British had rejected Soviet-sponsored governments in
both nations and had refused to sign their peace treaties.
Knowing of U.S. efforts to oust the pro-Soviet regime of Petru
Groza in Romania, the Foreign Office had added that
country to the agenda as an American request. If
successful the Americans would perhaps be able to
establish tripartite responsibility in Eastern Europe and,
thereby, better protect Western interests.

It was assumed that the Russians would staunchly
defend their puppet governments, and the British expected
an American-Soviet clash on the matter, with possible
Soviet reactions in the Balkans and Mediterranean. The
Russians previously had stated that "there was no cause to
show any favours to Italy which should not be extended to
Bulgaria, etc." Sir Orme Sargent suggested that, to aid
Britain's position, "we could play occasionally peace-maker
between the U.S. [and] the Soviet Government," taking a
middle stand on Romania and Bulgaria.

The British assessment of American intentions was not
far from the mark. Secretary Byrnes did plan to press for
the removal of Groza and the creation of more repre-

sentative governments in Romania and Bulgaria. W. Averell Harriman was first to try to convince Molotov that a solution to the Romanian political problem could be found "with the Russians at London in a calmer atmosphere." Molotov refused the offer, reaffirmed his support for the Romanian and Bulgarian governments, and told Groza that eventually the Soviets could convince the British and Americans to recognize his government and conclude the peace treaty. There soon followed editorials in *Pravda* and *Izvestia* praising the two governments and implying that Anglo-American actions in southeastern Europe would weigh heavily in the Soviets' assessments of Western intentions toward them and world peace.[2]

Of more importance to the planners in London was the issue of Italy and its African colonies. Both the British and the Americans agreed that it was absolutely necessary to deny the Soviets any influence in Italy. The country had to remain firmly within the Western orbit, and it therefore was important to please the Italians. This would require meeting their desires regarding the disposition of their colonies and the Yugoslav border, the amount of reparations, and the size of their armed forces. Similarly, American officials believed that it made no sense to weaken economically or militarily "a prospective friend in southeastern Europe and the Mediterranean."

The State Department concluded that it was "foolish to debate" Italian justifications and was willing to yield on nearly every issue. Especially important in keeping Italy happy was the placing of nearly all of Venezia Giulia in its hands. This region is the territory between the Po Valley and the Danubian basin; it contains the port cities of Trieste and Rijeka (Fiume) that link Europe to the Adriatic Sea. It constitutes a natural crossroads connecting the Italian peninsula, the Balkans, and central Europe. Both Yugoslavia, whose troops occupied part of Trieste and the eastern half of the region, and Italy claimed Trieste and most of the surrounding area. Italy had no troops there, relying on British and American occupation forces to protect its interests and citizens, who made up the majority of the population in the urban areas. Yugoslavia claimed to represent the largely Slavic rural population and Communists within the major cities. The State Department believed that the territory should have been divided along the

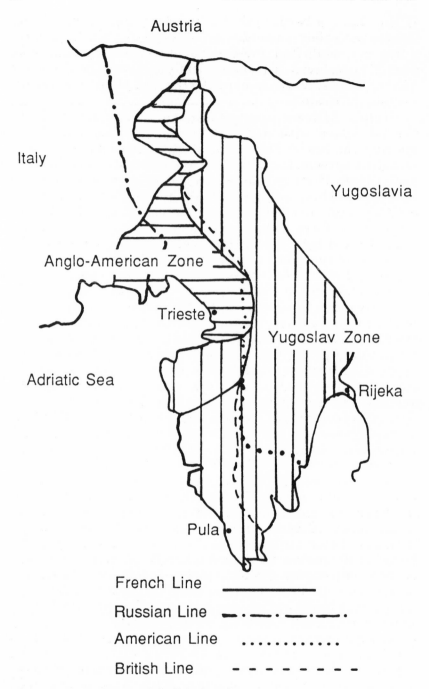

Map 2. Occupation zones of the Trieste region.

Wilson Line, a border ethnically determined in 1919, with Trieste put safely under Italian rule. Rijeka would be made a free city, while Zadar (Zara) would become an autonomous part of Yugoslavia. Western officials expected the Soviets to uphold Yugoslavia's demand for nearly all of the region, including Trieste.[3]

Italy's African colonies presented Britain and the United States with a problem. Beyond the necessity of keeping the Soviet Union out of any of the colonies, there was little agreement. The State Department's Near Eastern and African Division wanted to place the colonies under a UN trusteeship, while the European Division and the military recommended that Italy be the trustee. The Special Political Affairs Branch favored having the colonies administered by a special commission composed of the five members of the Council of Foreign Ministers and Italy. As Byrnes left for London, no decision had been made.

The plans of the British for Italy reflected their country's Mediterranean interests. They wanted to keep the Soviets out of the region, and, fearful of rivals in the Mediterranean, they sought a smaller Italian military than that wanted by the Italians. More important, Britain hoped to gain control over the lion's share of Italy's African colonies. With the threat of nationalism in Egypt and the possible loss of military bases there, British planners looked toward the colony of Cyrenaica, the eastern part of Libya, as a replacement. If such an arrangement became impossible, the Foreign Office recommended making Italy the trustee of its previous colonies.

Britain, like the United States, recognized that the Soviets would object to many aspects of their proposed treatment for Italy, but the Foreign Office hoped that the Russians would be willing to trade Italy for Romania and Bulgaria. Bevin instructed the Foreign Office to support the Soviet draft treaties for Romania and Bulgaria if the Soviets in turn supported British plans for Italy. From his perspective, it was the Americans and their inability to recognize a brick wall in southeastern Europe that loomed as likely problems in forming a deal on Italy.[4]

Byrnes did not intend to fight British policy unless it stood in the way of achieving American goals. In truth, he expected to lead while Bevin and, to a lesser extent, Molotov followed. After all, Byrnes was in Stalin's words the "best

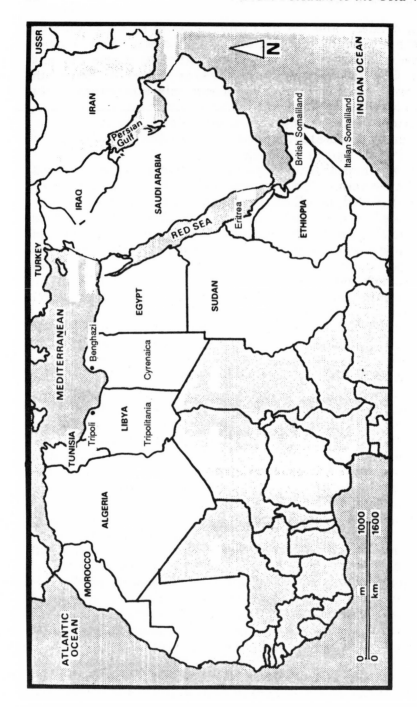

Map 3. Italian colonies in Africa. *(Historical Maps on File)*

horse trader," and his own talents would be supplemented by the economic, military, and atomic power of the United States. Among State Department officials, it was thought that Britain's ability to oppose or obstruct American interests would be limited by its economic dependence on the United States. It already was negotiating for a major American loan. England must follow the Americans, Harriman speculated; "she will do anything that we insist and she won't go out on a limb alone."

It was hoped that the same economic power would work on the Soviets. Their request for an American loan was, Bevin believed, an effective, if not the most effective, "hidden pressure" to gain "political demands from Russia." This was not Byrnes's only weapon. There was also the atomic bomb, whose power was as obvious as the American monopoly over it. Byrnes told friends that it just may make the Soviets more reasonable in their policies. He left for London confident that he would protect American interests and establish the beginnings of an enduring peace.[5]

Byrnes was too self-assured. Even the British, in their initial discussions on the draft agenda, considered proposals that would collide with American interests. The Foreign Office wanted to discuss Japan. The United States was acting "as independently as possible in controlling Japan," Bevin explained to the cabinet. He wanted to "put forward as soon as possible a plan" for an Allied Control Council that would ensure full British participation. Expecting the Chinese and Soviets to have similar attitudes, the Foreign Office solicited their support for adding the question of Japan to the agenda. Both nations replied favorably.

The final draft agenda, however, was missing any mention of an Allied Control Council for Japan. Almost as the delegates arrived in London, Bevin decided to delete the issue from the agenda. Reflecting Harriman's observation, the foreign secretary feared that it might anger the Americans and thereby threaten British economic negotiations with them. Nearly all observers believed that the success of the conference would depend on the major powers' ability to maintain their wartime relationship. If they did not, T. V. Soong, the Chinese foreign minister, told Bevin, "the outlook would be extremely bleak" for the future. Among those closely watching events in London, there was almost total agreement that success or failure would rest largely on Molotov's actions.[6]

The London Conference

The shaping of the postwar world began on the afternoon of September 11, 1945. The foreign ministers of the Big Three were joined by Georges Bidault of France and Wang Shih-chieh of China, and gathered in Lancaster House, a gilded and marble mansion near London's Hyde Park. Bevin, as host, called the delegates to order and presented the draft agenda. But, before the agenda could be considered, Byrnes offered a procedural point. He asked that all representatives be allowed to discuss all questions.

According to the Potsdam protocol, peace treaties could be considered and voted upon by only those nations that had signed the "terms of surrender." Neither China nor France had signed such terms with any of the East European nations, and possibly the Soviets would deny them even the opportunity to discuss the treaties. Byrnes, supported by Bevin, was in effect asking Molotov to allow the Chinese and French to deliberate and vote on the draft treaties. The formula for voting agreed upon at Berlin would be applied to the finished documents. If Molotov concurred, Britain and the United States would have a 4-to-1 advantage on the issue because France and China were expected automatically to support the Anglo-American position. Such a majority could prove invaluable in determining the clauses that would compose the final treaties. To nearly everyone's surprise, Molotov agreed, after ensuring that the Berlin formula for voting would be followed. The meeting had begun well for Bevin and Byrnes.[7]

Discussion of the agenda, however, quickly raised tempers and revealed a variety of negotiating tactics. Byrnes began by objecting to two supposedly American-initiated topics: Romanian internal affairs and the Black Sea straits. While the items were of interest to the United States, he saw no reason to treat them as separate issues. He requested that they be removed from the agenda, and they were.

Molotov asked why Japan was missing from the agenda. If Byrnes could make an issue of Romanian affairs, the Soviet minister could counter by bringing up Japan. After some heated discussion in which Molotov jabbed at British actions in Greece and Indonesia, eight topics were set as the agenda:

1) Italy's peace treaty and colonies;
2) treaties for Romania, Hungary, and Bulgaria;
3) a treaty for Finland;
4) the withdrawal of Allied troops from Iran;
5) the internationalization of inland waterways;
6) the repatriation of Soviet citizens;
7) decisions made at Potsdam regarding Germany; and
8) the work of the German Reparations Commission.[8]

The following days saw the spirit of Yalta erode as the ministers began work on the treaties. At one point, Byrnes observed that "none of them was in a very good mood." The mood, however, improved somewhat during a gala dinner at the House of Lords, during which he was able to conduct some of his best back-room diplomacy. The South Carolinian asked Molotov when he was "going to get his sightseeing completed and . . . get down to business." The Soviet minister laughed and asked if Byrnes had "an atomic bomb in his side pocket." "You don't know Southerners," Byrnes replied. "We carry our artillery in our hip pocket. If you can't cut out all this stalling and let us get down to work, I am going to pull an atomic bomb out of my hip pocket and let you have it." Later that evening he again chided his colleague about getting to work: "Mr. Molotov, I don't think that vodka you drink agreed with you. What you need under your chest is two or three Kentucky Bourbons. I know they would make you feel better and then we might get down to work." Again, all laughed, but none mistook the seriousness of Byrnes's words.[9]

The next formal session found Molotov with a better attitude, and work began on the Italian treaty. Discussions of the British draft were proceeding smoothly until the United States presented a proposal on the disposition of the African colonies. Its harshness toward Italy's role as a colonizing power surprised the other delegates, even the Soviets, who quickly agreed with the negative assessment.

The proposal had just been drafted, following a midnight decision, to prevent Soviet participation in administering any Italian colonies. It called for a collective trusteeship governed by a UN administrator and advised by a committee composed of a European, a native from the territory involved, and representatives of Italy, Great Britain, France, the United States, and the Soviet Union. It was a formula that would exclude meaningful Soviet influence in the region.

Only China supported Byrnes's proposal. The rest asked for time to consider such a novel concept. Then Bidault and Molotov spoke in favor of single trustees, the French minister suggesting Italy and the Soviet preferring to divide the colonies among the four European powers, with his country receiving Tripolitania. Molotov seemed adamant. In a private meeting with Byrnes, he emphasized that Russia was not an average member of the United Nations but a victorious power that "had the right to play a more active part [in] the fate of the Italian colonies than any rank and file member." What Byrnes and Bevin feared had occurred: a Soviet request for a trusteeship on the Mediterranean. They were equally determined to prevent any Soviet influence in the region.[10]

By September 15 sides had been chosen. Britain, France, China, and the United States opposed the Soviet Union's bid for a trusteeship. Referring to his country's "vital interests" in the region, Bevin voiced surprise at the Soviet request. He proceeded to support the American proposal "with the view of avoiding friction between the Great Powers." Gone was any hope of a trusteeship for Britain.

Undaunted by the opposition, Molotov launched into a loud and lengthy statement supporting the Soviet Union's request for a trusteeship. "Italy had attacked, and had inflicted enormous damage upon, the Soviet Union . . . Britain should not hold a monopoly of all communications in the Mediterranean. Russia was anxious to have bases . . . for her merchant fleet. World trade would develop and the Soviet Union wished to take her share in it." He promised that "the Soviet system" would not be introduced into Tripolitania. Democracy would be promoted, although, he added, not along the lines "recently followed in Greece."[11]

As the debate continued the Soviets introduced draft treaties for Romania and Bulgaria. Byrnes and his advisers found them unacceptable because they would "eliminate American participation in the reconstruction of the Balkans and would guarantee the USSR an even more important role than her physical position and power would insure." Unwilling to abandon democracy and "equality of economic opportunity" in southeastern Europe, Byrnes concluded that it was time "to let Molotov know that the U.S. would remain firm in its stand on the Balkans."[12]

Meeting alone with Molotov, Byrnes argued that, while the United States wanted governments friendly to Russia along its borders, there was no reason why those regimes could not be truly representative as well. He asked for a Polish-style broadening of the Romanian government of Petru Groza. When Molotov rejected the idea, Byrnes countered that the United States "could not conclude treaties with the existing governments." The Soviet minister said that the American attitude would foster "a very bad impression" within his government. He then resumed his efforts to gain a Soviet trusteeship of one of Italy's colonies. Former Secretary of State Edward Stettinius, he informed Byrnes, "had assured Ambassador [Andrey] Gromyko that the United States was prepared to support the Soviet Government in its request to receive a territory for administration under trusteeship." Byrnes argued that his predecessor's pledge affirmed the "principle" of a Soviet trusteeship but did not commit the United States to supporting a specific claim. Molotov correctly concluded that "the United States did not wish the Soviet Union to have any territory under trusteeship."[13]

The abrasive tone of the private meeting carried over into the following council sessions. Byrnes's aide Walter Brown called one "a knock-down drag-out affair" in which "for the first time Molotov was critical of the U.S." Angered by the Soviet minister's remarks and obstinacy, Byrnes composed a strong statement to precede the American amendment to the Soviet treaties for Romania and Bulgaria: "The United States will not negotiate a treaty of peace with Rumania until there has been established a government broadly representative of all democratic elements in the population and pledged to the earliest possible establishment through free elections of a government responsive to the will of the people, which can be recognized by the United States." It was an escalation of the war of words recently begun with

Molotov. Byrnes's closest advisers strongly opposed the statement. John Foster Dulles believed that it would "force a Soviet defense of Groza," make the Soviets more rigid, and hinder relations. Rejecting this view, Byrnes readied the statement for formal presentation.[14]

Meeting with Molotov the next morning, Byrnes read the statement. Clearly angered, the Soviet minister announced that all of Hitler's allies looked the same to the Kremlin, and, if the United States "refused to sign the treaties with Rumania and Bulgaria, the Soviet Union could not sign the treaty with Italy." President Roosevelt had been friendly toward his nation, Molotov noted, but that had changed. Later, when Byrnes presented the document to the council, Molotov again lashed out at the secretary, saying that the Soviet Union could not ignore such a statement and that a reply soon would be coming.

On the next day, while waiting for the response, the ministers referred the Italian peace treaty, including the trusteeship question, to their deputies. Byrnes asked that the deputies' draft be based "on a majority view," meaning that France and China would continue to discuss and shape the treaty. As on the opening day, he hoped to place the Soviets at a disadvantage. Molotov thought that it "was an interesting but new suggestion and he would like a day or two to consider it."[15]

The London Conference had reached a turning point. The United States had dominated the proceedings, putting forward its objections to the Romanian and Bulgarian regimes, formulating a procedure for drafting the treaties that gave the West an advantage, deflecting a Russian request for a trusteeship, and avoiding any discussion of Japan. The Soviets had been blocked by Byrnes's maneuvers. Success, however, rested on Molotov's next actions, for he was preparing his answers to the American statement on Romania and Bulgaria, and to the procedural issue.

Molotov's replies came over the next two days and completely reversed the momentum of the conference. At a council session on September 21, he made a strong defense of the Romanian and Bulgarian governments, and a sharp denunciation of American anti-Soviet attitudes. His next response was given at the Soviet embassy. Byrnes had been invited to meet with Molotov at 11:30; Bevin was to arrive at noon. The American expected that Molotov was going to withdraw from the conference. Instead, the Soviet minister attacked U.S. policy, arguing that Washington was being too easy on the Japanese. An Allied Control Council with Soviet membership was needed to formulate policy for Japan. Byrnes lamely replied that he could not discuss any Asian questions until his government and Tokyo were consulted.

As the Soviets probably knew, Byrnes was not telling the whole truth. Anglo-American discussions on Japan were already under way, with the secretary exerting strong pressure to have the British drop their support for an Allied Control Council and join the Far Eastern Advisory Commission. Unless they accepted the American position, Byrnes had suggested, their American loan might be endangered.[16]

Before Byrnes and Molotov could discuss the Japanese matter further, Bevin arrived. Molotov immediately turned to the official reason for the meeting. He announced that the Soviet Union would not participate further in the conference unless France and China were excluded from debating the peace treaties for Romania, Bulgaria, and Hungary. He had not only rejected Byrnes's request that all five deputies work on the treaties but also reversed the opening day's procedural decision.

The Soviets had selected their position with care. According to the Berlin protocol, neither France nor China should have any role in discussing, writing, or approving the peace treaties for Eastern Europe. Molotov was merely correcting the opening day's mistake. If the conference failed over this issue, it would be difficult to blame the Russians, who were upholding proper procedure. Moreover, any position taken by Britain and the United States would result in negative consequences. If they agreed to deny France and China a role in writing the treaties, they might save the conference and even encourage Soviet cooperation, but such a decision would alienate the other delegates.

Bevin and Byrnes were stunned by Molotov's announcement, but neither was speechless. They immediately voiced support for full French and Chinese participation in all council discussions. Byrnes struck a legalistic pose, judiciously arguing that it made no sense to undo everything accomplished by the five ministers. The volatile Bevin exploded and declared that the central problem facing the conference was "the philosophy and attitude of the Soviet Government." Anger and logic had no effect. Stone Bottom Molotov stood by his statement.

That afternoon the British and American delegations independently sought answers for the Soviet action. Opinions differed. "Molotov's objective is now clear," Ambassador Harriman announced; the Russians wanted to obtain Anglo-American recognition for the governments of Romania and Bulgaria and would not proceed with the conference until that was assured. Pierson Dixon and others, especially among the British delegation, disagreed. Dixon believed that the goal was to gain control over an Italian colony. A few in both delegations thought that the Soviets were trying to isolate France or to split the British and Americans over support for France.

Both delegations agreed that it was necessary to support France and China. England and the United States were "not in a position to lose more friends," concluded one British official. Some believed that Molotov was acting independently and others that he had specific instructions from Stalin. On the chance that the Soviet leader would overrule his foreign minister, it was decided that Prime Minister Attlee and President Truman should formally protest Molotov's action and request that Stalin save the conference by accepting the procedural decision made on September 11. Both sent messages, but Stalin stood firmly by his minister. If the impasse was to be removed, it would have to be done locally, through British and American concessions to the Soviets. The questions were, What did the Russians want? Were Bevin and Byrnes willing to make concessions?

Byrnes was in little mood to do so. He decided not only to support France and China but also to counterattack. He proposed convoking a general peace conference that would replace the five nations of the Council of Foreign Ministers with fifty nations, each clamoring for its share of the spoils. "We offered them five and they would not take it," he told his staff; "now we will give them 50."[17]

The British, unlike the Americans, looked for a possible compromise. Assuming that Byrnes's position on the Romanian and Bulgarian governments had precipitated

Molotov's action, the Foreign Office drafted a proposal to end the dispute while leaving France a major power. But for the plan to be successful the United States would have to be brought "into line about the Roumanian and Bulgarian Governments." It would not be easy persuading the Americans to change their position, the Foreign Office concluded.[18]

Meanwhile, the sessions grew more and more acid. Molotov almost walked out when Bevin called his actions "the nearest thing to the Hitler theory I have ever heard." He returned to his seat only after receiving an apology. Seeing that their discussions were accomplishing nothing, that they were at an impasse over the procedural point, the council agreed to end the conference on October 2 unless a last-minute breakthrough occurred.

On the afternoon of October 1, Bevin worked toward such a solution. He met with Byrnes and explained the Foreign Office's scheme. He asked the secretary of state to withdraw his statement on the nature of the Romanian and Bulgarian regimes, and to announce that the United States would recognize the governments once Finnish-style elections were conducted. Byrnes then asked "who was to say whether in fact the elections would be on the lines of Finland."

Bevin could only reply that they must "be prepared to exchange one set of crooks for another." Byrnes listened to his explanation and offered some modifications: (1) the Romanian opposition leaders, Iuliu Maniu and Constantin Bratianu, would have to be guaranteed cabinet posts; (2) the honesty of the elections would have to be verified by an independent commission; and (3) the United States would not withdraw its reservations about the two governments until the above criteria were met. Without the modifications, Byrnes explained, Washington could not support the plan. With them, Bevin realized, the Soviets were unlikely even to consider the proposal. Facing a dilemma, he decided to accept the secretary's amendments. It was better to remain close to the United States.

Upon presenting the new plan to Molotov, Bevin got what he expected. It was coldly dismissed. The Soviet Union found the Romanian and Bulgarian governments both democratic and representative, and would wait, however long, until Britain and the United States recognized the regimes. Molotov next offered Bevin a deal on the Italian colonies. Britain could have Cyrenaica in exchange for "only a corner of Tripolitania." After all, he said, "a Russian trusteeship for ten years would do no harm." Politely but firmly Bevin declined the offer. He left the meeting ready to conclude the conference.[19]

Before the sessions ended, the Soviet Union hosted a party at its embassy, providing one last opportunity for back-room diplomacy. This time Molotov was the catalyst. After baiting Bevin throughout the evening about Greece, he jokingly suggested that the Soviets might exchange a trusteeship over an Italian colony for the Belgian Congo. For those unable to see a connection between the Congo, where uranium was mined, and Soviet interests, Molotov made it obvious later when he blurted out, "You know we have the atomic bomb." In stunned silence the other delegates watched Ambassador Fedor Gusev usher the foreign minister from the room.[20]

In the shadow of Molotov's announcement the London Conference came to a deadlocked close on October 2. The ministers were unable to agree on either a protocol or on a final communiqué. Tired of arguing, they went home without fanfare to explain the failure. The cooperation that had characterized the Big Three during the war, the spirit of Yalta and Potsdam, was gone. A new configuration of world power was emerging, but, in October 1945, no one was sure of its shape, only that relations in the postwar world were beginning to harden.

In Search of a Russian Policy

Following the London meeting, each nation assessed its position. Wartime allies had become postwar rivals as national interests overcame the desire for agreement. Still, despite the failure at London, there remained in the capitals of the Big Three a desire to repair the damages, if it could be done without national loss. The United States, Byrnes told the American public, was not giving up on negotiations; it still sought a "just peace," but not at the price of sacrificing its principles. The secretary was applauded, and Justice Felix Frankfurter congratulated him for speaking "candidly to the American people without encouraging the Russophobes at home and exciting sensibilities abroad."[21]

Byrnes's position was affirmed by Truman in the president's Navy Day speech on October 27. With the strength of the armed forces as a backdrop, Truman outlined the principles of foreign policy that the United States would not abandon, including support for freely elected governments, without offering any solutions to existing Soviet-American problems. Nonetheless, the public was reassured and remained supportive of further negotiations and the idea of international cooperation.[22]

What the people did not know was that, at about the same time, Ambassador Harriman was meeting with Stalin to try and end the trouble created at London. The American overture had resulted from an apparent, sudden reversal of Soviet opinion regarding the conference and the nature of international cooperation.

When the London meeting concluded, the Russians blamed Bevin and Byrnes, whom they called pawns of anti-Soviet, reactionary forces. There seemed little opportunity for diplomatic progress, and some observers believed that the Soviets might adopt unilateral policies. *Pravda* showed a reverse in attitudes on October 6 by suggesting that progress had been made at London and that ups and downs were part of international negotiations.

George F. Kennan, the American chargé d'affaires in Moscow, thought that the door was open to solving the problems. Many in London and Washington, trying to explain the sudden change, credited Stalin. The more "reasonable" leader had reversed the policy of his anti-Western foreign minister. Whatever the cause, H. Freeman Matthews and others in the State Department believed that an effort should be made to resolve differences before the Soviets "crystallized" their position. Within days, Harriman arranged a meeting with Stalin to discuss the Council of Foreign Ministers and, if the Soviets desired, Allied controls for Japan.[23]

The two men met on October 24 at the Black Sea resort of Sochi, where Harriman presented a private letter from Truman. It focused on the need to restart the process of writing the peace treaties for Germany's allies; it made no mention of Japan. Washington officials had hoped to avoid Asian questions, but Stalin would have none of it. He

immediately commented that there was no reference to
Japan and that the Kremlin considered it a vital question.
The "Soviet Union would not be a satellite of the United
States in the Far East," he told the ambassador. Like
Molotov at London, he wanted an Allied Control Council to
help formulate policy. Until one was created, the Soviet
Union would not participate in the Far Eastern Advisory
Commission.

Harriman attempted to assure Stalin that the United
States was willing to reach an agreement on Japan. But, he
explained, General Douglas MacArthur must maintain
final authority over the defeated nation. Drawing attention
to the United States' double standard, Stalin said that he did
not question MacArthur's authority, since it was the same
as that of his commanders in chief in Romania and
Hungary. Later, the Soviet leader confided to Harriman
that his country would accept American unilateral action in
Japan but might adopt a similar "isolationist" policy. As
Admiral Richard Gates had predicted, it was becoming very
difficult for the United States to demand four-power
authority in Eastern Europe while telling the Soviets they
could not have it in Japan.

However, progress was made on the issue of the peace
treaties. While Stalin and Harriman were unable to agree
on which nations should be involved in writing and
approving the treaties, the Soviet leader acquiesced in
allowing the deputies of the Council of Foreign Ministers to
renew their work. He also accepted the idea of calling a
general peace conference as part of the treaty process.[24]

Harriman continued the discussions in Moscow with
Molotov, who took tougher positions than had Stalin. Of
particular concern to the State and War departments were
Soviet intentions in East Asia and the Middle East.
Renewed tension between Chinese Nationalists and Chinese
Communists, combined with Soviet actions in Manchuria,
Korea, and northern Iran, seemed to support the opinion
that the Russians were moving to fill any political vacuum
that might be forming along their eastern and southern
borders. For some in the State Department, a possible
solution to Soviet behavior in the Far East lay in Stalin's
linkage between Japan and Eastern Europe. If the United
States was willing to accept the Soviet position in the
Balkans, the Soviet Union might agree to the U.S. policy in

East Asia. Cloyce Huston, chief of the Southern European Division, wrote in a memorandum that better relations were possible if Washington supported "Soviet aims to establish free and mutually advantageous relations between Soviet Russia and her Western neighbors." Byrnes had no intention of changing his stand on Romania and Bulgaria. As a result, two weeks later, Huston was removed as chief and transferred to Norway.[25]

Byrnes, however, was willing to appear more open to compromise. Publicly, he announced that the United States did not disagree with East European governments friendly to Russia but only opposed those that closed themselves off from the friendship of others. On October 10 it was announced that Mark Ethridge, publisher of the *Louisville Courier-Journal,* would conduct a fact-finding tour of Romania and Bulgaria. Many observers thought that his mission showed mistrust of the State Department, while forming a new approach to the Balkan problems. They were wrong. Byrnes and the department expected Ethridge's observations to support those made by American officials. Lord Halifax reported to the Foreign Office that the tour represented "no change in policy." As expected, the publisher was critical of the political situation in Romania. He believed that Groza was a "singularly stupid" person, and, more important, found that Western influence was "disintegrating fast" in both Romania and Bulgaria.[26]

As November began, American relations with the Soviet Union seemed to be crumbling as the potential for Soviet gains in Iran and East Asia increased. But the Russians were not the only ones demanding Washington's attention. The British worried that their interests were being ignored by both the Americans and the Soviets. The former were acting unilaterally, while the latter sought a foothold in the Mediterranean and had launched a major propaganda attack on Britain. "If we are not careful our victory in war may lead to us being plucked by our Allies," Bevin told Pierson Dixon.

In evaluating the London Conference and Soviet behavior, Bevin concluded that Britain should not make any move toward compromise. The Russians understood only strength, and the foreign minister assumed that any approach to Moscow would be seen as a sign of weakness. If there was to be an effort to improve Anglo-Soviet relations, it

should come from the Soviets. The Foreign Office opposed
Harriman's overture toward Stalin and told the State
Department that the meeting was a mistake and a waste of
time. Privately, British officials worried about an
American-Soviet deal that would further reduce their
country's status as a major power and place it at a
disadvantage in negotiations.[27]

Despite their distaste for Byrnes and the "jungle-like"
diplomacy of the United States, the British were compelled
to smooth relations with the Americans. Even though
economic negotiations were still under way, Prime Minister
Attlee was determined to promote a postwar atomic
partnership. The wartime Anglo-American cooperation
seemed to have lapsed, with Washington denying access to
atomic information and technology. Britain needed to
develop its own nuclear power and weapons. Equally
important, Attlee believed that America's atomic monopoly
significantly increased international discord and the
hostility of the Soviet Union toward the West. To deal with
both issues, he wanted to confer with Truman on
international controls and to affirm that Britain would
share in all military and domestic aspects of nuclear
energy.

An American, British, and Canadian conference,
therefore, was set in Washington for November 11. The
meeting consisted of four bitter days for the British.
Eventually, agreements were reached covering both of
Attlee's concerns but not along the paths he wanted. In a
public ceremony on November 15, the three countries
promulgated the Washington Declaration, a pledge of
support for the formation of a UN commission on atomic
energy and the sharing of nuclear information once
"effective, reciprocal, and enforceable safeguards" were
instituted. Secret Anglo-American agreements were also
concluded that affirmed the two governments' promise to
cooperate with each other in developing nonmilitary atomic
technology.[28]

While the meeting had helped to improve Anglo-
American relations and resolve one major issue, it had only
further convinced the British that the Americans were
treating them as the "poor relation." Nor did it seem to have
a positive impact on the Soviets. The Russian media
denounced the conference and the Washington Declaration

as two more cases of U.S. "atomic diplomacy." Harriman reported that the nuclear agreement had only increased the prospect of Soviet "aggressiveness and intrigue" at future international meetings.[29]

As the British delegation departed, Byrnes, who had opposed sharing U.S. nuclear secrets with anyone, increasingly worried about the status of American-Soviet relations. He and Truman were concerned about the tightening hold of the Russians on Eastern Europe and their potential for gains in East Asia and the Middle East. Both were aware that commentators such as Walter Lippmann were calling American foreign policy adrift and without direction. The *New Republic* believed that the administration should promote the "unity of the United States, Great Britain, and Russia—unity on which the entire structure of the United Nations must stand or fall."

To Byrnes and Truman, it now seemed necessary to open discussions with the Soviets, if possible directly with Stalin, before the first of the year and the opening session of the General Assembly of the United Nations. The president and his secretary were concerned about the hostile response to the Washington Declaration and feared that such aggression would threaten the development of the United Nations. Truman considered sending Harry Hopkins to Moscow again. But he was too ill to travel, and Truman's staff could not think of a suitable alternative. Byrnes, wanting to gain Soviet approval of a UN atomic energy commission, contemplated meeting with Molotov and Stalin in Moscow. Such a trip also might serve to restart the activities of the Council of Foreign Ministers, better American-Soviet relations, and save the U.S. position in East Asia. By Thanksgiving, Byrnes was convinced of the benefits of a quick, Big Three meeting in Moscow before the end of the year. His next step was to persuade the Soviets.[30]

To encourage the Soviets to approve such a meeting, Byrnes was willing to offer them a partial atomic partnership. Immediately a special committee was created to consider and recommend the extent of such collaboration, and what information and materials could be shared. Britain was completely left out of the discussions about the meeting. Told only after the conference had been arranged with the Soviets, Bevin refused to participate. However, fearful that Byrnes and Molotov would meet without him,

Bevin soon decided to attend the gathering, which was to begin in mid-December.[31]

Prior to leaving for Moscow, Byrnes and American officials took stock of the state of international affairs, especially the relationship of the United States to the Soviet Union. Since the end of the Potsdam meeting, the building of a stable postwar system had not gone according to American wishes. Truman had been optimistic that the Soviets would eventually see the benefits to be gained from following the American vision of a postwar world based on multilateralism and the extension of free trade. But they had not, and the question facing Byrnes and the president was why the Soviets were not more cooperative. Was it their Communist ideology? Was it a desire for expansion and power? Was it the "little fellows" around Stalin who wanted to "strut their stuff" and were hostile toward the West? State Department officials were unsure but provided Byrnes with a nineteen-page document on Soviet capabilities and intentions.

The memorandum took the position that, like many nations, the Soviet Union based its foreign policy on four fundamentals:

1) its economic and military capabilities;
2) the ideology and goals of its leaders;
3) the foreign situation in those regions where it had interests; and
4) the policies and actions of other major powers—in this case the United States and Britain—as understood by its leadership.

Examining the dynamics of Soviet decisions more closely, the State Department concluded that the country's economic and military capabilities were not supportive of a truly aggressive foreign policy. The Soviet economy needed to be almost completely rebuilt, and even with American aid the process was estimated to require at least five years.

Despite the huge number of Russian soldiers, the State Department believed that the United States commanded overwhelming military superiority for at least ten years and that the Soviet Union would pose no threat until 1965. The key to America's military strength rested on its economy, technology, and the atomic bomb. According to the memorandum, until the Soviets rebuilt their economy and gained nuclear parity, the United States did not need to "be acutely concerned about the current intentions of the Soviet Union" and had "considerable latitude in determining its policy toward the U.S.S.R."

Regarding the ideology and goals of the Soviet leaders, the State Department recognized that as good Communists they must believe in the "inevitability of conflict between the U.S.S.R. and the non-Soviet powers." However, these leaders, especially Stalin, were realists and pragmatic. They had not let ideology drive foreign policy since the 1930s, and there was no indication of a change to come in their approach. Opportunism more than ideology guided them. They would attempt to exploit global revolutionary situations but not to the extent that their actions would threaten to bring a confrontation and possible war with the West.

How the Soviets might respond to American actions was also considered at length. The State Department projected three possible scenarios. The first called upon the United States to promote harmony among the Big Three. This would be "a deliberately reassuring and moderate policy" that recognized Soviet security needs, treated the Soviets as nuclear partners, and provided economic support. At the same time, the United States would continue to show leadership in solving international problems and promoting economic recovery in Europe and Asia. Positive American leadership would help keep revolutionary situations from developing. Faced with a lack of revolutionary opportunities and with real gains to be made from better relations with the United States, Soviet leaders would continue to de-emphasize ideology and work to resolve external problems through big-power cooperation and open diplomacy.

The second approach was the opposite of the first, to develop the "maximum alignment of power against the Soviet Union" to deter the Russians from any thoughts of aggression. If this policy were implemented, the memorandum stated, the Soviets would react by retreating from open diplomacy and adopt an ideologically aggressive, expansionistic, and anticapitalistic policy. Deterrence, not friendship, would become the basis for an international system of hostile blocs.

Between the first and second alternatives, the State Department suggested a third possibility: to keep

"American-Soviet relations somewhat indeterminate and fluid." In applying this approach the United States sometimes would offer concessions and friendship while at other times opposing Soviet interests and working to construct an anti-Soviet bloc. According to the memorandum, the probable consequence of the third option would be to create a limited adversarial relationship between the United States and the Soviet Union, neither peace nor war.[32]

In December 1945, Truman and his secretary of state opted for the first approach. Byrnes's trip to Moscow was a symbol of American efforts to maintain good relations with the Soviet Union. A partial nuclear partnership and economic aid was possible, provided the Soviets responded in an equally positive fashion. Byrnes told friends that he was going to see if Stalin was preparing for peace or war. He was willing to meet the Soviets more than halfway, but the future of American policy would depend on how they responded. The United States could always fall back to either the second or the third alternative. Nevertheless, Byrnes, Truman, and many others were hopeful, if not optimistic. Marquis Childs wrote in the *Washington Post* that "as Secretary Byrnes sets out for Moscow, our hopes rise a little. This means another chance to come together. . . . In going to Moscow he should feel confident of support from back home. . . . Good luck Mr. Secretary, Happy Landings, and a better world."[33]

The Moscow Conference

Anxious to begin the conference, Byrnes and his delegation braved flying through a blizzard to arrive in Moscow. Unfortunately, they landed at the wrong airport and were welcomed by a small Soviet delegation placed there in case of such an event. After very brief greetings, the tired and cold Americans were hurried to their embassy. Bevin, less enamored of the conference, waited in Berlin until the storm was over and arrived at the right airport the following day. He was met by a larger delegation.

Moscow had changed since its last Big Three meeting, in 1943. Lenin had been returned to his tomb, people filled the streets, and British and American officials were not accorded special treatment. Drinks were no longer free, and caviar was so expensive that it was completely off the menu, complained one delegate. While the city sported a new coat of paint, Soviet diplomacy and secrecy remained the same.[34]

On December 16, Byrnes, in the lavish setting of Spiridonvka Palace, opened the meeting by presenting eight topics for the agenda:

1) formation of a UN atomic energy commission;
2) drafting of the peace treaties for Italy, Romania, Bulgaria, Hungary, and Finland;
3) establishment of a unified and independent Korea;
4) formation of an Allied Control Council for Japan and the Far Eastern Advisory Commission;
5) removal of Japanese troops from northern China;
6) withdrawal of Soviet troops from Manchuria;
7) removal of Allied troops from Iran; and
8) establishment of governments in Romania and Bulgaria that the United States and Britain could recognize.

Molotov immediately asked for modifications. As if to de-emphasize its importance, he wanted the Atomic Energy Commission to be last on the agenda. He also asked to discuss Indonesia, British troops in Greece, and American troops in China. Whenever the Soviets disliked something on any agenda and did not wish to discuss it, a British delegate concluded, they would make "a counter-suggestion by putting forward some item they know will annoy us."[35]

After an hour and a half of sometimes heated debate, Molotov got most of what he wanted. All issues were divided between formal and informal sessions. All troop withdrawals, whether from Iran, Manchuria, China, or Greece, were relegated to the informal, private sessions. The formal-session agenda stood at six topics, with atomic energy last. It was agreed, however, that any topic could be discussed at any time.

If Molotov's intention by moving atomic energy was to encourage American concessions on other topics, he had miscalculated. Byrnes decided to reduce the degree of nuclear cooperation to be offered to the Soviet Union. He instructed Benjamin V. Cohen and James B. Conant to rewrite the proposal and to delete references to the immediate sharing of nuclear information and materials. The final product rephrased the paragraphs of the Washington Declaration, pledging the provision to other nations of atomic information and technology. The Soviets, already having rejected such an arrangement, could be expected to object to the newest version as well.[36]

Tough bargaining began on December 18. Byrnes worked to convince Molotov that Mark Ethridge was a liberal who had a "sympathetic attitude toward the Soviet Union" and had written an "absolutely independent" and factual analysis of the unrepresentative nature of the regimes in Romania and Bulgaria. Molotov barely glanced at the report, which had been translated into Russian, before dismissing it by saying that no American could judge Eastern-style democracy. The Soviets were holding firm in supporting their Balkan regimes.

The Soviets held firm also on who should participate in drafting and considering the peace treaties. Byrnes asked Molotov to distinguish between "judges and witnesses." Those named in the Potsdam protocol were judges and had all the power to write and approve the treaties. The others to be invited to the peace conference would be witnesses, able only to give opinions. Molotov demanded complete compliance with the Berlin protocol, so that only those nations listed therein could participate in drafting and approving the peace treaties.[37]

Byrnes was disappointed and frustrated by Molotov's responses. He feared that their negotiations might conclude like those in London. Bevin was even more dismayed. He found the Soviet minister's positions, especially on Iran, "unhelpful if not sinister." Bevin had asked him to lay his cards on the table and explain Russian actions in Iran, but Molotov merely repeated that the Soviet Union was not involved in the rebellion, had no designs on Iran, and would evacuate its troops six months after the end of hostilities. Unable to get positive responses, Byrnes and Bevin looked forward to meeting with Stalin. They hoped he would prove more cooperative than Molotov.

They were wrong. At nearly every point the Soviet leader supported his minister's positions. On Iran, Stalin seemed even more irate, saying that it was hostile toward the Soviet Union and that his forces would stay in northern Iran to protect Russian oil fields in Baku "until the date set by the treaty." He stirred British and American concerns when he reminded Byrnes that a Soviet-Iranian treaty of 1921 permitted his troops to remain in Iran as long as he wished.[38]

On December 21 the gloom began to lift, as Molotov and Byrnes worked to find a solution to the Korean issue. Four days earlier the United States had proposed a unified Korea under an American-Soviet administration until a four-power trusteeship could be established. The trusteeship would rule the country for four years or until its people were ready for independence. On December 22 it was concluded that an American-Soviet commission would be established to work with Korean democratic parties and social organizations to develop a provisional government like the one suggested. The trusteeship would last "for a period up to five years," after which a unified Korea would receive its independence. Byrnes was pleased; the basic language of the American proposition had been accepted by the Soviets.[39]

The agreement on Korea began a series of decisions in which the Soviets reversed previously held positions. Without explanation, Molotov accepted the American proposal for the Far Eastern Advisory Commission and Allied Control Council for Japan, along with Byrnes's concept of the peace conference. He even provided a list of nations to be invited that included India and excluded the Baltic states. Half of the agenda was completed, almost totally along American lines. Byrnes was in a joyful mood, predicting his return home for Christmas.

Soviet willingness to compromise next extended to enlarging the Romanian government. Molotov declared that the Big Three might persuade Groza's government to incorporate "one or two ministers without portfolio . . . from non-party statesmen." But Britain and the United States must "agree not to delay the conclusion of a peace treaty." The new Soviet stance on Romania matched the British line of thought and approached the Polish-style solution suggested by Byrnes at London. The secretary now wanted more and demanded that the two pro-Western opposition parties be identified as the source of the added statesmen. He also wanted Romanian guarantees that a general amnesty would be granted and all civil and political rights would be respected.

When Molotov rejected the conditions, Byrnes took his request to Stalin. He reasoned that the real obstacle to the Romanian question was the foreign minister, not Soviet policy. His assessment appeared correct when Stalin offered a more favorable proposal. "In a pinch it might be possible," he told Byrnes, to include two from the opposition parties, provided that the leaders of the opposition were barred from participating in the broadened government. Unexpectedly, Stalin added that he would quietly advise the Bulgarians to enlarge their government as well, although there must be no hint of Soviet pressure.

Stalin, however, was not finished meeting American goals. He accepted U.S. troops in China and the proposed formation of a UN atomic commission. He asked only to be informed about China and that the commission be placed under the control of the Security Council. Overjoyed, Byrnes agreed. It was two days before Christmas, and it appeared that nearly all the topics were resolved in favor of the United States. All that was still necessary was cleaning up a few small details.[40]

The details mushroomed, and Byrnes's joy soon dissipated. It seemed that Molotov was back to his old negotiating tricks. While he accepted the proposal for the Atomic Energy Commission, he strayed from the spirit of the understanding on Romania and Bulgaria. He stated that the Soviet Union demanded that the individuals to be added to the Romanian regime had to come from the "loyal opposition." Those to be excluded, he announced, should be named publicly in the protocol. Byrnes opposed the term "loyal opposition" and objected to ostracizing "men in their own country." Unable to convince Molotov, he asked that an interim communiqué be released on Christmas Eve to announce the end of the London deadlock and the calling of a general peace conference. It would be a present for the world, Byrnes proclaimed. Neither Bevin nor Molotov thought that the announcement was necessary, but they agreed to the request.[41]

Looking for his own Christmas present, Bevin met privately with Stalin in the hope of duplicating Byrnes's success and reaching an agreement on Iran. He asked for the establishment of a three-power commission to set up Iranian provincial assemblies that officially would be under the control of the central government but in fact would be autonomous. Allied troops would be withdrawn according to a schedule established by a three-power liaison group. If Stalin agreed the resulting arrangement would leave Soviet influence in northern Iran and British influence in the south.

Stalin replied that the plan had merit and promised to deliver minor amendments the next morning. But, before Bevin could congratulate himself, the Soviet leader asked him why his government had opposed a Russian trusteeship in Tripolitania. Was not Britain "prepared to trust the Soviet Union in Tripolitania"? If it wanted influence in Iran, why would it not allow a Soviet foothold in North Africa? "Could not the interests of the Soviet Union be taken into account?" According to Stalin, Britain already had "bases all over the world, even more than the United States." The British and the Americans had their spheres of influence, "but the Soviet Union had nothing." Bevin could hardly believe his ears. He reminded Stalin "that the Russian sphere extended from Lubeck to Port Arthur." Unable to agree on who had influence and to what extent, both men saw it was time to attend a gala dinner in the salon of the Order of Saint Catherine.[42]

The following morning, Byrnes and Molotov continued their verbal sparring, trying to find acceptable language for the request to enlarge the Romanian government. Molotov was willing not to name those excluded from the government if they were known at least to those monitoring the expansion. In return he asked Bevin and Byrnes to accept his latest phrase describing those permitted to participate: "two representatives loyal to the present Government—truly representative of those groups of the National Peasant and Liberal parties not at the present participating in the present government." The British and the Americans accepted most of the wording but wanted some minor modifications. After several more hours of discussions, they finally agreed that those "truly representative of the groups" not in the government but who were willing "to work loyally with the Government" would be asked to join.

However, the language for the "quiet suggestion" to the Bulgarian government escaped the three ministers, and, after a day of debate, they agreed to remove Bulgaria from the formal agenda. They had thus resolved all the issues and could go home. Byrnes was pleased; for him the conference had been a success. Bevin was less happy. British interests had been all but ignored by both the Soviets and the Americans. And the Iranian issue still was not settled.[43]

Bevin appeared close to finding a solution. On Christmas morning, he received Stalin's comments on the Iranian proposal and had begun to incorporate them into the British draft when Byrnes arrived. After reading Stalin's points the American expressed his concern that the Soviets had deleted the specific date for the withdrawal of Allied forces from Iran, March 2, 1946. He said that inclusion of the date was necessary, as was Iran's ratification of any agreement constructed by the Big Three. The secretary was unwilling to support a proposal that did not reflect the U.S. position. Bevin, as he had during the closing days of the London Conference, believed that he had no choice but to accept the American demand.

Byrnes next visited the Soviet foreign minister. Almost as if he knew of the secretary's conversation with Bevin, Molotov asked for his opinion of the British proposal. Byrnes confessed that he "did not especially like" it but could accept it. Molotov made no response, but later, when the ministers met to consider Bevin's proposal, he totally rejected it.

Bevin refused to give up, reminding Molotov that Stalin had all but accepted his plan. The Soviet minister stood firm. Bevin then looked to Byrnes for support and was shocked by his reply. "There would never be a time when all questions could be settled," Byrnes explained. He thought they should turn to writing a final communiqué and protocol. Molotov smiled and observed "that if Mr. Byrnes and Mr. Bevin did only wish to deal with remaining questions, he could not concur." The meeting was over and, unless Bevin could get his proposal on Iran reconsidered, so, too, was the conference.

An angry Bevin requested a meeting with Stalin, who was unavailable, and the British minister was forced to see Molotov again. The Soviet minister refused to reconsider the proposal and launched into a lengthy statement about Iranian abuses against the Soviet Union. His patience at an end, Bevin left, saying, "I do not want to be faced with faits accomplis." He had been willing to stay until the Iranian issue was resolved to Britain's satisfaction, but, ignored by

Stalin, rebuffed by Molotov, and deserted by Byrnes, he had to leave it unresolved and to accept the closing of the conference.[44]

Success at the Moscow Conference, December 1945. Left to right: Ernest Bevin, Vyacheslav M. Molotov, and James F. Byrnes. (Robert M. Cooper Library, Clemson University)

The end came after an all-night session debating whether to include Bulgaria in the communiqué and protocol. When the drafts of the two documents arrived from the Russian typists, Molotov burst out laughing. By mistake, he said, the typists had included the Soviet proposal on Bulgaria even though it had been removed from the agenda. He asked Byrnes and Bevin if they could accept Stalin's offer to advise the Bulgarians to broaden their government. Byrnes countered by suggesting that the Soviets accept the American language, which paralleled the statement for Romania and promised recognition once the advice had been followed. To everyone's surprise, Molotov agreed. Back went the drafts for retyping, and finally at "3:30 am, amid the usual battery of pressmen," the protocol and communiqué were signed. The Moscow meeting was completed.[45]

The conference left the Soviets and the Americans pleased; it clearly had been a meeting of the Big Two. The British left Moscow angered at their treatment and feeling more and more the junior partner of the United States. For Bevin there were no complimentary gifts, while Byrnes flew home with an autographed picture of Stalin. General E. Ian Jacob expressed the feelings of many within the delegation when he stated that "it is awful to think that the foreign policy of a great country like the U.S.A. should be in the hands of a shanty Irishman from Carolina."

Despite British dissatisfaction, much had been accomplished to overcome the hostilities that had surfaced at London. Through tough, give-and-take bargaining similar to that of Yalta, the conference had produced solutions for drafting and signing the peace treaties, for broadening the Romanian and Bulgarian governments, and for controlling atomic energy. Soviet-American relations in Asia had been improved without threatening U.S. interests, especially in Japan. The Moscow Conference indicated that the Big Three could continue to cooperate and reach compromises without the pressures of war. Edward R. Murrow told his radio audience that the meeting signified an end of national methods of international relations and "a beginning of an era of world methods."[46]

Notes

1. Gormly, *Collapse of the Grand Alliance,* 16–58; Dixon, *Double Diploma,* 189.

2. *FRUS: Diplomatic Papers, 1945* (Washington, DC, 1967), 5:606–8; Roberts to C. F. A. Warner, September 1, 1945, F.O. 371, N13185/78/15; minute, September 10, 1945, F.O. 371, R15867/120226/37, both in PRO; Gormly, *Collapse of the Grand Alliance,* 41–47.

3. Roberto G. Rabel, *Between East and West: Trieste, the United States, and the Cold War, 1941–1954* (Durham, NC, 1988), 1–17, 26–51; memorandum, "U.K. Policy—Italy," September 20, 1945, F.O. 371, U7597/50/70, PRO; *FRUS: Diplomatic Papers, 1945* (Washington, DC, 1968), 4:1034–57; Gormly, *Collapse of the Grand Alliance,* 34–36.

4. Gormly, *Collapse of the Grand Alliance,* 36–38; memorandum, "Italian Peace Treaty—Colonies," August 18, 1945, F.O. 371, U6368/50/70; Cabinet Papers, ORC (45) 18, "Future Policy toward Italy," ORC (45) 23, August 30, 1945, ZM4588/1/22, all in PRO.

5. Messer, *End of an Alliance,* 77–85; Herken, *Winning Weapon,* 39–49.

6. Memorandum, "Cabinet Meeting," August 9, 1945, F.O. 371, F5743/364/23; memorandum, September 11, 1945, F.O. 371, F6699/364/23; memorandum, "Conversation between Bevin and T. V. Soong," August 10, 1945, F.O. 371, F7205/186/10, all in PRO.

7. *FRUS: Diplomatic Papers, 1945* (Washington, DC, 1967), 2:114–17; *FRUS: Berlin, 1945* 2:1972; memorandum, August 10, 1945, F.O. 371, U6135/5559/70, PRO.

8. *FRUS: Diplomatic Papers, 1945* 2:114–28.

9. Ibid.; Walter Brown diary, September 13, 1945, James F. Byrnes Papers, Robert M. Cooper Library, Clemson University, Clemson, South Carolina (hereafter cited as Byrnes Papers).

10. Byrnes, *Speaking Frankly,* 94; *FRUS: Diplomatic Papers, 1945* 2:162–65.

11. *FRUS: Diplomatic Papers, 1945* 2:164–66, 188–89; Byrnes, *Speaking Frankly,* 95; Dixon, *Double Diploma,* 183; minute, September 15, 1945, F.O. 371, U7574/51/70, PRO.

12. *FRUS: Diplomatic Papers, 1945* 2:202–16, 225–36, 239–61.

13. Walter Brown diary, September 16, 1945, Byrnes Papers; *FRUS: Diplomatic Papers, 1945* 2:182–85, 194–220; memorandum, September 21, 1945, F.O. 371, U7839/51/70, PRO.

14. Walter Brown diary, September 17, 1945, Byrnes Papers; Dixon, *Double Diploma,* 184; Byrnes, *Speaking Frankly,* 106–7.

15. *FRUS: Diplomatic Papers, 1945* 2:202–16, 225–36, 239–94.

16. Walter Brown diary, September 22, 1945, Byrnes Papers; Byrnes, *Speaking Frankly,* 102; Herbert Feis, *Contest over Japan: The Soviet Bid for Power in the Far East* (New York, 1968), 36–38; *FRUS: Diplomatic Papers, 1945* 2:336–39, 360–70; memorandum, September 29, 1945, F.O. 371, F6699/364/23, PRO.

17. Memorandum of conversation with Bevin, Byrnes, and Molotov, September 22, 1945, F.O. 371, U7384/5559/70, PRO; *FRUS: Diplomatic Papers, 1945* 2:313–15, 329; Byrnes, *Speaking Frankly,* 102–3; Gormly, *Collapse of the Grand Alliance,* 76–79; Truman, *Memoirs* 1:516–18.

18. Gormly, *Collapse of the Grand Alliance,* 76–79; Dixon, *Double Diploma,* 191–92; memorandum, October 1, 1945, F.O. 371, U7669/5559/70, PRO.

19. Memorandum, October 1, 1945, F.O. 371, U7669/5559/70; memorandum, October 1, 1945, N13613/18/38, both in PRO; Dixon, *Double Diploma,* 193–94; *FRUS: Diplomatic Papers, 1945* 2:417–27, 440–47, 482–85.

20. Colonel H. K. Calvert to General Leslie Groves, November 13, 1945, Folder 20, Manhattan Project Files, 1942–45, Manhattan Engineer District Files, Modern Military Branch, National Archives, Washington, DC (hereafter cited as Military). Hugh Dalton, chancellor of the exchequer, heard it differently: "Here's to the Atom Bomb! . . . We've got it" (Dalton diary, October 17, 1945, Hugh Dalton Papers, London School of Economic and Political Science, London).

21. *New York Times,* October 3, 1945; Gormly, *Collapse of the Grand Alliance,* 86–88.

22. *New York Times,* October 28, 1945.

23. Jonathan Knight, "Russia's Search for Peace: The London Conference of Foreign Ministers, 1945," *Journal of Contemporary History* 13 (1978): 155–56; *FRUS: Diplomatic Papers, 1945* 2:562–63; Gormly, *Collapse of the Grand Alliance,* 89–90.

24. *FRUS: Diplomatic Papers, 1945* (Washington, DC, 1969), 6:751–56, 567–75, 783–85, 787–93; Feis, *Contest over Japan,* 56–66; Harriman and Abel, *Special Envoy,* 512–13; minutes of Top Policy Group, Department of the Navy, October 8, 1945, Secretary of the Navy Papers, Military.

25. Gormly, *Collapse of the Grand Alliance,* 91–93.

26. *FRUS: Diplomatic Papers, 1945* 5:633–37; Lord Halifax to Foreign Office, March 5, 1945, F.O. 371, AN885/245/45; Record of conversation between Wright and Mark Ethridge, November 30, 1945, F.O. 371, R20247/21/7, both in PRO; Mark Ethridge and C. E. Black, "Negotiating on the Balkans, 1945–1947," in *The Kremlin and World Politics,* ed. Philip Mosely (New York, 1960).

27. Minute, October 22, 1945, F.O. 371, N15653/13/38; minute, October 6, 1945, F.O. 371, N13432/18/32; Foreign Office to Lord Halifax, October 6, 1945, U7856/5559/70, all in PRO.

28. James L. Gormly, "The Washington Declaration and the 'Poor Relation': Anglo-American Atomic Diplomacy, 1945–46," *Diplomatic History* 8 (1984): 125–43.

29. *New Times* (Moscow) 11 (November 1, 1945): 14–22; *New York Times,* November 25, 1945.

30. Gormly, *Collapse of the Grand Alliance,* 106–7; Liebovich, *Origins of the Cold War,* 116–20; Larson, *Origins of Containment,* 237–39.

31. *FRUS: Diplomatic Papers, 1945* 2:578–85; Gormly, *Collapse of the Grand Alliance,* 106–7; Byrnes, *Speaking Frankly,* 109–12.

32. Memorandum, December 10, 1945, RG 59, DS 711.61; *Department of State Policy Manual, 1945,* December 15, 1945, RG 59, DS 711.00; Robert L. Messer, "Paths Not Taken: The United States Department of State and Alternatives to Containment, 1945–1946," *Diplomatic History* 1 (1977): 297–319.

33. *Washington Post,* December 13, 1945.

34. Byrnes, *Speaking Frankly,* 110–11; Harriman and Abel, *Special Envoy,* 523; Gormly, *Collapse of the Grand Alliance,* 110–11.

35. *FRUS: Diplomatic Papers, 1945* 2:610–29.

36. Ibid., 610–29, 663–64; Gormly, *Collapse of the Grand Alliance,* 112–14.

37. *FRUS: Diplomatic Papers, 1945* 2:632–40, 643–47; Byrnes, *Speaking Frankly,* 115–16; Harriman and Abel, *Special Envoy,* 523–24.

38. Harriman and Abel, *Special Envoy,* 532; *FRUS: Diplomatic Papers, 1945* 2:644, 647, 680–91; Byrnes, *Speaking Frankly,* 113–14; Ernest Bevin to Foreign Office, December 19, 1945, F.O. 371, U10223/6550;

Ernest Bevin to Foreign Office, December 21, 1945, F.O. 371, U10272/6550/70, both in PRO; Dixon, *Double Diploma*, 202.

39. *FRUS: Diplomatic Papers, 1945* 2:617–20, 627, 639, 641–43, 696–700, 716–17.

40. Ibid., 716–19, 727–34, 750–58; Byrnes, *Speaking Frankly,* 116–17.

41. *FRUS: Diplomatic Papers, 1945* 2:761–76; Ernest Bevin to Foreign Office, December 26, 1945, F.O. 371, U10377/6550/70, PRO.

42. Ernest Bevin to Foreign Office, December 26, 1945, F.O. 371, U10377/6550/70, PRO; Dixon, *Double Diploma*, 202–4.

43. *FRUS: Diplomatic Papers, 1945* 2:781–95, 805–6.

44. Ibid., 777–79, 795–99, 805–6; Dixon, *Double Diploma*, 205; Ernest Bevin to Foreign Office, December 27, 1945, F.O. 371, E10191/103/34, PRO.

45. Dixon, *Double Diploma*, 20–26; Byrnes, *Speaking Frankly,* 121; *FRUS: Diplomatic Papers, 1945* 2:813–14.

46. Gormly, *Collapse of the Grand Alliance*, 129–31; Bullock, *Bevin,* 212–16.

IV

Dealing with the Soviets, January– June 1946

Secretary of State Byrnes returned from Moscow exhausted and in no mood to greet critics. Yet he realized that the public and, more important, those near President Truman were questioning the merits of his diplomacy. Popular radio personality Walter Winchell and a number of newspaper editorialists were suggesting that American interests were harmed by the secretary's style of negotiating. According to the *Chicago Tribune*, he was "silly" for trusting the Russians. National approval of the Moscow agreements had fallen nearly 10 percent almost overnight.

Therefore, it was a grim and serious official who landed in Washington on December 28. Although tired, he needed to address the people, to explain the success of the conference in a speech that would permit him to continue the diplomacy he had begun overseas. Having told his aides to reserve airtime on the major radio networks, Byrnes was more than irritated to hear that Truman wanted to see him as soon as possible. "Goddammit to Hell, I can't do that," he swore at Assistant Secretary of State Dean Acheson, "I've got to work on this speech."[1]

Criticism of Byrnes

Truman's insistence on an immediate meeting highlighted the threat of voices close to the president who were hostile to

Byrnes and the Soviets.   Having concluded that the Roosevelt-style, horse-trading approach to dealing with the Kremlin was inappropriate for an expansionist and ideologically motivated nation, these critics opposed the tone and substance of the Moscow accords.   Led by Admiral William Leahy, who disliked both the secretary of state and the Soviets, various political and private friends of Truman conducted a campaign to control or remove Byrnes and to shift American policy toward a more combative stance. They were joined by many in Congress and within the State, War, and Navy departments.

Initially, it appeared that Byrnes was going to overcome his enemies. His meeting with Truman on the presidential yacht, *Williamsburg,* was a success—no doubt disappointing Leahy and others on board. Angry about Byrnes's failure to keep him informed, the president complained that he had first read about the agreements in the newspapers. The secretary soothed his ire by explaining the difficulties of relaying coded messages between Moscow and Washington compared to the ease with which the press could broadcast news. He assured Truman that the accords were in the best interests of the United States.

Byrnes was proud of his accomplishments at Moscow, where he had worked to allay Soviet suspicions and mistrust. He had achieved meaningful agreements, ones that very nearly duplicated those drafted by the State Department prior to the conference. Only two results were unsatisfactory: First, the Bulgarian accord was "flawed" because no provisions guaranteed the enlargement of the government or the protection of civil and political rights. Second, the Soviets had refused to deal with the present government in Iran, blocking a solution to the problems of that country.

The briefing lasted slightly over one hour. Truman emerged satisfied, ordering his aide to ensure that CBS honored the secretary of state's request for broadcasting time. He did not even ask to see an advance copy of the speech. Exhausted from nearly nonstop activities over the past three days and needing to put finishing touches on his remarks, Byrnes declined the president's invitation to stay and play poker.[2]

The next day, December 29, the secretary publicly recounted the Moscow agreements. He admitted that much still needed to be resolved, including the Iran issue. "We must not slacken in our efforts," he told the public, but move forward "with patience, good will, and toleration . . . to build and maintain a just and enduring peace." The speech generated support, and public opinion rose concerning both the conference and Byrnes. Former Secretary of State Cordell Hull wired his "heartiest congratulations." Truman, writing to Secretary of War Henry Stimson, commented that, while the domestic scene was "still a very bad headache," the international outlook was "very much improved." Leahy, still critical, wrote in his diary that he was in "the bad graces of the State Department." The spirit of the Moscow accords, however, was not to last long. By the beginning of February the formula that stressed "patience, good will, and toleration" in working with the Soviets was undergoing a metamorphosis.

In his memoirs, Truman credits himself for changing American policy when he called Byrnes into his office on January 5 and read him the "riot act." After reviewing the Moscow agreements and reading Mark Ethridge's report on Eastern Europe, the president found Soviet behavior unacceptable and leading the world toward war. He restated his complaint that he was "kept totally in the dark." Soviet actions in Iran were an "outrage," and the Red Army intended to attack Turkey. "Unless Russia is faced with an iron fist and strong language another war is in the making." It was time, Truman told Byrnes, to "stop babying the Russians." Among other things, he wanted his secretary not to recognize the Romanian and Bulgarian governments, while maintaining complete control of Japan and the Pacific and establishing a strong central government in Korea.[3]

The president was not alone in taking credit for shifting U.S. policy. In his account of the postwar years, Senator Arthur Vandenberg also claimed responsibility for stiffening Byrnes's diplomatic backbone. Neither account is totally accurate. Truman's report of a meeting on January 5 is clearly in error, for he did not receive Ethridge's comments until nearly one week later. Moreover, it is unlikely that the fiery Byrnes would have taken such a lecture without resigning. Nor did policy toward Korea, Iran, Romania, Bulgaria, or the Soviet Union change at that time. As for Vandenberg's assertion, the secretary adopted his sterner approach before the senator's speech of February 27. The shift regarding the Soviets was not caused by one or two individuals or actions; rather, it resulted from a complex combination of domestic and foreign events and considerations. Both the president and Vandenberg played a part, but so too did the press, public opinion, Russian behavior, and Byrnes's own evaluations.[4]

Despite the surge of support for the Moscow agreements following his speech, many in the government still disapproved of Byrnes and his diplomacy. They were determined to prevent more Yalta-style gifts to the Soviets. Almost from the end of that earlier conference, conservatives had questioned the resulting accords and the style of diplomacy practiced there. They contended that Yalta provided too many advantages for the Soviets in Eastern Europe and the Far East. Opposition intensified in early 1946, when the Russian press revealed that Roosevelt had returned the Kuril Islands and Sakhalin to Soviet control. Because the United States had recently denied such a charge, Byrnes was repeatedly asked about the truth of the printed statement. He finally admitted that the account was correct and that the former president had made secret arrangements with the Kremlin. Such revelations only further tarnished the memory of Yalta and those who had participated in it. By early February, even the liberal press was calling the summit a mistake and blaming the deceased president's illness and his advisers.

As the debate continued, Byrnes's image as an honest statesman eroded. George Elsey, Truman's aide, thought that the secretary now had "the reputation of being a liar." Press accounts of a major rift between the president and Byrnes surfaced. The latter met the stories with quick denials, but from the White House came only silence. Inside and outside the administration, pressure was building for Byrnes to adopt a tougher policy, closer to that practiced in London.[5] In September 1945 he had stood up to Molotov, willing to see the London Conference fail rather than concede. Yet, despite widespread approval of his stance, he had gone to Moscow and had sought more than just to resolve outstanding issues.

Byrnes had intended to evaluate the Kremlin's intentions and commitment to peace. At the Moscow meeting he had expected positive signs from the Soviets as proof of their goodwill, telling Ernest Bevin that he had met the Russians more than halfway, and now it was their turn to match his efforts. By early February, it was increasingly clear that they would not. Across the globe, he and other American officials saw Soviet obstructionism and expansionism occurring with increasing frequency. Full-scale propaganda attacks were launched against Britain, and the Americans were accused of violating the agreements on Bulgaria and Korea. It appeared that the accords were falling apart almost as Byrnes defended them to Truman and the public.

Watching the Soviet Union

In southeastern Europe, implementation of the Moscow agreements was having mixed results. The Romanian government had been enlarged and recognized by the United States and Britain. Throughout the region, however, the Soviets and local Communists were making "concerted efforts" to consolidate their positions. Even in Romania there seemed little positive political change. The State Department and the Foreign Office helplessly watched as Moscow linked the economies of the region "to ever closer dependence on the Soviet system" and isolated or eliminated pro-Western politicians and groups.[6]

The Soviets appeared to be having the largest success in Bulgaria, where the Moscow agreement to broaden the government was bogged down, and American and Russian officials blamed each other for the impasse. The fatherland front, as pro-Soviet governments became known, had asked that two members of the opposition join the regime, but the request was rejected. According to the Russians, the American representative, Maynard Barnes, had encouraged the opposition not to cooperate until further concessions were made, particularly the removal of the Ministries of Interior and Justice from Communist hands. The fatherland front had refused.

In January, while attending the London meeting of the United Nations, Deputy Foreign Minister Andrey Vyshinsky met with Byrnes and asked him to instruct Barnes and the Bulgarian opposition to drop their demands and join the government. Although minor, Vyshinsky said,

the issue "was poisoning relations between the powers."
Byrnes, supported by Bevin, adopted what he termed a
"neutral" position. The responsibility for broadening the
government rested with the Soviets and the Bulgarians.
They needed to take action to ensure the expansion of the
regime. The deputy totally disagreed. The Kremlin and the
fatherland front had fulfilled their part of the bargain, and
the impasse needed to be removed by the United States and
Britain. By early February the Soviet and Bulgarian press
were openly stating that it was Western unwillingness that
kept the government from being enlarged.

On February 22, back in Washington, Byrnes was in the
process of shifting to a stiffer policy. Without notifying the
Russians, he had abandoned his neutral position and
informed the Bulgarians that his government expected the
opposition to participate when "mutually acceptable
changes and policies" had been approved. The United
States now required political reform before the opposition
joined the regime. Without the modifications and broader
participation, Washington would not consider recognizing
the government. Two weeks later the Bulgarians and the
Soviets responded, flatly rejecting the American position
and pointing out that it went beyond the scope of the original
agreement. The matter was small, as Vyshinsky had said,
but, in the charged atmosphere of early 1946, it added to the
poisoning of East-West relations.[7]

Nor was it just events in southeastern Europe that
soured Byrnes's view. Throughout January and February a
variety of Soviet actions seemed all too familiar. From about
the beginning of the opening session of the United Nations,
it appeared that the Russians were involved in
confrontation. Highlighting the debates was Iran's protest
on January 19 against Soviet intervention in its affairs.
Believing that London had a role in the complaint, the
Russians responded by asking the United Nations to
investigate British actions in Greece and Indonesia.
Charges and countercharges followed, providing a heated
atmosphere for a clash between Bevin and Vyshinksy. Each
claimed that the other represented a threat to peace.
"Incessant propaganda from Moscow . . . sets us one
against another," the British minister announced. With
Byrnes and the U.S. delegation quietly watching from the
sidelines, the American press made Bevin a hero for taking

on the Soviets. One magazine pointedly suggested that the
government swap Byrnes for him.[8]

As the foreign ministers sparred over Greece,
Indonesia, and the Soviet war of nerves against Turkey and
Iran, the West watched another reflection of Soviet plans:
the 1946 election campaigns. Observers closely studied
Russian campaign speeches for clues to the direction of
policy. The Kremlin seemed determined to convince its
people that the West was no longer a friend but an enemy.
Increasingly, terms like "capitalistic encirclement" and
suggestions of Soviet unilateralism laced the speeches of
Communist officials. Such language was expected of
known hard-liners such as G. M. Melenkov and L. M.
Kaganovich. What worried the State Department and the
Foreign Office was that moderates and Stalin voiced similar
positions.

Stalin's February 9 speech was deemed especially
important. The Soviet leader reasserted that war was the
"inevitable result of the development of world capitalism
and political forces on the basis of modern monopoly
capitalism." Future war might be avoided if peaceful
means could be established to redistribute raw materials
and markets, but it was "impossible to do under present
capitalist conditions." While much of the address dealt with
domestic and economic affairs, American evaluators
focused on the parts suggesting that Stalin was moving
away from cooperation with the West. *Time* noted that his
remarks contained no threats and were defensive in content
but still believed that the speech constituted the most
"warlike pronouncement uttered by any top-ranked
statesman since V-J Day." What concerned the editors and
other American observers was Stalin's "truculent
exaggeration of the danger of attack from the capitalist
world" and his call for the Russian people to prepare
themselves for "all contingencies." Recording the
American response to the generalissimo's words, Lord
Halifax called it the event of the week.[9]

To most Kremlin watchers the speech showed Soviet
hostility. Supreme Court Justice William O. Douglas called
it "a Declaration of World War III." Even Walter Lippmann
considered the address dangerous, and opinions in the State
Department mirrored such alarm. Assistant Secretary
Acheson believed that the speech showed Stalin to be moving

away from cooperation, along "an ominous course."
H. Freeman Matthews considered it proof of the leader's
anti-Western views and wanted other officials to read the
transcript. Less alarmed, the Foreign Office quipped that
Americans were aroused because Stalin had attacked their
god of capitalism.[10]

The election rhetoric, Vyshinsky's antics at the United
Nations, and Soviet actions in southeastern Europe and
Iran prompted evaluations of Kremlin policy. Within the
State Department, experts Charles Bohlen and Dr. Gerold
Robinson undertook the task. Finishing their assessment
in February, they concluded that the policy was not
ideologically driven by communism but related to economic,
social, and political "internal situations and conditions"
unlikely to change in the immediate future. The report,
supporting Byrnes's earlier approach, confirmed that
Washington's central diplomatic goal toward the Soviet
Union should be to encourage its participation in the
international system. The experts rejected as positive
methods both unilateral moves and a balance of power,
tactics that undermined multilateralism and only paid lip
service to the United Nations. At best, they surmised, such
techniques only would delay a Soviet-American clash.

Bohlen and Robinson supported a diplomatic attitude
that continued Big Three cooperation while slowly placing
more and more reliance on the United Nations.
Recognizing that the suspicious Russians were not easy
partners, the analysis concluded that the most productive
course was to hold Big Three meetings prior to larger
international gatherings. It was also necessary for the
United States to allay the Soviets' fears and meet them
halfway in negotiations.[11]

Even as the report was readied, Bohlen's perspective
was rapidly becoming less popular. Ambassador W.
Averell Harriman, recently returned from Moscow, Loy
Henderson of the foreign service, Assistant Secretary of War
John J. McCloy, George Kennan, Matthews, and others
were already advocating a much less conciliatory policy.
Outside the State Department the desire to use a balance-of-
power approach or unilateral action was strong. In the
War Department the view that Soviet behavior was
nonideological and based on physical and geographical
security requirements was fast losing support.

In January 1946 the Joint War Plans Committee projected that, instead of seeking buffer zones along its borders, the Soviet Union wanted to dominate "the Eurasian landmass" and all of its approaches. The military attaché in Moscow went further. According to his January report, the Kremlin wanted nothing less than world domination and the destruction of capitalism. In February the War Department advised Truman that the United States should not compromise on principle and should provide bilateral support to nations threatened by Soviet expansion. To meet the perceived threat the Joint Chiefs desired a policy with a global sense of responsibility, backed by American military force and still paying lip service to the United Nations.[12]

This attitude matched long-standing views of Secretary of the Navy James V. Forrestal and Admiral Leahy, both of whom had emphasized the ideological and expansionist nature of Soviet plans. Dissatisfied with State Department evaluations, Forrestal had commissioned, in late 1945, a private study of Russian policy. Conducted by Smith College Professor Edward Willett, the analysis concluded that the Soviets were committed to "global, violent proletarian revolution" and were a real threat to world peace. In opposing Byrnes's policy, the secretary of the navy ensured that Willett's study received a wide distribution throughout Washington.

Supporting the opinion that firmness would produce better results was Kennan's "long telegram" of February 22. He discounted physical and geographical security as directing Soviet actions. Instead, he stressed the basic dynamics of the totalitarian nature of the government. Its ingrown and isolated leadership needed external enemies, and so cooperative long-term relationships were precluded. Consequently, the United States should oppose Moscow's expansionism and interests. Although rejecting the possibility of civilizing the Russian Bear, Kennan did not ignore the benefits to be gained by negotiating with it. The Soviet leadership did not want war and was "highly sensitive to the logic of force." When faced with determination, the Kremlin would back down. Recognizing that the American people might not understand the tougher stance their government should take, the telegram also recommended educating the public about "the realities of the Russian situation."[13]

Bohlen thought that Kennan's analysis was too pessimistic, but the latter's evaluation and recommendations were finding a very favorable and wide reception. Passages from his telegram were soon leaked to the press by those anxious to educate the public. On February 27, Vandenberg stood before the Senate with his hands firmly clenching the lectern and demanded: "What is Russia up to now? We ask it in Manchuria. We ask it in Eastern Europe . . . in Italy . . . in Iran." He argued that the Soviets were busily promoting their own goals and called upon the United States to be equally forceful in supporting its interests and principles. America needed to avoid vacillation and compromise and must stand up for right and justice. The rousing speech received a standing ovation from the gallery and strong editorial support across the country. Some writers saw it as a direct challenge to Byrnes's policy and requested Washington to stop appeasing the Soviets.

The West Toughens

On February 28, Byrnes answered his critics and shifted American policy in an address prepared prior to Senator Vandenberg's and edited by Truman. After reading it, the president told his secretary to "stiffen up" and "not to make any compromises." The speech, given to the Overseas Press Club, challenged Moscow to follow proper forms of international behavior. While supporting the United Nations and welcoming the Soviet Union as a great country and ally, Byrnes advocated unilateral U.S. moves to promote and protect American goals. He stated that there were actions that no government should be allowed to take: occupying territories without consent, delaying peace treaties, expropriating property without agreements, and conducting a war of nerves against others. Listeners did not need the secretary to name the country that was following these paths. The United States had implicitly yet publicly stated that the Soviets not only would be held accountable for their actions but also would possibly face retaliation. As Kennan later told audiences across the nation, Washington needed to set "will against will, force against force, idea against idea . . . until Soviet expansionism is finally worn down."[14]

Public expressions of concern about Russian intentions continued. On March 1, John Foster Dulles spoke of his experiences at the United Nations. Calling for stronger American leadership, he speculated that the Russians did not want to cooperate. But Dulles's words were only a prologue to former Prime Minister Winston Churchill's speech at Fulton, Missouri, on March 5. There, accompanied by Truman, Churchill addressed two related themes: the Soviet threat and the need for an Anglo-American partnership to protect the peace. He undermined reliance on the United Nations and the Yalta view. Not only had Moscow dropped an "iron curtain" on Eastern Europe, but it also was threatening peace in Germany, Italy, Turkey, Iran, and the Far East. The message was clear. Ruthless, brutal, and untrustworthy Russia was not going to be civilized. With the idea of cooperation thus shattered, Churchill called upon "the fraternal association of English-speaking peoples" to prevent war and further Soviet aggrandizement.[15]

The speech brought mixed reactions. While many affirmed Churchill's view of the Soviets and their threat to the world, fewer supported his call for an Anglo-American partnership. Most approving were those previously critical of Byrnes. *Time* and the *New York Times* were joined by the *Wall Street Journal*, *US News & World Report*, the *Christian Science Monitor*, and other publications in lauding Churchill as the greatest statesman of the era. According to *Time*, Byrnes had the voice of a "turtle" and the former prime minister that of a "lion."[16]

Even within the conservative press and the ranks of those applauding Churchill's realism came questioning of his Anglo-American partnership, his rejection of compromise, and his depreciation of the United Nations. The moderate and liberal press went further and used these points to criticize the speech. The *Boston Globe*, *Newsweek*, and the *New York Herald Tribune* found Churchill's assessment off target and advocated more, not less, reliance on the United Nations. Polls of congressional opinion reflected the view of most Americans that the Soviets were dangerous and a threat to world peace, but the United States should not yet abandon the concept of an international organization and negotiations with the Kremlin.

In their responses to the controversy surrounding the Fulton speech, Truman and Byrnes were less than honest with the public. Both had read and approved Churchill's address before it was presented yet in the following weeks denied any prior knowledge of its contents. They rejected the former prime minister's "unequivocal" and hostile view of the Soviet Union and declared unflinching support for the United Nations and attempts to reach agreements with the Russians. The liberal journal *Nation* concluded that "a vast gulf between Churchill and the Byrnes-Vandenberg positions" existed. Still, neither Truman nor his secretary backed away from the view that the United States would stand up to Moscow whenever and wherever necessary to protect American principles and the rights of other nations.[17]

Behind the scenes, Byrnes had already started to implement a more aggressive approach. Throughout February, prior to his Overseas Press Club speech, he had objected to Soviet policies on the principles he was to announce publicly. Regarding Bulgaria, he had blamed the Kremlin and the fatherland front for nonimplementation of the Moscow agreement and placed the United States on the side of the opposition. Despite recognition of Romania's enlarged government, he had dispatched several telegrams to Moscow denouncing the lack of other political and civil reforms in that country. Washington had strengthened its stand against Soviet economic policies in southeastern Europe while linking any loans with the implementation of American principles in Eastern Europe.[18]

Southeastern Europe was not the only place where U.S. policy was assuming a tougher tone. Byrnes was preparing a new stand on Korea that abandoned the position taken at Moscow. In late 1945 he had thought that Korea might be a place where Soviet and American interests would not clash and that the Moscow agreement pledging Korean independence and unification after a joint trusteeship was a positive one. South Koreans, however, wanted immediate freedom and opposed any trusteeship. The American commander in chief for the country, General John Hodge, a strong opponent of communism there, initially stated that the Soviets had insisted on being trustees. Never, he wired

Washington, had U.S. popularity been so high as when the Koreans blamed Moscow for their lack of independence. But that was soon to change. In early January, Tass printed the full account of the discussions at Moscow on the subject. The story clearly showed that the idea of a trusteeship was American and almost completely reversed public opinion. Anti-American riots broke out as Washington confirmed the accuracy of the Russian article to an unhappy Hodge.

Upon returning to Washington after stopping in Korea, Ambassador Harriman explained to Byrnes and other officials, including the secretary's strongest critics, that the Soviet intention in Korea was to dominate the region as in Eastern Europe. This opinion was duplicated in the War Department. General Hodge told his staff that there was no doubt the Kremlin meant "to have Korea become a Soviet state" and that it was "just one pawn in their great ambition."[19]

Already under attack for involvement in the secret diplomacy and concessions of Yalta, Byrnes quickly backed away from considering Korea as a place where the United States and the Soviet Union could cooperate. Believing that the Russians and Korean Communists were purging those who did not support Soviet goals, the State Department instructed Hodge to deny political participation to any "groups dominated by totalitarian leftists, such as communists." By mid-February the State Department told the commander that, if the initial meetings of the Joint Commission proved ineffective, as expected, he was to create unilaterally an advisory group whose goal would be the formation of a provisional government. Washington was no longer committed to a trusteeship and now looked toward establishing "a free and independent Korea."[20]

Trouble over Iran

American policies in southeastern Europe and Korea took place on an official level, away from the public posturing reflected in the speeches of February. But in March, almost simultaneously with Churchill's address, the extremes merged as Iran again became front-page news. This time, Byrnes was determined that he and the United States, instead of Great Britain and Bevin, would receive credit for standing up against Russian aggression.

Since the January UN meeting, which had witnessed the confrontation between Bevin and Vyshinsky, the Iranian issue had simmered out of sight. The Azerbaijani rebels of northern Iran, with Soviet support and encouragement, seemed to be consolidating their control, while Iranian Prime Minister Ahmad Qavam was in Moscow with Stalin and Molotov, trying to negotiate the removal of Red Army forces. When Qavam referred to March 2 as the date for the withdrawal of forces, Stalin objected. According to the latter, the presence of troops was no longer dictated by the wartime agreement but by the Iranian-Soviet Treaty of 1921, which permitted occupation for as long as Moscow deemed necessary. Later during the discussions, Molotov presented the premier with a list of conditions that needed to be met before any forces would leave. It contained not only the conclusion of an Iranian-Soviet oil contract but also Iran's recognition of provincial autonomy for Azerbaijan.

Having received reports of the negotiations, the United States and Britain watched anxiously as the March 2 deadline approached and passed without the Soviet troops' departure. Concern rapidly turned to alarm when the American consul in Tabriz, the capital of Azerbaijan, reported that Red Army forces and armor were moving toward Turkey, Iraq, and Tehran. Displayed on a State Department war-room map, the maneuvers seemed to indicate a Russian thrust to occupy all of the Near East. Upon being briefed, Byrnes appeared almost pleased, announcing: "Now we'll give it to them with both barrels." He had found an opportunity to display toughness with the Soviets, but exactly how was a problem. Direct military action was impossible because the United States had no forces in the region. That left only public diplomacy.[21]

Byrnes worked on two levels in handling the Iranian crisis. The first was a series of notes to Moscow and Tehran firmly opposing the continued presence of Soviet troops. Frequently, parts of these messages, although confidential, found their way into the American press and won widespread support. The second, and more visible, diplomatic effort took place at the United Nations as Byrnes upheld the Iranian complaint against the Soviet Union.

Once it was apparent that Soviet forces were not withdrawing on schedule, the State Department dispatched a moderate but firm message to Moscow. It declared that the United States "could not remain indifferent" to the occupation of Iran and wanted the troops immediately removed. At the same time, Byrnes attempted to pressure the Soviets by asking that they inform Washington about their actions. A second note, sent after alarming reports from the Middle East began to arrive, asked the Soviets for an explanation. While neither statement constituted an ultimatum, Washington clearly intended to support Iran and to hold the Kremlin accountable for its actions.[22]

Not only was Byrnes letting the Soviets know of the U.S. determination to back Iran, but he also was working to ensure that Iran would not give in. Since January the Kremlin had placed increasing pressure on Prime Minister Qavam to negotiate a settlement that would result in the evacuation of troops. In return, however, Moscow wanted a significant amount of autonomy for Azerbaijan and the formation of an Iranian-Soviet oil company. Unwilling to accept these conditions, Qavam returned to Iran in early March, but the war of nerves continued. Byrnes feared that the prime minister might buckle and therefore make concessions. To give encouragement, even as tanks were rumored to be moving on Tehran, the secretary used the American press. Journalists with close contacts in the State Department were told that the forthcoming UN meeting in New York would see a "showdown" on Iran pitting the United States and the principles of the United Nations against the Soviet Union.[23]

Byrnes wanted Iran to file a formal protest against the Soviet Union for threatening the peace and interfering in its affairs. He and many American and British officials believed that the United Nations and world opinion offered the best means to force the Russians to withdraw. But more seemed at stake than merely changing their behavior in the Middle East; many thought that the very existence of the United Nations and international cooperation was at risk. Byrnes suggested that, unless there was a successful conclusion of the Iranian issue, the world organization would "die in its infancy of inefficiency and ineffectiveness." His view was echoed by much of the American press.[24]

Byrnes was also interested in recapturing support for himself. Nearly all of the recent evaluations of the Soviet Union concluded that it did not want war and, when faced with firmness and hostile world opinion, would change its international behavior to a more acceptable pattern. The secretary of state, after being attacked for compromising with the Soviets, saw the crisis as a means of demonstrating his strength and resolve—but only if Iran kept its protest on the agenda of the Security Council and before the world. On March 18 the secretary finally moved closer to achieving his goals, when the Iranian ambassador to the United Nations, Hussain Ala, formally presented a complaint to the organization and asked that it be placed on the agenda of the Security Council as soon as possible. Accepted by the council, the Iranian resolution was scheduled to be considered on March 25.

The Soviet reaction was to call for the removal of the complaint while trying to settle the issue bilaterally with Qavam. On March 19 the Russian ambassador to the United Nations, Andrey Gromyko, requested that the resolution be postponed until talks between Tehran and Moscow were completed. Immediately there was a chorus of protests. Ambassador Ala, Byrnes, and even Truman strongly opposed any delay and pointed out that no such negotiations were currently taking place. The following day, with pressure on Qavam still building, the Soviet ambassador in Tehran presented a new proposal for consideration. It offered the removal of troops following a letter from Qavam's government accepting the formation of an Iranian-Soviet oil company.[25]

At the same time, the Soviets publicly announced reductions in their troop strength in Germany, further demobilizations, and the beginning of the removal of forces from Manchuria. On March 21, Stalin reaffirmed the Soviet commitment to peace and support for international cooperation and the United Nations. Three days later the Russians presented Qavam with a new and slightly tougher proposal for the removal of troops. On March 25, Tass announced that an agreement had been reached between the two countries and that Soviet forces would soon begin to leave. Complete withdrawal would take from five to six weeks, the Soviet news service stated, "if nothing unforeseen should take place." On the same day, Stalin gave a rare, personal interview to a Western reporter and confirmed the agreement, noting that it removed any need for UN consideration. In reality, there was no such accord, and both Stalin and Qavam knew it.[26]

For the premier, who had yet to respond to the Soviet proposal of March 20, the new offer and Stalin's interview made it clear that, unless an agreement was quickly reached and the complaint removed, the Russian position might stiffen further. In New York, Gromyko privately told U.S. Ambassador to the United Nations Edward Stettinius that, if the Security Council heard the Iranian complaint, the Soviet Union could not participate. Stettinius was unmoved; the resolution stayed on the agenda.

As the Security Council began its discussion of the Iranian issue, Gromyko stated that Moscow and Tehran had reached a settlement. He asked that the complaint be removed. Determined to be tough, knowing that no agreement had been made, Byrnes rejected the ambassador's request and asked for proof of any settlement. Since none was available, the issue stayed on the agenda. When Gromyko lost a motion to postpone discussion until April 10, he stalked out of the meeting. With the Soviet Union no longer represented, the council listened to Iran's complaint. Having won an important battle in the diplomatic war, Byrnes eased the impact of the victory by moving that any decisions be delayed until early April, when the Soviets and the Iranians could report on their negotiations.[27]

On April 3, Gromyko again stood before the Security Council and presented his nation's position. Referring to the March 24 Iranian-Soviet "agreement," he emphasized that Red Army troops were leaving the country and therefore it was not necessary for the United Nations to consider the issue further. Once more the Iranian ambassador refuted the Russian position, as he lashed out against intervention in Tehran's affairs. Faced with two opposing reports, the council deferred consideration until May 6.

Satisfied with the handling of the Iranian issue, Byrnes returned to Washington. The problem continued to simmer but increasingly far from the limelight. Over the next few days, Qavam and Moscow finalized an agreement. The Soviets would evacuate their troops unconditionally and

allow Tehran to deal with Azerbaijan. In exchange, Qavam
would form an Iranian-Soviet oil corporation, provided his
parliament approved. The crisis was over.[28]

The secretary was very pleased with the results. Byrnes
had successfully used the United Nations and world opinion
to hold the Soviet Union accountable for its actions. The
Russians had been forced to change their tactics. He had
also returned to public and official favor and demonstrated a
new brand of tough diplomacy. Charles Bohlen and
H. Freeman Matthews took special notice of the role played
by the world organization and public disapproval. The
United Nations had proven "a particularly effective
instrument in counter-acting Soviet aggressiveness," and it
would, wrote Matthews, "continue to provide one of the most
useful channels for keeping Soviet ambitions within
legitimate bounds as well as . . . an effective means of
rallying public support" for American policies.[29]

The State-War-Navy Coordinating Committee (SWNCC)
recognized the usefulness of the United Nations as well but
also emphasized the necessity of American and British
actions. "Peaceful coexistence," recorded a SWNCC
memorandum, depended upon demonstrating by diplomatic
and, if necessary, military means to the Soviets that their
behavior would lead only to disaster. In another part of the
memorandum, the committee came very close to calling for
an Anglo-American alliance, concluding that the Russians
could be denied "the hegemony of Europe" only if the United
States supported a politically, militarily, and economically
strong Britain.[30]

As the events of early 1946 indicated, a new relationship
between the United States and the Soviet Union had
emerged. Washington was no longer reassuring and
moderate toward the Kremlin, no longer willing to avoid
unilateral actions. While open hostility was officially
absent, it seemed obvious that former President Franklin
Roosevelt's view of world stability based on Big Three
cooperation and harmony would not serve as the basis of the
postwar international system.

While the United States and Byrnes toughened their
stance toward the Soviet Union, concern arose within the
Kremlin. Like their wartime allies, the Soviet leaders were
evaluating their international position. Events indicated to
the Russians, as to the British and the Americans, that the

collaboration of the Grand Alliance was over. Rather than friends, Moscow saw its onetime allies as rivals, even enemies, and was anxious to ensure that its people accepted the change.

Traditional Russian isolationism had been broken by the war. The result was an infusion of Western ideas and culture. Many elements within Soviet society hoped that the trend toward better and more open relations would continue after the war. Their hopes proved unfounded. The February election speeches and changes in the structure and membership of the Communist party indicated that the country's leadership decided to dampen admiration of the West. At the same time, there was reemphasis on Soviet ideology, the hostility of the capitalistic world, and the unity of the Russian people. Frank K. Roberts, British chargé d'affaires in Moscow, concluded that Stalin did not "intend to have any 20th century Decembrist movement" and that the Central Committee of the Communist Party was going to educate the populace about the dangers of "bourgeois ideas and philosophies."[31]

In shifting public opinion against the West, the Soviet press ignored the Iranian crisis and concentrated instead on Churchill's Fulton speech. At first the Soviets had nearly ignored the address and merely noted any comments critical of its themes. But, on March 11, *Pravda* printed a full-scale attack. The article focused on the former prime minister's call for an Anglo-American coalition and suggested that the Soviet Union might withdraw from international cooperation. A similar article in *Izvestia* linked the Labour government with Churchill. Official criticism rose to another level when Stalin responded, claiming that the former prime minister was like Hitler and never had been a friend of the Soviet people.

In evaluating the criticism of Churchill and the general nature of Soviet propaganda, British and American observers believed that the Russians were trying to drive "a wedge" between the United States and Britain, being "genuinely alarmed by the recent signs of American rapprochement with Britain" and fearing a possible Anglo-Saxon atomic bloc. Roberts reported that there was frequent talk on the Moscow streets of war with the West. He called it a "flutter of nerves" and a "hysterical reaction" but added that the fear was nonetheless real. Russian housewives, he noted, were lining up to buy extra supplies of food and other necessities.[32]

Stalin and other officials soon assured the people that the Soviet Union was not really threatened. The generalissimo concluded in a press interview that "neither nations nor their armies" wanted war and that the recent alarm was caused by small political groups that sought to sow the "seeds of discord and uncertainty." Efforts to reduce internal and external tensions in late March did not mean that Moscow accepted the views and actions of the United States and Great Britain. Stalin informed newly appointed American Ambassador Walter Bedell Smith that the Soviet Union was being mistreated by the West and that Russian motives and actions in the Balkans and Iran had been misrepresented. The Soviet leader was especially angry at Churchill, who, he believed, "tried to instigate war against Russia, and persuaded the U.S. to join him in armed occupation of part of our territory in 1919, and lately he has been at it again." Ambassador Smith then asked if Stalin "really believed that the U.S. and Britain were united in an alliance to thwart Russia." Without hesitation the reply was "Yes." After blaming the United States and especially Britain for the cooling of relations among the powers, Stalin reasserted his belief in Big Three cooperation. He thought that Western and Soviet goals were "not incompatible" and the world should not be alarmed over "differences of opinion and arguments," as these would "with patience and good will . . . be reconciled."[33]

Stalin ended his conversation with Smith by advocating a Soviet-American relationship similar to that projected by Bohlen and Robinson in February and advocated earlier by Byrnes. But, in April 1946, many U.S. officials no longer believed in Stalin's goodwill or that differences could be resolved. If Stalin had hoped to engender conciliation with his interviews and announcements of troop removals from Iran, Manchuria, and Bornholm Island, he had miscalculated. Instead of interpreting these actions as friendly gestures, American and British statesmen decided that they were the result of confrontation and Western firmness. It was with this tough attitude that Byrnes prepared for his next round of meetings with the Soviets at the Paris meeting of the Council of Foreign Ministers.

Notes

1. Messer, *End of an Alliance,* 157; John Lewis Gaddis, *The United States and the Origins of the Cold War, 1941–1947* (New York, 1972), 286–96; Arthur H. Vandenberg, *The Private Papers of Senator Vandenberg,* ed. Arthur H. Vandenberg, Jr. (Boston, 1952), 232–33.

2. Gormly, *Collapse of the Grand Alliance,* 134–37; Vandenberg, *Private Papers,* 157.

3. Truman, *Memoirs* 1:551–52.

4. Ibid., 247–51; Messer, *End of an Alliance,* 157–65, 189–91.

5. *Newsweek* 28 (January 14, 1946): 25–26; ibid. (January 21, 1946): 4, 27; Messer, *End of an Alliance,* 166–77; Liebovich, *Origins of the Cold War,* 121–22.

6. Gormly, *Collapse of the Grand Alliance,* 139–44; Michael M. Boll, *Cold War in the Balkans: American Foreign Policy and the Emergence of Communist Bulgaria, 1943–1947* (Lexington, KY, 1984), 164–73.

7. Boll, *Cold War in the Balkans,* 165–88; Gormly, *Collapse of the Grand Alliance,* 140–42; memorandum, January 27, 1946, F.O. 371, N1471/140/38, PRO.

8. Harbutt, *Iron Curtain,* 146–50; Bruce R. Kuniholm, *The Origins of the Cold War in the Near East: Great Power Conflict and Diplomacy in Iran, Turkey, and Greece* (Princeton, 1980), 304–8; *Newsweek* 27 (February 11, 1946): 32; Richard A. Best, Jr., *"Cooperation with Like-Minded Peoples": British Influences on American Security Policy, 1945–1949* (New York, 1987), 115.

9. Robert V. Daniels, ed., *A Documentary History of Communism,* vol. 2, *Communism and the World* (Hanover, NH, 1987), 137–39; *Time* 47 (February 18, 1946): 29–30; Lord Halifax to Foreign Office, February 17, 1946, F.O. 371, AN423/1/45, PRO.

10. Lord Halifax to Foreign Office, February 17, 1946, F.O. 371, AN423/1/45, PRO; Hugh DeSantis, *The Diplomacy of Silence: The American Foreign Service, the Soviet Union, and the Cold War, 1933–1947* (Chicago, 1980), 172–73; Larson, *Origins of Containment,* 250–55.

11. Memorandum, February 14, 1946, RG 59, DS 711.61; Gaddis, *Long Peace,* 51–54; Daniel Yergin, *Shattered Peace: The Origins of the Cold War and the National Security State* (Boston, 1977), 165; Messer, "Paths Not Taken," 297–320.

12. *FRUS: General; The United Nations, 1946* (Washington, DC, 1972), 1:1165–66; Best, *British Influences,* 71–73, 77–79; Melvyn P. Leffler, "The American Conception of National Security and the Beginnings of the Cold War, 1945–48," *American Historical Review* 89 (1984): 351–58, 365–67.

13. *FRUS: Eastern Europe; The Soviet Union, 1946* (Washington, DC, 1969), 6:696–709; James V. Forrestal, *The Forrestal Diaries,* ed. Walter Millis and E. S. Duffield (New York, 1951), 127–32, 137–40.

14. Gaddis, *Long Peace*, 52–54; Messer, *End of an Alliance*, 189–94; Harbutt, *Iron Curtain*, 172–76; John Balfour to Foreign Office, July 17, 1946, F.O. 371, N9816/140/38, PRO.

15. *New York Times*, March 2, 1946; Harbutt, *Iron Curtain*, 179–96; Jeremy K. Ward, "Winston Churchill and the 'Iron Curtain' Speech," *History Teacher* 1 (1968): 5–13; Henry B. Ryan, "A New Look at Churchill's 'Iron Curtain' Speech," *Historical Journal* 22 (1979): 895–920.

16. Harbutt, *Iron Curtain*, 197–208; *Time* 47 (March 25, 1946): 32.

17. Harbutt, *Iron Curtain*, 197–208.

18. *FRUS: Eastern Europe, 1946* 6:62–64, 66–68, 71–72; Boll, *Cold War in the Balkans*, 169–72; Harbutt, *Iron Curtain*, 165–68.

19. Gormly, *Collapse of the Grand Alliance*, 137–39; Stephen Pelz, "Decision on Korean Policy," in *Child of Conflict: The Korean-American Relationship, 1943–1953*, ed. Bruce Cumings (Seattle, 1983), 106–10; William W. Stueck, Jr., *The Road to Confrontation: American Policy toward China and Korea, 1947–1950* (Chapel Hill, 1981), 20–28. See also James I. Matray, *The Reluctant Crusade: American Foreign Policy in Korea, 1941–50* (Honolulu, 1985); and Bruce Cumings, *The Origins of the Korean War: Liberation and the Emergence of Separate Regimes* (Princeton, 1981).

20. *FRUS: The Far East, 1946* (Washington, DC, 1971), 8: 623–27, 657–58, 685–87.

21. Harbutt, *Iron Curtain*, 217–23; Messer, *End of an Alliance*, 195–200.

22. Stephen L. McFarland, "A Peripheral View of the Origins of the Cold War: The Crises in Iran, 1941–47," *Diplomatic History* 4 (1980): 343–48; Harbutt, *Iron Curtain*, 216–19; Kuniholm, *Near East*, 316–26.

23. Kuniholm, *Near East*, 326–8; Harbutt, *Iron Curtain*, 219–23, 226–27.

24. Harbutt, *Iron Curtain*, 230–36; Kuniholm, *Near East*, 320–30.

25. Kuniholm, *Near East*, 239–331; Harbutt, *Iron Curtain*, 240–44, 325–29.

26. Harbutt, *Iron Curtain*, 245–60; Kuniholm, *Near East*, 331–42.

27. Kuniholm, *Near East*, 340–42.

28. Harbutt, *Iron Curtain*, 660–66.

29. Draft report by Charles Bohlen and Gerold Robinson, "What to Do with the USSR," February 14, 1946, RG 59, DS 711.61/1–1446; H. Freeman Matthews, "Memorandum for the Secretary of State," January 17, 1947, DS, Matthews File.

30. *FRUS: General, 1946* 1:1170.

31. Gormly, *Collapse of the Grand Alliance*, 150–53; Harbutt, *Iron Curtain*, 209–14.

32. Harbutt, *Iron Curtain*, 214–16; Gormly, *Collapse of the Grand Alliance*, 150–53, 159–62.

33. *FRUS: Eastern Europe, 1946* 6:732–36; Yergin, *Shattered Peace*, 190–92.

V

Stalemate in Paris, April 25– May 16, 1946

As relations among the Big Three deteriorated throughout the early months of 1946 the deputies to the Council of Foreign Ministers were meeting in London. Following the Moscow Conference the powers instructed their representatives—Fedor Gusev for the Soviet Union, James Dunn for the United States, and Ronald Campbell for Great Britain—to begin writing draft peace treaties for Hitler's European allies. Molotov, Byrnes, and Bevin had finally established May 1 as a tentative date to begin a general peace conference.[1] Now all that was needed to place Europe back on the path of stability was to invoke the conference, in which the nations at war with Hitler's satellites would accept and sign the treaties. No one believed that the task would be easy, but nearly everyone agreed it was necessary. The *Manchester Guardian* speculated that the Russians would obstruct the process at nearly every turn and even might force the writing of less-than-perfect treaties but concluded that a "bad peace was better than no peace at all." More optimistically, *Life* wrote that the process "offered another fair chance to sweep up some of the plaguing problems" the world faced and could "bring hope to a world whose peace aims are drifting into war talk." It asserted that "there is still time and Paris [the city selected for the conference] in the spring is a good place to begin."[2]

Initial Discussions

Meeting fifty-four times in Lancaster House in the center of London from January through April, the deputies considered the treaties for Italy, Romania, Bulgaria, Hungary, and Finland. Turning to Italy, they adopted a pattern similar to their previous London meeting. As in September, the U.S. and British delegations found themselves in general agreement and opposed by the Soviets. Aware of the great similarity between British and American views, Jacques Reinstein of the U.S. delegation thought it necessary to disagree occasionally to prevent the Russians from complaining too bitterly of an Anglo-American bloc.[3]

It soon appeared that Gusev had been instructed to make progress difficult. After watching him maneuver, Dunn concluded that the Soviets had "no interest whatever in helping to provide any return to stability" or in changing their "puppet stooge governments" in the Balkans. Both he and Campbell believed that the Russian goal was to delay reaching decisions until almost May. By holding the treaties hostage until the "last moment," the Soviets might force the West to compromise in order to complete them. Supported by the Foreign Office and the State Department, the two deputies agreed not to stand for such blackmail and favored making a separate peace with Italy, if necessary.[4]

By March, Dunn and Campbell's prediction about Soviet tactics seemed to be coming true: The date set for the peace conference was approaching, and the treaties remained unwritten. Britain and the United States faced a tough decision. Should a conference be called if the documents were not completed? Should a Big Four meeting of foreign ministers be called to resolve the problems? Should a separate peace with Italy be signed by the West, acknowledging the division of Europe into two zones? The last option was immediately dismissed. Neither Washington nor London was willing to assume the responsibility for ending big-power negotiations. In regard to the other alternatives, there seemed to be interconnected problems. Opening a conference without sufficient progress on the treaties only invited public failure, and clearly the deputies had reached a deadlock. The situation might be resolved by a four-power discussion among the foreign ministers. But, with the Big Three in the midst of the Iranian crisis and with Soviet forces possibly advancing toward Tehran, was that course advisable? It might appear as Western weakness and only encourage Soviet obstructionism.

In Washington, Byrnes considered the options and chose convoking the Council of Foreign Ministers as soon as possible. Anxious to proceed with the peace negotiations, he wanted a mid-April meeting in Paris to thrash out treaty differences. With their problems resolved, a May 1 conference was still feasible, and gathering in Paris would be more diplomatic than in London. The French, including the French Communists, were eager to host the meeting. Bringing Molotov to Paris, Byrnes speculated, might pressure the Soviet minister into completing the drafts and accepting France as an equal partner at the conference to follow. The secretary of state approached the British with the idea on March 6.

Bevin and the Foreign Office were of a different opinion. They saw little to be gained and much to be lost, especially if Byrnes chose to appease Molotov. The British appreciated the increasingly hard line Washington was taking toward the Soviet Union but remained unsure about the duration of the change and the secretary's commitment to it. Responding to Byrnes's query about a mid-April meeting, Bevin tactfully tried to decline, pointing to two obstacles that barred his participation. First, some "light" from the Soviets needed to be shed on the Iranian crisis before they sat down with Molotov. Second, the Dominion and Commonwealth ministers were arriving in April to consider a wide range of issues, including foreign policy, and his attendance at that discussion was vital.

Seeing his excuses fail to change Byrnes's position, Bevin modified his approach. He was willing to meet, but only if two conditions were fulfilled: A "moderately satisfactory reply" must be received from the Soviets concerning their actions in northern Iran, and Germany must be added to the agenda as the first topic. Again, his tactics had little effect. The secretary was determined to see Molotov. He rejected placing Germany on the agenda and pressed Bevin for a more positive answer. Worn down, the foreign minister finally agreed to the soundness of an April meeting, asking only that it be held after the Iranian crisis was over. Unaffected by Bevin's concerns, Byrnes forged ahead. Even as the United Nations heard Iran's complaint, he moved to arrange the summit. By the first week in April the schedule was set. A formal peace conference would open in May, and the Council of Foreign Ministers would convene on April 25. Both gatherings would be in Paris.[5]

Byrnes prepared for the council meeting with the same frame of mind he had before the London Conference of September 1945. He was going to succeed or hold the Soviets accountable for the failure. The secretary was determined to oppose Molotov and not budge. There would be no concessions to Moscow, he informed the cabinet. If necessary, he would write the peace treaties without Soviet participation or approval. In his own mind, he planned to accomplish what President Woodrow Wilson had failed to do: conclude the treaties and obtain Senate approval. Byrnes had participated in the 1918 debate over the Treaty of Versailles and recently had been reminded about the dangers of domestic opposition. To avoid political criticism and ensure bipartisan support for his actions, he asked prominent congressmen, Republican Arthur Vandenberg and Democrat Tom Connally, to accompany him to Paris. Both agreed, saying privately that they intended to "keep a bit of the good old iron" in the secretary's spine. To further insulate himself and the treaties from critics within the administration, before leaving he gave Truman his resignation. Citing poor health, which was probably not true, Byrnes asked that he be allowed to conclude the negotiations before the president announced his replacement.[6]

The tougher U.S. stance toward the Soviet Union and Byrnes's determination to finish the treaties received official and unofficial confirmation. Stories about the possibility of a separate peace with Italy surfaced. The *New York Times* noted in April that the Truman administration was taking great trouble to stress its firmer policy. American diplomats informed their British and French colleagues that Washington was not going to make concessions to the Russians, whose behavior had changed the U.S. public's mood.[7]

Drafting the Peace Treaties

Paris in April was a city approaching the gaiety of its prewar days. Tulips bloomed in the parks while vendors and colorful parasols dotted the sidewalks. The world watched the delegations arrive and take up residence in the most luxurious hotels: the Americans at the Meurice, the British at the George V, and the Soviets at the Plaza-Athénée. However, the apparent recovery of Paris was deceptive: France teetered on the brink of turmoil. Suffering from a lack of coal and food, its economy was faltering, a condition that intensified the already heated political debates for the June 2 national election. American Ambassador to France Jefferson Caffery called the situation "seriously deteriorated" and feared a Communist party victory.

Aware of the volatility and closeness of the upcoming election, the three powers sought opportunities to indicate support and respect for France. Amid public fanfare the Soviet Union provided shiploads of needed grain, hoping to increase existing sentiments in Moscow's favor. In Washington, State Department officials lobbied for the approval of a $650-million loan before the election. France and England held "the key to the whole Western European situation," Undersecretary of State William L. Clayton testified. "If we can bring about a condition of economic and social stability . . . there is a good chance of saving Western Europe from a collapse and . . . economic and social chaos."[8]

The Council of Foreign Ministers officially began its second meeting as scheduled, on April 25, 1946, at the Luxembourg Palace in Paris. Foreign Minister Georges Bidault's goal was to assert France's role as a major power and to succeed where Georges Clemenceau had failed: in separating the Rhineland and the Ruhr from Germany. Bidault wished to have Germany added to the agenda and got nearly all he wanted. Soon after the delegates entered the palace and started to work in the refurbished Victor Hugo Salon, Molotov reversed his London position. France would be allowed to participate fully in all discussions. Pierson Dixon, a British veteran of the London and Moscow meetings, observed that "we had a feeling the Russians would open with conciliation, with an eye on the French election. And they did, accepting the French proposals on procedure, which let the French into all discussions. . . . The Russians care nothing for consistency . . . and show no trace of shame or even amusement at a volte-face however violent." Germany was to be considered after work on the peace treaties had been completed.[9]

Having established their agenda and procedures, the ministers turned their attention to Italy. Almost immediately they confronted issues that had stalemated the deputies: reparations, colonies, and Trieste. The Soviet Union and France wanted reparations; the United States and Britain were opposed. Each advocated a different solution for the disposition of the colonies and the Yugoslav-Italian border. An unsmiling, businesslike Molotov immediately announced that his government demanded $600 million in reparations, with one half to be paid to the Soviet Union and the remainder to Yugoslavia, Greece, and Albania. It represented "justice," he stated, not revenge. Unexpectedly, Bidault gave his support. France, too, had been invaded by Italy and had suffered damage.

Concerned about reestablishing the nation's economy, Britain and the United States wanted to limit Italian reparations. While accepting them in principle, Byrnes and Bevin thought that even $300 million was too high; it exceeded Italy's ability to pay. His government, Byrnes pointed out, already had funneled $500 million into the Italian economy. Bevin noted that Britain also was providing relief. Unable to agree, the ministers sent the issue back to the deputies.[10]

The discussions so far had produced concern and disagreement but little ill feeling. That changed, however, when the ministers took up the issue of Italy's colonies. As with reparations, not much was new since the London Conference. Resubmitting the proposal for an international trusteeship, Byrnes called it still "the best solution." Bidault disagreed and asserted that Italy should be named as a sole trustee over its prewar colonies. Trying to adopt the guise of statesman, Molotov observed that both plans had merit and suggested a "compromise." The American version should be followed, but with Italy joining one of the four powers to administer its colony. He thought that Italy and the Soviet Union should be named trustees for Tripolitania, and Italy and either the United States or Great Britain for Cyrenaica.

Bevin offered a fourth alternative. Afraid of a Soviet foothold in North Africa and on the Mediterranean, he called for Libyan independence and opposed any Italian trusteeship. Britain had liberated the area and promised the natives that it would not allow a return of Italian rule. As for the colony of Somaliland, Bevin recommended that it be combined with Ogaden and British Somaliland to form "Great Somalia," which England would administer.

This was a new position for Britain. During the London Conference, it had been willing to accept either Italy as a trustee or even the "ridiculous American plan" in order to keep the Soviets away from the Mediterranean. But now, facing the loss of military bases in Egypt, the Joint Chiefs had selected the eastern portion of Libya as a replacement. Bevin told the cabinet that for imperial defense some control over Cyrenaica was "essential." The Foreign Office projected two possible methods for maintaining influence in the region: a direct trusteeship over Cyrenaica or independence for Libya. In either case the British meant to use Idris el-Sayed, leader of the Senussi Muslim brotherhood, as their Libyan spokesman. Independence seemed the alternative more likely to be accepted by the council.[11]

Bevin's offer was met with deadly silence and dagger stares from Byrnes. Molotov and Bidault coldly reserved comment until they saw a written proposal. The secretary then launched into a lengthy speech advocating his plan as the most logical because the British would not permit an Italian trusteeship and the Soviets would not allow a British one. The United States was even willing to pay the costs. Bevin had expected negative reactions from the French and the Soviets, but Byrnes's reply angered him. He had briefed the secretary on the proposal the day before, and now Byrnes not only acted as if it were all new but also seemed to dismiss it.

When the ministers next discussed the colonies, on May 2, Molotov had read Bevin's proposal and was ready to respond. He denounced Britain for trying "to keep all the Italian colonies for herself and even take something from Ethiopia." The British had "too many colonies and did not need more"; London was simply "too selfish." The Italian colonies "might be difficult for England to digest," Molotov warned. Eyes glaring, Bevin rose to reply, stating that his government sought only what was best for the peoples of Libya and the economic development of Somaliland. It was, he said, "too bad some regarded it with suspicion"; the Soviet empire covered "one-seventh of the earth's surface." Smugly, Molotov contended that his nation's territory had been acquired legally. Bevin retorted angrily that "perhaps England had made a mistake" by not having concluded a secret treaty during the war. With a bitter atmosphere filling the room, the ministers adjourned.[12]

Returning to the salon that afternoon, they considered the issue that Senator Vandenberg had predicted would create the real fireworks: Trieste and the Yugoslav-Italian border. As with reparations and colonies, the debate on the boundary was not new. During the London Conference the ministers had disagreed and appointed a special committee to investigate the territory. After more than one month of on-site investigations and hundreds of interviews, the committee could not reach a consensus. All that had changed was the degree of specificity about the proposed border and the desires of the people living in the disputed area.

As expected, the Soviet-sponsored boundary awarded almost all of the contested land, including Trieste, to Yugoslavia. While it permitted a sizable Italian population in the Communist country, it left almost no Yugoslavs living across the border. At the other end of the spectrum the U.S. proposal allocated most of the territory to Italy, leaving many Yugoslavs living under Italian control. The British solution was similar to the American, while the French recommendation lay somewhere between the British and the Soviet lines.[13]

Seeing no solution ahead, Bidault hoped that a change in procedure might help. On May 2 he suggested that they hold smaller, informal meetings in their offices. It was one of the few ideas upon which the ministers could agree. Unfortunately, the informal gatherings only duplicated the formal ones. Disagreements on reparations, colonies, and boundaries continued, and the tone of discussions became more ominous. Molotov pointedly informed his colleagues that the "Soviet Union would stay on its own feet whether or not it received a hundred million dollars worth of reparations" but that no decisions on the Italian treaty "could be reached without a clear reply on the reparations question." Angered, Byrnes proclaimed that the United States "was not going to do as it had done after the war and that was pay out hundreds of millions of dollars for the reparations account of others." Bevin was more blunt, declaring that, if Molotov meant that the Italian treaty would cost $100 million, then there "would be no treaty."[14]

Back in formal session the ministers continued to discuss the Yugoslav-Italian border. Noting that "[p]erfection was impossible in human endeavor," Bidault pointed out that the French line, although not perfect, best reflected the ethnic distribution. Each of the other statesmen agreed with the minister's point but still rejected the line. There were, they argued, other considerations.

Molotov wanted to support the claim of an ally and eliminate "the historic injustice against the Southern Slavs." The Soviet line, he said, met the needs of Yugoslavia, including the acquisition of Trieste. Not only did that country deserve the city because of its Allied status, but also it made no sense economically to sever Trieste from the surrounding region. Offering an inducement, Molotov "wondered if it might not be possible to meet the wishes of Yugoslavia . . . [now and] the wishes of Italy in other questions . . . including the question of the colonies and that of reparations."

For Bevin and Byrnes the criterion of ethnicity was balanced by economic and geographic considerations. The United States believed that its proposed border would make a reasonable ethnic distribution and maintain for Italy some valuable assets, including vital coal mines. Trying to bridge the gap between the Soviet and American lines, Byrnes suggested that they hold a plebiscite and let the people decide. If those in one area wanted to live under Italian or Yugoslav rule, they would so vote. Molotov objected that the result might prove to be very "bizarre," a chessboard effect providing no political or economic unity. Bevin and Bidault did not like the idea either and feared that the Yugoslavs and local Communists might control elections and create results unfavorable to Italy.[15]

Later, in a private meeting with Byrnes, Molotov was still in a trading mood. He was willing to agree to a plebiscite if it were held for all of Venezia Giulia and if the majority would determine the disposition of the area. But, Molotov continued, if the whole region could be given to Yugoslavia, it would be "possible for him to take a more favorable attitude toward Italy's desires in regard to the colonies and reparations." He explained that the Soviet Union would permit Italy to be the sole trustee over one or two of its former colonies and would only demand an "excessively modest" $100 million in reparations. Yugoslavia, Molotov guaranteed, would renounce its claims against its neighbor in return for Trieste. Byrnes found nothing of substance in the offer and quickly rejected it.

Molotov now began a tirade against American "imperialist expansion." Calling the assertion absurd, Byrnes calmly and patiently refuted the minister's allegations. But, when the 1919 Siberian intervention was mentioned, the secretary got up and left. He was increasingly convinced that no solutions were possible and it was time to end the conference. Despite having Truman's approval for closing the session, Byrnes did not make such a request; instead, the ministers considered the treaties for Romania, Bulgaria, Hungary, and Finland.[16]

Throughout the early months of 1946, the Foreign Office and the State Department had watched a flurry of activity as the Kremlin tried to ensure that Soviet and Communist influence would be well entrenched by the time the peace treaties were concluded. Just as during the London Conference, the Foreign Office wanted to finish the treaties soon and worried that U.S. efforts to modify the political status quo might quicken Sovietization. Christopher Warner of the Russia Committee wondered if it was possible to suggest to the Americans that in the cases of Hungary, Romania, and Bulgaria "discretion" was required, "not to appease [the Russians] but to spare our friends."[17]

Britain and the United States decided to accept the majority of the Soviet-drafted treaties and use economic clauses to try to maintain some influence. The Russians were attempting to incorporate southeastern Europe into "ever closer dependence on the Soviet system," while Western interests were being "pushed rudely out . . . and eliminated." Washington hoped to slow the inclusion of Eastern Europe in a Soviet colonial system by working freedom of trade and navigation and most-favored-nation clauses into the treaties. Such clauses might ensure that Western economic enterprises would receive the same favors that East European states offered the Soviets. The British supported the effort but believed that the Americans overemphasized the possible results. The U.S. position was, in their opinion, simply a case of "airy optimism."[18]

On May 7, as the ministers began to discuss the treaties for Romania, Bulgaria, and Hungary, they found general agreement on borders, political clauses, and military matters. But, on the economic issues, Molotov was as obstinate as ever. He refused to allow either a reference to Bevin's proposal of an international commission for the Danube or even a general statement supporting freedom of navigation on the river in both the Romanian and the Bulgarian documents. Such considerations were, he repeatedly explained, an issue for a separate conference.

Byrnes's attempt to write "equality of economic opportunity" into the treaties also failed. He wanted his colleagues to accept the principles of the Atlantic Charter and Article 20 of the Berlin protocol, which guaranteed equal access to trade, raw materials, and industry. Molotov agreed with the concept but believed that it should be considered through normal diplomatic channels and not by the council. Angered by his obstinacy, Byrnes coldly stated that the issue had been referred to the deputies in September. If the deputies did not constitute diplomatic channels, "he did not know where they could submit it." Frustrated by the Soviet minister's argument, he finally asked: "What was the sense of continuing this ring-around-a-rosy?" Unmoved by the secretary's anger, Stone Bottom Molotov maintained his position.[19]

With progress impossible on the Italian or southeast European treaties, Byrnes wanted either to announce the date of the peace conference or to highlight the Soviets' behavior as the obstacle and make them responsible for "world turmoil." On May 8 he proposed that the deputies prepare a report indicating their points of agreement and disagreement and that it be submitted to the conference for consideration. The secretary asked that June 15 be established for the opening of the negotiations, explaining that it "was the anniversary of V-E Day, and the world was expecting the restoration of peace." Beginning the conference then "would give the world something to celebrate."

Byrnes's colleagues conceded that a list of agreements and disagreements was a good idea but dissented about calling the peace conference. They wanted to try to solve their outstanding problems first. Molotov forcefully rejected calling a conference until they had approved the completed treaties.

Immediately, Bevin, Byrnes, and Bidault took exception to the Soviet view. The first two argued that the treaties did not need to be completed or approved before the conference. Bidault stated that, because France "had not had the good fortune to participate in as many such conferences," he "was not entirely disillusioned and had not lost hope that the Foreign Ministers could reconcile their points of view." He suggested a three-step procedure. First, before ending the present meeting, the ministers should make every effort to resolve disputed questions. Second, the deputies should continue after the close of the conference to work on settling any remaining issues. Finally, the ministers should reconvene in mid-June to hear the deputies' recommendations and consider solutions to their differences. During the June meeting, they would name a date for the peace conference.

Bevin seconded Bidault's plan with one modification: The peace conference should begin one month after the close of the proposed June meeting. In supporting the French proposition the British minister was forced to "choose between deferring issuing the invitations to the [peace] conference until a later date, and impairing Great Power unity by proceeding to call the conference in the face of Russian opposition." As he later explained to the cabinet, "The consequence of this latter course would be serious, and I was not prepared at that time to take such a step."

Byrnes, anxious to protect the peace conference, accepted the French and British positions but wanted to name either July 1 or July 15 as the opening date. Bevin and Bidault easily accepted the 15th. So, too, did Molotov, but only if the treaties were approved by that time. Bevin correctly pointed out that the Russian condition would allow any one of them to ensure that "the Peace Conference would never be held." The formal meetings seemed deadlocked; perhaps the informal discussions would produce better results.[20]

That afternoon the ministers began another series of informal sessions. Almost at once Molotov exploded a bombshell. He dropped the Soviet position on the Italian colonies and strongly promoted France's. The Soviet Union, he said, now supported "the new democratic Italy" as the sole trustee for its former colonies. When it appeared that Byrnes also was moving toward Bidault's proposal, Bevin asked that Britain govern Cyrenaica. As he explained to Prime Minister Attlee:

> Molotov took us all by surprise by definitely dropping his claim to be in the African continent and backing the French proposal that all the Italian colonies should be returned to Italy.
>
> Byrnes immediately showed signs of weakening and it was at once obvious to me that, from the moment Russia was ready to withdraw her claim to be in Africa, American interest in collective trusteeship would drop to zero. . . .
>
> With the Egyptian situation and Palestine in my mind I felt it imperative that I should at once spring a claim for Cyrenaica.

Bevin's action, at least temporarily, blocked further agreement on the question.[21]

As the informal talks continued, "concessions" were offered to narrow differences. Playing his part, Byrnes announced that his government was willing to accept $100 million for reparations to the Soviet Union. Furthermore, Washington would allow more than external Italian assets as sources of payment. The secretary remained adamant, however, that Italian current production should not be used as reparations. Molotov was joyful. Now, he said, all they needed to do was concur on sources. Unable to agree, the ministers sent the issue to the deputies.[22]

Molotov then offered a possible solution to the dispute over the calling of the peace conference. He boldly stated that the Soviet Union's position was misunderstood. Moscow did not require that every issue be resolved before the conference; only the fundamental questions needed to be answered. In light of this admission the ministers reviewed their discussions. They discovered there were no such questions left regarding the treaties for Finland, Hungary, Bulgaria, and Romania. Only Italy's reparations, the disposition of its colonies, and the Yugoslav border remained.

Hope continued to flicker that a breakthrough might be made. On May 13, Byrnes forged on, suggesting a new approach to the colonial dispute. Because the Soviets "could not find acceptable Mr. Bevin's proposal for a trusteeship over Cyrenaica," he suggested that the four powers administer the colonies for one year while they sought a permanent solution. If they could not find one in that time, they would turn the question over to the United Nations. Neither Bidault nor Molotov accepted the plan, calling it a step backward from their earlier agreement.

Undeterred, Byrnes made a second offer "in the spirit of compromise." The United States was willing to agree to the border proposed by France for Yugoslavia and Italy. Bevin also accepted the line. It was, he said, "a wise and fair decision." Molotov, however, refused, steadfastly supporting the Yugoslav claim on Trieste. For Byrnes any hope of a breakthrough vanished. He wanted to finish business and return to the United States. Left on his agenda were only two issues: a date for the peace conference and the four-power policy on Germany. It was clear to him that the ministers had reached the end of their ability to negotiate.[23]

The German Problem

Although writing the peace treaties for Hitler's allies had been the first priority, Germany was an issue that towered over that of Italy and southeastern Europe. By May 1946 the four powers had accepted unofficially that Italy belonged in the Western orbit, while Romania, Bulgaria, and Hungary lay in the Soviet circle. In haggling over the treaties, the ministers were merely trying to get the best deal, each either protecting his country's sphere of influence or preventing the opposing sphere from being totally closed. But the geographical area of Germany was not yet defined nor ascribed to anyone's control. It was an issue that required careful diplomacy and might permanently split the four powers. On May 15, as they prepared to discuss the defeated country, the ministers faced a three-part problem.

The first issue, security, was highly emotional, especially to the French and the Russians. As Bidault and Molotov pointed out on more than one occasion, they had been victims of German aggression several times during the past century. For these ministers and their fellow citizens, the fear of a German resurgence was real. "During 150 years Germany had seven times invaded France and there was hardly a French adult who did not remember the last two," Bidault explained to his colleagues; "for France, the German question was primarily a security and political problem."

Second was the issue of how to treat Germany economically. To many Europeans, for security reasons the best solution appeared to be to keep the country weak and divided. In early May, Bevin had told the cabinet that a "worse situation would be a revived Germany in league with or dominated by Russia." But a deprived nation presented another serious problem, especially for the Americans and the British. A punitive treatment that placed economic shackles on Germany and deprived the fatherland of territory would create conditions that would make the country a source of increasing instability and disruption. Believing that the decisions made at Potsdam were part of the difficulty, one British official concluded that the agreements would "complete the ruin of every class which might be on our side, that is to say everybody with anything to lose." Both the State Department and the Foreign Office believed that impoverishment would boost the German Communists. Equally disturbing to American and British planners was the thought that an economically weak Germany would not be able to contribute to the rehabilitation of Europe.[24]

The short-run costs of occupying a weakened territory, including maintaining an adequate standard of living for its citizens, was the third problem. Britain, facing its own financial crisis, bemoaned the drain of an unproductive Germany. One observer in the Foreign Office speculated that it "seemed quite likely" that "a solvent Germany" would be preferred over one that was demilitarized. The Americans complained that their zone contained only scenic wealth. Like the British, they believed that one solution to the immediate problem of cost was to stress German economic unity.

The issues overlapped and collided. To satisfy public opinion and maintain security, Germany should be kept weak. But an economically drained nation was not desired by the United States and Great Britain. In May the American commander in chief in Germany and representative to the Allied Control Council, General Lucius Clay, halted all reparations payments from the American zone, citing the lack of national economic stability. "If economic unity is obtained," he stated, "there is no reason why the reparations plan should not be implemented promptly." The general's action was aimed at both the French and the Soviets, who seemed to oppose efforts to treat Germany as an economic whole. As reparations stopped, however, the Kremlin showed signs of supporting a stronger and unified nation. Throughout Germany, Communists, clearly with Soviet backing, were advocating more production and control of the Ruhr. France remained steadfast, wanting to use the council meeting to gain favor for its control over the Ruhr, Rhineland, and Saar.[25]

Before leaving for Paris, Bevin had conferred with the cabinet on French goals and Britain's German policy. While his government's position was still undecided, it was definitely opposed to France's scheme. To Bevin the best option, one that would create the least discontent, was to make a new German province of the Ruhr and Rhineland, with industries and mines placed under the control of a "socialised German corporation" and linked to the provincial government. Another option was to form the nation without including the Soviet zone. While this plan solved many economic problems of the British zone and would encourage the Germans to look to the West for leadership, Bevin noted that this course contained significant risks. It would mean departing from the Potsdam agreement, and he did not think that the Americans were ready for such a move. The French also were very likely to oppose it, and, without their support, Britain would be left "out on a limb." The foreign minister therefore believed that it was too early to consider a divided Germany. A workable solution was still possible with the Soviets, who, he thought, were unsure of their policy, too. Should it become necessary to abandon German unity, he told the cabinet, they must ensure that the Soviets receive the blame for the break.

Agreeing that the French position should be blocked, the cabinet gave Bevin permission to advocate a loose economic federation of the four zones with a weak German central administration. Such a course would help the economy of the British zone and move toward national unity. As for other German issues the cabinet concluded that it was best to wait and keep avenues open.[26]

American policymakers faced a similar dilemma. Like the British, they saw German policy tied to relations with the Soviet Union and to the economic future of Europe. If the defeated country was kept divided the Soviet Union would have no reason to fear its resurgence and consequently would have fewer excuses for the total domination of Eastern Europe. But to weaken Germany would threaten the rebuilding of Europe. If the United States supported development of the nation's economy, however, it would only confirm to the Soviets the hostility of the Americans.

Byrnes flew to Paris with two plans in hand. The first and more dramatic was a proposal for a treaty to guarantee the demilitarization of Germany for twenty-five years. It was not a new idea; Senator Vandenberg had suggested a similar course in January 1945. Reflecting the juncture of German and Soviet issues, it had two goals: to keep Germany disarmed and to test the Kremlin's commitment to peace and cooperation. The plan had been sent to Britain, France, and the Soviet Union in February, giving each, Byrnes hoped, time for consideration. The treaty would allow only a small civil police force, with the four powers inspecting Germany to ensure that, if violations occurred, they would be dealt with quickly and effectively. The treaty was to last for twenty-five years, with the possibility of renewal if the German people had not reconstructed their lives "on a democratic and peaceful basis." With their former enemy completely demilitarized, neither France nor the Soviet Union would have reason to fear or block German economic rebuilding and unification. Rejection of the proposal by the Russians would be further proof that their goal was not security but expansion and would provide a means to pillory them in the world press.[27]

Byrnes's second plan was to obtain a more unified Germany and begin the process of ending occupational control. American officials in Moscow, George Kennan and Ambassador Walter Bedell Smith, believed that the Soviets were creating a satellite in their zone and recommended that the United States consider unifying the western zones into a friendly state. At the same time, General Clay and other American representatives informed Byrnes that Russian propaganda was increasingly successful in convincing the Germans that the Soviet Union and local

Communists would best protect their interests.   U.S.
observers strongly recommended that the secretary of state
take a more aggressive stance to promote a unified
Germany with its own central administration.   Byrnes
decided to propose a central government and the formation
of a commission to study possible settlements that would
end occupational controls.[28]

Once in Paris, Byrnes had lost little time in promoting
the demilitarization treaty. On April 28 he invited Molotov
to dinner and afterward discussed the proposal. First he
reviewed the history of the idea, reminding the Soviet
minister that it had been mentioned in September and again
in December and that Stalin had liked the plan.   The
secretary hoped that the treaty would "serve as a
reinsurance against any Soviet fears of a renewed attack by
Germany and . . . remove any element of doubt of the United
States bearing its full share in safeguarding the peace." He
also informed Molotov that many Americans were unsure
of Russian motivation, "whether it was search for security
or expansionism."   The Soviet minister's response made
little sense. Molotov suggested that the treaty actually
postponed the demilitarization of Germany while his
government wanted it right away, believing that a special
commission should immediately investigate the extent of
disarmament in the zones. Only after verification that it
was complete would the Kremlin favor such a treaty.[29]

Having accomplished nothing in the private talk, Byrnes
officially presented the scheme at the end of the next day's
meeting. He launched into a lengthy speech about the
American commitment to Europe and desire for peace and
security and how the U.S. demilitarization proposal
achieved that security. Molotov had not changed his mind
in twenty-four hours and formally responded as he had
privately.   Byrnes, prepared for the Soviet response,
attempted to show how the minister misunderstood the
intent of the proposal. Reading out loud, the secretary
emphasized that the plan called for the immediate
demilitarization of Germany by the occupying powers. He
added that he saw no reason why an inspection could not
take place right away. From Byrnes's perspective, if his
logical explanation was rejected, then clearly the Soviet goal
was not an independent and unified Germany. But it was

not just Molotov who responded less than positively to the proposal.

Bevin wanted more time to consider the idea. He stated that, because the Americans had classified the proposal "top secret," very few had read it. His government agreed in principle but needed to examine the plan further before commenting. Byrnes told Bevin that he could ignore the top-secret classification, knowing that the proposal was soon to be made public. Bidault also found the idea acceptable but asked for more time to study it.

Bevin then took issue with the Soviet request to check on demilitarization. He believed that a council-mandated inspection would imply that something was wrong in the zones and suggested that any investigation be made through the Allied Control Council. When Molotov continued to call for a special commission, Bevin noted that it "seemed quite clear to him that . . . there should be no discussion of the U.S. draft treaty by the Council." Tired and hungry, he thought that it was "better to leave it at that" and to adjourn. For once, everyone agreed.[30]

The topic of Germany emerged again in the closing days of the conference. On May 15, Bidault presented the French proposal on the Ruhr, Rhineland, and Saar. The Ruhr, Germany's industrial area, was to be placed under an international regime. Only "non-German political control would prevent its being used for German rearmament," the minister explained. The Rhineland was also to be separated, with the river's left bank occupied by French, British, Belgian, and Dutch forces; the Saar would return to France.

Bevin's response changed the shape of the debate. The French proposal was not unlike that favored by Britain, except "on the question of political separation." He emphasized that Germany needed to be considered as a whole, not just as zones. A first step would be to raise the level of production for its industries. Byrnes said that he agreed with Bevin and Bidault and had a plan that covered both goals. A special committee of deputies would be appointed to consider German problems and draft a settlement for the country. The committee would clarify agreements made at Potsdam and project "the eventual provision of peace terms." To deal with short-range issues the proposal listed specific questions for the deputies to consider. Most related to treating Germany as an economic whole and creating a central administrative structure. In both cases the special committee would consider the future status of the Ruhr and Rhineland. It would be ready to make recommendations on the immediate issues when the ministers resumed their work on June 15. Proposals on long-range considerations, Byrnes said, would be ready in mid-November.[31]

The American proposal received mixed responses, and everyone seemed cautious. Bidault saw "no objection" to the procedure but wanted the council to agree on French control over the Saar first. Molotov took his usual route: He was unsure and confused about parts of the plan and had several questions. Bevin supported it but thought that the instructions to the deputies should be modified. The discussion quickly degenerated into a series of thrusts and parries. Unable to agree, the ministers adjourned.[32]

They met only one more time, on the afternoon of May 16. Moving beyond the German issue after Molotov stoutly reaffirmed his unwillingness to discuss Byrnes's plan, Bidault suggested June 15 for the next council session and recommended that they wait until then to select a date to begin the peace conference. Everyone agreed, and Byrnes urged that they adjourn to the bar. The ministers filed across the hall to a buffet. Molotov and Byrnes each enjoyed a glass of bourbon; Bidault and Bevin drank champagne. After twenty days of debates, meetings, luncheons, dinners, and parties, the one concrete accomplishment the secretary could claim was that Molotov thought that American whiskey was as good as vodka. In the morning, Bevin, Molotov, and Byrnes left for home.[33]

Each man was returning to a nation reflecting the attitudes he had displayed at the conference. Still angry at Molotov's actions and aware of public sentiments, Byrnes addressed the people on May 20. His speech was hardly reminiscent of that given after the Moscow Conference. Although he pointed out that negotiations required patience, tolerance, and understanding, he stressed that America was tired of Soviet behavior. The Kremlin needed to realize that its "quest for security may lead to less rather than more security." He blamed the Russians for the lack of progress and promised to refer the treaties to the United Nations if Soviet obstructionism prevented a summer peace conference. There was "no iron curtain" that the world's hope for peace could not penetrate. "We must take the offensive for peace as we took the offensive for war." Public response was overwhelmingly positive.[34]

The Soviet stance was similar. Since mid-May the press had unleashed harsh attacks on American policy and leaders. Upon returning to Moscow, Molotov told Ambassador Smith that he was willing to make very few compromises on the peace treaties. In public he charged that the United States and Great Britain were threatening the peace and planning an aggressive war for world domination. Across the Soviet Union, officials were emphasizing ideology and patriotism, the *Zhadanovschina*. Evaluating their rhetoric and domestic policies, an observer in the Foreign Office commented that the Russians were "really disturbed by American strength and the great changes in American policy." With Byrnes and Molotov each proclaiming the other an obstacle to peace, the chances of success at the council meeting in June seemed remote.[35]

Notes

1. The procedural problem that had deadlocked the London conference had centered on which nations would be allowed to draft and approve the peace treaties for Finland, Hungary, Romania, and Bulgaria. Discussions following the London meeting also included the issue of what countries would be allowed to participate in the treaty-making process but not be a part of the drafting and final approving of the treaties.

At the Moscow Conference the following decisions were reached:
1) The Italian treaty would be drafted by the United States, Great Britain, the Soviet Union, and France.
2) The Romanian, Bulgarian, and Hungarian treaties would be drafted by the United States, Great Britain, and the Soviet Union.
3) The Finnish treaty would be drafted by Great Britain and the Soviet Union.
4) The Council of Foreign Ministers would call a conference to consider the drafted treaties, and that conference would include the five members of the Council of Foreign Ministers and those nations that had "actively waged war with substantial military force against [the] European enemy states."
5) The final approval of the peace treaties would be decided by those nations that had drafted the original treaties. This system allowed

input from a number of nations not part of the Council of Foreign Ministers but left real decision making in the hands of the Big Three, with France included in approving the treaty for Italy.

See *FRUS: Diplomatic Papers, 1945* 2:815–16.

2. Bullock, *Bevin,* 260; "No Peace Yet," *Life* 20 (April 26, 1946): 36.

3. Ward, *Threat of Peace,* 260.

4. *FRUS: Council of Foreign Ministers, 1946* (Washington, DC, 1970), 2:16–19; Ward, *Threat of Peace,* 86–88.

5. *FRUS: Foreign Ministers, 1946* 2:25–27, 33–36; Ward, *Threat of Peace,* 88–89.

6. Ward, *Threat of Peace,* 89–90; Messer, *End of an Alliance,* 179, 199–203. After studying Byrnes's medical records and behavior over the next several months, Messer concluded that he had no health problem and was using it as an excuse for leaving office.

7. Gaddis, *Long Peace,* 32; Ward, *Threat of Peace,* 88–90; Gormly, *Collapse of the Grand Alliance,* 154–56.

8. *Newsweek* 27 (May 6, 1946): 40, 43; ibid. (May 13, 1946): 40; ibid. (April 29, 1946): 45; *FRUS: The British Commonwealth; Western and Central Europe, 1946* (Washington, DC, 1969), 5:413, 421–24, 430, 438–46; Pollard, *Economic Security,* 74–77.

9. *FRUS: British Commonwealth, 1946* 5:369; Dixon, *Double Diploma,* 208; Bullock, *Bevin,* 261; Ward, *Threat of Peace,* 90–91; *Newsweek* 27 (May 6, 1946): 40, 43; ibid. (May 13, 1946): 40, 42, 44.

10. Ward, *Threat of Peace,* 91; *FRUS: Foreign Ministers, 1946* 2:114–20, 286–88.

11. *FRUS: Foreign Ministers, 1946* 2:155–65, 194; William Roger Lewis, *The British Empire in the Middle East, 1945–1951: Arab Nationalism, the United States, and Postwar Imperialism* (Oxford, 1984), 270–74, 276–80; cabinet memorandum, "Policy in Libya," C.P. (46) 354, September 23, 1946, PREM 8/515, PRO; Bullock, *Bevin,* 262–64.

12. *Newsweek* 27 (May 13, 1946): 42; *FRUS: Foreign Ministers, 1946* 2:221–22; Bullock, *Bevin,* 263–64.

13. Ward, *Threat of Peace,* 92–94; *FRUS: Foreign Ministers, 1946* 2:149–53, 178–84, 207–8.

14. *FRUS: Foreign Ministers, 1946* 2:215–22.

15. Ibid., 225–35, 237–45; Rabel, *Between East and West,* 85–95.

16. *FRUS: Foreign Ministers, 1946* 2:247–49; Ward, *Threat of Peace,* 95–96.

17. Minute, November 14, 1946, F.O. 371, R4468/31/87; memorandum, November 14, 1946, F.O. 371, R16712/86/67; memorandum, "Balkans," December 12, 1945, F.O. 371, R21263/5063/67, all in PRO.

18. Memorandum, September 6, 1946, F.O. 371, UE4020/413/53; memorandum, August 28, 1946, F.O. 371, N11284/5169/38; Foreign Office to Lord Inverchapel, October 18, 1946, F.O. 371, UE4108/413/53; minute, December 1946, F.O. 371, N1309/710/63, all in PRO.

19. *FRUS: Foreign Ministers, 1946* 2:261–64, 266–70, 272–83; Ward, *Threat of Peace,* 96–98.

20. Ward, *Threat of Peace,* 98–99; *FRUS: Foreign Ministers, 1946* 2:301–7, 312–19, 323–32; Bullock, *Bevin,* 263.

21. Bullock, *Bevin,* 263–64; "Policy on Libya," C.P. (46) 354; *FRUS: Foreign Ministers, 1946* 2:333–41.

22. *FRUS: Foreign Ministers, 1946* 2:331–45; Ward, *Threat of Peace,* 97.

23. Ward, *Threat of Peace,* 97–98; *FRUS: Foreign Ministers, 1946* 2:348–52, 360–68.

24. Rothwell, *Britain and the Cold War,* 308–11, 314–18; Bullock, *Bevin,* 267–68; Pollard, *Economic Security,* 95–98.

25. Rothwell, *Britain and the Cold War,* 295; Pollard, *Economic Security,* 95–98; John Gimbel, "On the Implementation of the Potsdam Agreement: An Essay on U.S. Postwar German Policy," *Political Science Quarterly* 87 (June 1972): 250–58.

26. Rothwell, *Britain and the Cold War,* 304–25; Bullock, *Bevin,* 266–68.

27. Gaddis, *Long Peace,* 53–54; Ward, *Threat of Peace,* 93–94; Gimbel, *American Occupation,* 52–80.

28. *FRUS: Foreign Ministers, 1946* 2:190–93.

29. Ibid., 146–47; Ward, *Threat of Peace,* 94.

30. *FRUS: Foreign Ministers, 1946* 2:166–73; Ward, *Threat of Peace,* 94.

31. *FRUS: Foreign Ministers, 1946* 2:394–402.

32. Ibid., 394–402, 426–33; Bullock, *Bevin,* 270–71.

33. *FRUS: Foreign Ministers, 1946* 2:434–36; Ward, *Threat of Peace,* 98–99; *Newsweek* 27 (May 20, 1946): 40; ibid. (May 27, 1946): 36; *Time* 47 (May 20, 1946): 21.

34. Ward, *Threat of Peace,* 99–101; Gormly, *Collapse of the Grand Alliance,* 154–58.

35. Gormly, *Collapse of the Grand Alliance,* 159–62.

VI

The Foreign Ministers Try Again, June 15–July 12, 1946

While Molotov and Byrnes returned to nations supporting their hard-line positions, Bevin returned to a country divided over its relations with the United States and the Soviet Union. A large minority, including some members of the Labour party, opposed what they saw as the minister's anti-Soviet and pro-American goals. They sought a more independent, "socialist" foreign policy and called for more understanding of Russian needs and fears. While a minority opinion, it exerted influence in the party and in the cabinet and appeared to hinder any approach favoring the United States and openly hostile to Moscow. Some journalists were already writing of a revolt against Bevin within his party.[1]

In May and June, as the Paris negotiations had dragged on, the Foreign Office recommended to the foreign minister that Britain engage the Soviet Union and the Communists in a propaganda campaign aimed at promoting British interests in Germany, Eastern Europe, and the Middle East and combating Soviet lies. The cabinet rejected the request, believing instead that Britain should champion "the achievements of our own political philosophy rather than attacking that of [the] Russians."[2] The decision disappointed many in the Foreign Office but did not disturb Bevin unduly. He had Prime Minister Clement Attlee's confidence and commanded significant influence in the cabinet and the Labour party. While not ready to signal publicly a break with the Soviet Union and Big Three

cooperation, Bevin was determined to place the blame for
their disagreements and disunity on the Kremlin. In taking
a critical view, he could depend on support from the
majority of his party, fellow ministers, and the Conservative
party, led by Winston Churchill.

The Council of Foreign Ministers at Paris, June–July 1946. Seated, facing the
camera, far right: James F. Byrnes; far left: Vyacheslav M. Molotov. Senator
Tom Connally is seated to the left of Byrnes. (Robert M. Cooper Library,
Clemson University)

Bevin joined Churchill before Parliament in calling the
Soviet Union an obstacle to the completion of the peace
treaties and the search for stability. Both statesmen agreed
that Russian opposition made it necessary to work with the
United States if a settlement was to be achieved. Churchill
offered Stalin a "friendly hint":

> The American eagle sits on his perch, a large strong bird with
> formidable beak and claws. There he sits, motionless, and
> Mr. Gromyko is sent every day to prod him with a sharp sickle,
> now on his beak, now under his wing, now in his tail feathers.
> All the time the eagle keeps quite still. But it would be a great
> mistake to suppose that nothing is going on inside the breast of
> the eagle.[3]

As the foreign ministers arrived in Paris during the
second week in June the seriousness of their task was

evident. If they continued to disagree on the treaties, the peace conference that could provide the foundation for European security was doomed. Instead, there surely would follow a showdown between the West and the Soviet Union. Even Paris reflected the changed atmosphere. In May the weather had been cool, brisk, and refreshing, signaling a new season, but by mid-June it was sultry and humid. Parisians, too, acted differently. No longer was there fanfare or pomp and pageantry. No crowds lined the streets to wave or watch the flagged limousines speed back and forth from the Luxembourg Palace. It was, some journalists thought, the "last call for peace."[4]

When the Council of Foreign Ministers returned to the negotiating table, an air of steady resolve settled over the room. It was evident in Georges Bidault's welcome that much remained to be done. He stated that they needed to "concentrate their efforts," because it was clear that "the Great Powers must act together to make peace as they had in making war," concluding that "hope must be maintained." Upon turning to the agenda, they had reason to believe that hope indeed might survive. To nearly everyone's surprise, Molotov agreed to add the German question and even to discuss the Austrian treaty if time permitted. Bidault said that the approval of the agenda could be "a favorable augury" of things to come.[5]

Treaties for Italy and Southeastern Europe

For the next five days the council discussed the Italian treaty with only slightly encouraging results. Progress was made on a variety of peripheral issues but not on those that had defied agreement during earlier sessions. Trieste quickly became an especially volatile topic, for street battles there heightened tensions. Italian and Slavic nationalists fought each other in a series of increasingly bloody clashes. Rumors circulated that both sides were planning a military coup. Responding to the violence, the USS *Fargo*, the largest vessel of the American Mediterranean fleet, docked in Trieste's harbor. *Newsweek* concluded that the ship's "batteries of six-inch guns tacitly emphasized the determination of Secretary of State James F. Byrnes and Foreign Secretary Ernest Bevin not to deliver the city's overwhelming Italian majority to the safekeeping of Marshal Tito, the playmate of Russia."[6]

Reports of the Kremlin's intentions offered little encouragement that a confrontation might be avoided. The Russian press continued to denounce British and American plans and actions. Ambassador Walter Bedell Smith reported that, although the Soviets were "quite as anxious" as the United States to "avoid a complete break-up," they gave no sign that they were "preparing to recede at this time from their former intransigent attitude." Similar reports were received by Bidault and Bevin. Within the council, debates were becoming increasingly heated and laced with sharp-edged words and ominous implications. Molotov and Bevin frequently engaged each other in bitter verbal duels. French officials were quietly pessimistic about the chances for a successful outcome of the conference and believed the Soviets to be "much more intransigent than at the last meeting." Seeing their formal sessions approach another deadlock, Byrnes, on June 20, suggested that they revert to informal meetings in an effort to overcome their disagreements.[7]

Gathering informally that afternoon, the ministers dove into the colonial issue. Byrnes immediately modified his last position. Respecting French concerns, he suggested that Libya be considered for independence only after ten years of trusteeship. But this slight concession changed nothing. After restating the Soviet Union's desire for a trusteeship, Molotov said that he favored the previous U.S. proposal, which provided for a one-year trusteeship. Bevin agreed, while Bidault continued to press for an Italian trusteeship. Finally, they decided to ask the trusteeship commission to redraft the American proposal for a temporary trusteeship of Italy's colonies. No one claimed to prefer this solution over a permanent one, but, for the sake of moving forward on the peace treaty, they agreed to consider the U.S. plan.[8]

During more informal meetings over the next two days, the ministers examined the question of the Italian-Yugoslav border and the disposition of Trieste. Bidault asked the other delegates to consider new approaches to the problem, but no new ideas emerged. Molotov reasserted that he could not abandon an ally; Yugoslavia must have Trieste. Byrnes responded that the United States could not accept Yugoslav control of the city.

With anger and frustration building, Byrnes brought the underlying issue forward on June 21. There were, he informed his colleagues, "only two questions of any real difficulty before the Council": Trieste and reparations. He asked the group to set July 15 as the starting date for the peace conference and to resolve their differences over the next three weeks. To support his selection of the 15th, Byrnes pointed out that the United Nations was to meet in early September. If the date was set beyond mid-July, the conference would come into conflict with the UN meeting and could not be held.

Molotov, seeing a possible opening, agreed that they were "all anxious to convoke a Peace Conference," but that consideration of a date should not take place until significant progress was made on the treaties. To put it bluntly, he was holding the conference hostage until Soviet "requests" on Trieste and reparations were met. It seemed clear to everyone that the Russians were "in no hurry to reach agreement . . . on the various problems relating to Italy, the Balkans, Germany and Austria."[9]

Hoping to strike an agreement on Trieste, Molotov met privately with Byrnes on June 24. Verbal fencing began at once. The Soviet minister announced that he understood the French position but was unsure of the American one. Byrnes firmly informed him that the United States had compromised enough in accepting the French line; he believed that the issue now should be referred to the peace conference for a decision. Because the Soviets had rejected Bidault's suggestion for the temporary internationalization of Trieste, the American delegation had not considered it. Placing responsibility on Molotov, the secretary declared that "he felt it was now up to the Soviet Delegation to make a new proposal. . . . If we could settle Trieste, the other questions would not be too difficult."

Molotov agreed that "the other four treaties present no particular difficulty" and made a new offer. Trieste and the surrounding countryside should be placed under Yugoslav control within a statute established by the four powers. Byrnes disagreed with the basic concept of the Communist government's authority over the city but said, if necessary, he might favor a neutral UN-appointed administration. Not wanting to discount Molotov's idea totally, he promised to consider it more closely.[10]

The following day, just prior to the twenty-sixth formal meeting, Byrnes took the Soviet minister aside and officially rejected the proposal. The United States could not accept Yugoslav sovereignty over Trieste. Rather than act offended, Molotov presented another alternative: Since the Soviets "were seeking a solution which would remove the cause of discord," his government "was prepared to accept extreme measures provided they could reach agreement on other questions." Did the secretary mean that "if Trieste was settled, the problem of reparations could be disposed of in a positive fashion"? Suddenly, it appeared that Molotov was willing to abandon Yugoslavia's claim to Trieste for $100 million in Italian reparations.

Byrnes confirmed Molotov's understanding: "If they could settle Trieste the United States Delegation was prepared to modify its views on reparations." Furthermore, he was willing to allow reparations payments out of Italian current production, provided the Soviet Union supplied the raw materials to produce the goods. Molotov believed that such an arrangement, although difficult, could be worked out. He then asked whether, once work on the peace treaties was completed, the United States would sign all five documents, including the one for Bulgaria. When Byrnes replied that he saw no problem, Molotov responded "that in the circumstances he was willing to take another extreme step." He thought that Italy and Yugoslavia could hold dual sovereignty over Trieste, each appointing a governor. He believed that the approach might be acceptable to the contending nations.

Byrnes disagreed. Two governors would be impractical and a constant source of friction and conflict. The United States could not accept Yugoslav authority in any form over the Italian population of Trieste. He also asked that the Soviets "persuade the Bulgarian government to carry out the Moscow decision." As they parted, Molotov reminded the American that the Bulgarian impasse resulted from the actions of the Opposition and not the Bulgarian government. He also reaffirmed that the Soviet Union thought that its Trieste proposal was "quite good."[11]

Molotov later suggested his plan for dual sovereignty to the other ministers, but with little success. Listening to him and Byrnes, Bidault observed that the problem was "difficult but not insurmountable." Nonetheless, the ministers agreed to put aside the Trieste question and work on the Romanian, Hungarian, and Bulgarian treaties, where the chances of a favorable outcome seemed better. Except for minor modifications, only one issue stood in the way of the Balkan treaties, the question of equal economic rights.

British and American officials objected to clauses that gave economic advantages to neighboring East European states and would hamper Western trade with the region. The U.S. delegation attempted to modify such passages to ensure that every nation would receive the same treatment, while the British promoted freedom of navigation on the Danube. Bevin asked that the four powers "declare their intention" to keep the river open and to "take the necessary steps to secure the adherence of all the riparian states of the Danube" to the principle of free navigation.

Both efforts failed, but on other topics the ministers quickly moved through a variety of clauses. They even agreed to the size of the Bulgarian navy—one ship. Half in jest, Byrnes asked if they could end "a good afternoon and settle the question of the Dodecanese [islands]." Did Molotov agree that they should go to Greece? When the Soviet minister assented, Byrnes "asked for a minute or two to recover." Arthur Vandenberg called it a "breathless round of agreements."[12]

Solving Fundamental Problems

Nearly everyone hoped that the changed attitude would continue. Soon, however, uncooperative Soviet behavior returned, and deferral and disagreement again became the standard response. While they could concur on what Molotov called nonfundamental issues, on those that had separated them for ten months there was little harmony. Byrnes blocked any Italian reparations settlement unless the Soviets would give up Yugoslav sovereignty over Trieste. Molotov refused to permit a peace conference until the questions of most importance to him, including reparations, were settled. As June drew to an end the impasse seemed insoluble.[13]

The logjam began to break on July 1. Molotov suddenly announced that the Soviet Union accepted the French proposal for internationalization of Trieste and the surrounding countryside if the border between the international zone and Yugoslavia were placed between the French and Soviet lines. Circulating a map showing the new border, he added that it was drawn according to ethnic considerations. Byrnes was not impressed and quickly pointed out that the United States could not accept the transferring of any territory west of the French line to Yugoslavia. Bevin took a slightly less obstinate position. He was willing to discuss a border west of the French line, but not the Soviet one.

Although Molotov was willing to modify his offer, there followed a most unproductive discussion on possible boundaries for the international zone. As the talks moved away from any possible compromise, Bidault interjected that "he was willing once more to take the plunge" and sacrifice himself in an attempt to bring the ministers closer to an agreement. At "the risk of irritating everyone," he proposed that all territory east of the French line would belong to Yugoslavia. The international zone for Trieste would include all the land west of the French line from Dunio southward to Cittanuova d'Istria.[14]

Without rejecting Bidault's solution, Bevin and Byrnes hedged, suggesting that the lower border to the international zone should extend farther south. Molotov countered by asking for the border to be much farther north. Bickering followed until, quite unexpectedly, Molotov simply stated that the council should "accept, without amendment," Bidault's proposal. Agreeing with his Soviet colleague, the French minister asked that they take a fifteen-minute recess to consider the situation. Returning twenty-five minutes later, Bevin and Byrnes accepted the proposed eastern border of the international zone but were still unsure about the western one. They agreed to take up the question at the next session.[15]

Slowly, the ministers inched toward further agreement. Accepting the creation of an international zone, they disputed its size and type of administration. Byrnes wanted to refer these two issues to the peace conference. Bevin was willing to let the conference discuss both questions but believed that the United Nations should decide the statutes for the zone; the size of the zone should be determined by the ministers. Molotov wanted the council to establish the "basis for the statutes" and the size of the zone before sending the proposal to either the peace conference or the United Nations. He suggested that they place the zone under the administration of the four powers. Neither Bevin nor Byrnes agreed; they both thought that the responsibility belonged to the conference and the world organization. The secretary flatly told Molotov that, unless the United Nations drew up the statutes and appointed the governor, the United States would reject the internationalization of Trieste.[16]

The next day, Byrnes offered a plan for statutes in order to ensure that the United Nations would have authority over the zone and appoint the governor. Molotov astonished the others when he calmly accepted it, provided some minor amendments were made. In record time, changes were suggested, debated, and adopted. Trieste and the Yugoslav border were no longer obstacles to the calling of the peace conference. The Soviet Union had abandoned its ally; Trieste would not belong to Yugoslavia.[17]

Having answered one major question, the ministers next considered the British proposal calling for Italy to renounce all claims to its former colonies. France and England would administer the colonies "pending . . . final disposal," and the United Nations would settle the issue if the council could not determine their disposition within one year. Bidault and Byrnes supported the draft, finding it "the least bad" plan. Only Molotov remained unconvinced, and finally he, too, offered a bargain: "He was prepared to make concessions in this matter in hope that when the Council considered the question of reparation to the Soviet Union they would be able to come to an agreement on that in the same way as on these other problems." Thus another fundamental obstacle blocking the beginning of the peace conference was overcome.[18]

With the Trieste and colonial issues resolved the only major question still facing the ministers was that of Italian reparations. Before the matter could be discussed the council had to set a date for the peace conference. Byrnes immediately saw an opportunity to bargain with Molotov: He asked the Soviet minister either to accept July 23 or to suggest another day. Bidault and Bevin seconded the American position. Molotov countered with dates that he knew would be rejected—September 1 or 15. In control, Byrnes calmly disallowed both choices as too late because the conference would then interfere with the meeting of the General Assembly. He suggested July 20 instead. Molotov offered August 25 or a little sooner. His colleague, however, stood firm: "There was no reason for putting off a decision any longer, even for one day." Putting his cards on the table, Molotov said that, if such was the case, then "the Council should decide the remaining outstanding question, that of reparations." Smiling, the secretary of state reminded the Soviet minister that they had agreed on the agenda and that reparations was third on the list.

Byrnes, however, was willing to compromise and move the subject to second place. Germany would become the third item. Molotov argued that they had solved the Trieste problem, the foremost issue for the United States, and the colonial problem, the foremost issue for Britain, and asked why could they not now decide a matter of equal importance for the Soviet Union, reparations. Byrnes steadfastly refused to consider compensation until a date was chosen. Frustrated, Molotov demanded that both topics be postponed until the next day.[19] Bevin interceded, asking the Soviet minister to agree to a date now and take it as "an act of faith" that they would discuss reparations at their next meeting. But Molotov wanted more than faith. Both issues should be discussed in the following session, and reparations should be placed first on the agenda. Byrnes bluntly rejected Molotov's idea. He believed that they should adjourn, and they did.[20]

During the afternoon of July 4 they met again to consider a time when they would be finished drafting the treaties. The Americans and British projected July 14; the French, July 20; the Soviets, no sooner than July 25. Without fanfare or debate the ministers agreed on July 29 to begin the peace conference. With the date set, the road was open to resolving the question of reparations. Previously, they had reached agreement on the broad outline of Italian reparations. The country would pay $100 million to the Soviet Union, the amount coming from three Italian sources: 1) factory equipment and tools that had been used to produce war matériel; 2) assets in Romania, Bulgaria, and Finland; and 3) current production. All that remained to be decided were the small details: Over what period of time should reparations be made? Should payments from current production begin immediately or be deferred for several years? Should there be a limit on the amount of foreign assets transferred to the Soviet Union? Solutions, however, were not easily found, and hours of haggling and horse-trading followed.

Back and forth they argued, with Molotov usually a minority of one. He despaired that, if they "continued arguing, they might in the last analysis say not that Italy should pay reparations to the Soviet Union but vice versa." Finally, after midnight and seven long hours, an agreement was pasted together. The $100 million would be paid over seven years with no payments coming from current production for two years. There was no limit on the value of external assets transferred to the Soviet Union. Finally, the Russians agreed to provide Italy with raw materials on commercial terms, their value being deducted from that of the delivered goods. Exhausted, the ministers were prepared to leave when Molotov announced that his government could not accept the notice of the peace conference if China was listed as an inviting power. It was an issue, he said, they could discuss at the next meeting.[21]

What appeared to be a minor matter mushroomed into two days of heated, acrimonious confrontations. Molotov first objected to China as an inviting nation. Then he announced that the invitations could not be issued until the council established procedures for the peace conference. In a seemingly unending series of steps, the Soviet minister presented plans for the conference's organization and voting procedures. He explained that there should be a total of nine commissions and that each treaty commission should be composed only of those nations that had declared war on the government involved. All decisions should be reached by a two-thirds majority vote.[22]

It seemed clear to the other delegations that the Russians were trying to protect their interests, especially in the Balkans, by enabling a bloc to veto the decisions of the majority. With the Soviet Union having three votes (one for the USSR as a whole and two for the republics of Belorussia and the Ukraine), and with Poland, Yugoslavia, and Czechoslovakia in its corner, the Russians would need only one or two additional votes to block unfavorable clauses. To make matters worse, Stone Bottom Molotov was quite capable of ignoring all logic and arguments and deadlocking their present conference unless he got his way.

Over the next two days, during formal and informal meetings, the ministers almost resorted to violence. Molotov was in his element. Repeatedly he stated that the Moscow agreements required excluding China as a member of the council and establishing rules and regulations for the peace conference. Bevin was especially upset. At one point, he asked the Soviet minister to show him where in the Moscow decisions, or in any other document, the council was given the right to dictate to the conference. Later he appeared ready to attack the Russian. "Bevin rose to his feet, his hands knotted into fists, and started toward Molotov, saying, 'I've had enough of this, I'ave. ' " Charles Bohlen, who witnessed the event, thought that "for one glorious moment it looked as if the Foreign Minister of Great Britain and the Foreign Minister of the Soviet Union were about to come to blows." But security guards rushed forward, and cooler tempers ended the confrontation. Everyone's nerves were approaching the shattering point. Even Molotov looked more "worried, yellowed than usual and the bump on his right temple" stood out more.[23]

To overcome Molotov and save the peace conference, the other ministers fell back on their only weapons: concessions and reparations. Over a series of discussions in which pleading and reasoning gained no ground, Bidault, Bevin, and Byrnes slowly retreated. Worn down, they agreed to obscure China's role in inviting nations to the peace conference: Notices would be sent in the name of the Council of Foreign Ministers without reference to any of the constituent powers. On the question of rules and procedures for the conference the ministers harmonized their views. They would suggest regulations but not make them binding. Even the four powers would not be required to uphold them once the conference started. Molotov won on the issue of the two-thirds vote, although it was agreed that the minority had the right to present its views and ask for a decision from the entire assembly. Bevin, Byrnes, and Bidault now believed that they had made enough concessions, and, when Molotov seemed uninterested in ending his obstructionism, Byrnes angrily threatened to withdraw his support for the reparations agreement.[24]

Settlements for Germany and Austria

If the council had ended by establishing procedures for the peace conference the ministers would have left Paris only slightly irritated. Unfortunately, their sessions were not yet finished. Germany and Austria still were left on the agenda. Tempers were to become even shorter. Addressing the German question, Molotov commenced a fierce attack on British and American policies. It was a well-planned onslaught, complete with statements ready for the press.

The Soviet Union's view toward the ongoing demilitarization of Germany was outlined, and Byrnes's proposal of a twenty-five-year demilitarization treaty was rejected. Molotov did not deny the good intentions of the United States but considered the length of time specified totally inadequate to ensure security from an aggressive neighbor. In fact, he believed that the American measures "might harbour the danger of Germany's resurgence as an aggressive power." Germany needed to be totally disarmed for forty years. Nor did the treaty, Molotov added, provide for reparations to the Soviet Union. Not content with disparaging the U.S. proposal, he next attacked British and American actions in their zones. In violation of the Potsdam agreement, they had not totally disarmed or disbanded German military or paramilitary units. Also, neither "the remnants of German fascism" nor the country's war potential had been eliminated. Immediate measures were necessary to strip the land of its ability to make war. The Soviet minister ended by condemning the decision made by the United States to halt reparations payments from its zone.

Byrnes was unruffled as he responded to the lengthy diatribe. The American twenty-five-year treaty was a working document, and he "was glad to hear today . . . Mr. Molotov's objections to the draft." Point by point, he showed the inadequacies of the minister's reasoning, along with his understanding of the proposal and the issue of reparations. The secretary asked the council to create a commission of deputies to deal with many of the issues and to "prepare a draft of a proposed settlement for Germany." Exhausted and unable to agree on Byrnes's request, the council adjourned, planning to continue the discussion at the next session.[25]

The ministers met again on July 10. No one expected a dull time. Bevin and Bidault began by accepting Byrnes's call for a special commission and by reviewing their nations' views on Germany. Bidault reaffirmed France's desire to weaken its former enemy by removing the Rhineland, Ruhr, and Saar, while Bevin stressed the importance of treating Germany as an economic whole. However, the British minister also hinted that, if full reciprocity between zones was not forthcoming, his government would be forced to take some action that would "be injurious to future collaboration." Although he had not yet decided upon merging the British zone with the American, Bevin clearly was inching toward such an arrangement.

Poker-faced, Molotov listened and then presented a new position on Germany that caught the others totally by surprise. After again making the demand for reparations and total disarmament, he stated that "the destruction of Germany should not be our objective" and called for a united, industrial, and prosperous state that included the Rhineland and Ruhr. He asked that a central German administration be established. Once the country was demilitarized, the Ruhr placed under four-power control, a central government established, and a schedule set for reparations payments, Molotov continued, a treaty could be written. In the meantime, teams should be created to investigate disarmament and draw up plans to eliminate Germany's military industries. With each of the other ministers now reaffirming his own position, Byrnes suggested that they meet the next day to try to agree on instructions to send to the deputies. Molotov said he was willing.[26]

Released to the press nearly as the Soviet minister spoke, his proposal appeared to change the foundation upon which Moscow's policy toward Germany was based. The Soviet Union now meant to act as the defeated country's friend and benefactor, promoting unity and self-government. Immediately, British and American officials examined the new position, determining its dangers. "It looks," wrote an observer in the Foreign Office, "as if 'the apostles of the brotherhood of man' have rushed in and sprung a very fast one." Both delegations believed that the proposal launched a major propaganda effort to woo the Germans. Byrnes thought that it was a very "effective speech . . . timed to win favor of the German people." He later wrote that "he realized at once the strength of this appeal. It was clearly calculated to play on the widespread German fear of the so-called 'Morgenthau Plan,' which had been widely discussed in the American press." British and U.S. officials also worried that much of the German press responded well to the Soviet gambit. Typical of the responses was "the Liberal Democratic Party's *Der Morgen* headline: 'What Molotov demands for Germany' as contrasted with what the Western powers 'demand *from* Germany.' "[27]

The Soviets' proposal and their desire to obtain reparations out of Germany's current production was an attempt to incorporate that country's industry into the Russian economy. "The Russians have, it is to be imagined," wrote one British official, "no intention of ever leaving Eastern Germany." The Foreign Office doubted that there now existed any basis for a quadripartite policy for the country. Even cautious Bevin increasingly was willing to consider joining the British and American zones. Finally, after lengthy discussions with his advisers, Bevin advised Attlee on July 25 to approve the plan to combine the two zones, to halt reparations shipments to the Soviet Union, and to increase British propaganda to educate Germans about the benefits of the merger.[28]

Byrnes and Senators Arthur Vandenberg and Tom Connally were of the same opinion. They saw with alarm that Molotov's statement had received wide distribution. It was, the secretary commented, the first shot in the "battle for the minds of the German people." Meeting with General Lucius Clay and Robert Murphy, the American political representative to Germany, he concluded that the United States needed to take a stronger lead in promoting the defeated country's interests and should move forward to merge the British and American zones, thereby establishing "bizonia."[29]

When the ministers met again, their patience and goodwill clearly were at low ebb. Referring to the haggling over Germany, Bidault observed that they were riding on a merry-go-round and spouting soliloquies. For two days they discussed and debated, expressing a variety of concerns about Germany, usually with one eye on each other and one on public opinion. Byrnes was determined to win the second round in the fight for the approval of the Germans. In speeches given before the council and made available to the press, he emphasized that the United States "never sought to impose a peace of vengeance" on Germany and, indeed, hoped to see it unified and industrialized. He also attempted to place the blame for the lack of progress at the feet of the Soviets. He asked them to proceed toward an economic unification by immediately lifting zonal barriers.

Should the Soviets refuse, Byrnes planned to raise prospects of a unified British and American zone and a divided Germany. None of the zones, he pointed out, could "be regarded as fully self-sustaining," and, if two were treated "as an economic whole," conditions would be improved in both. General Clay, who had helped shape the secretary's views, observed that "all four delegations" recognized that the United States "would strive alone or with such others as joined with us" to bring about economic unity and stability. The differences centered on the future of Germany and perhaps Europe. The Americans firmly believed that German economic unity would foster prosperity, which in turn would lead to a democratic political system. Political unity without prosperity would help the Communist party.[30]

Molotov's and Byrnes's declarations were not the only explosive events to be sensed in Paris and around the globe. The world was also being rocked by atomic tests, Operation Crossroads, at Bikini Atoll in the Pacific. While the first test, Able, on July 1 was regarded by many observers as less than spectacular, the second test, Baker, later in the month, restored the image of a powerful and decisive weapon. While a French designer introduced a new bathing suit named after the site of the tests and an American jeweler advertised "Bursting Fury—Atomic Inspired Pin and Earring. . . . As daring to wear as it was to drop," other, more thoughtful commentators speculated on the importance of the tests and the U.S. decision not to share atomic information. *Pravda*, for one, acknowledged the enormous power of the bomb and charged that Washington was plotting an atomic war. The *Daily Worker* merely denounced the United States for "atomic diplomacy." Still another reaction occurred within weeks: the test firing of former German, now Soviet, self-propelled missiles. Launched from Peenemünde, in Soviet-occupied Germany, the V-4s flew over Sweden and Finland toward the Arctic Circle, some crashing along the way. *Newsweek* commented that the flights "fitted as neatly as an atomic bomb in the bay of a B-29 into the modern diplomacy of negotiating for peace and simultaneously preparing for war. The rockets that gleamed in the night over Sweden also hung over the Paris peace conference."[31]

The last moments of the council meeting were tied up in debating the treaty for Austria. Byrnes, Bevin, and Bidault were prepared to have the deputies begin work, but, as usual, Molotov blocked the way with a range of obstacles. After hours of fruitless debate the discussions slowed, and the ministers' willingness to continue lapsed. At last, without fanfare or pleasing speeches, Bevin asked if anyone wanted to consider further issues. Bidault motioned, "No"; Molotov stared blankly out the window; and Byrnes shook his head. "All right," Bevin bluntly announced, "we shall meet at the peace conference." With that the four ministers rose and walked out of the Luxembourg Palace. Byrnes was soon back in Washington, informing President Truman of what had taken place in Paris.[32]

The heat of the Parisian summer and Molotov's obstructionism had taken its toll. Nevertheless, the Western delegates, through a combination of demands, compromises, and arduous negotiations, had produced a series of agreements that permitted the holding of the peace conference. None was completely pleased with the results. Byrnes explained to the press that "peace could not be achieved by waving a magic wand," that the draft treaties were "the best which human wit could get the four principal Allies to agree upon . . . in this imperfect world and war weary world." The secretary of state announced that "some progress on the road back to peace" had been made. But he also made it clear that the United States opposed Soviet policies in Germany, and, if there was to be true peace, the Russians had to trust the West and stop creating obstacles to European recovery and stability.

Both the liberal and the conservative American press agreed that the proposed treaties and relations between East and West were not as good as desired. In sentiments echoed across the nation, one editorialist stated:

> The most disappointing aspect of the treaty-making . . . is . . .
> that its logically primary purpose—to build a Europe
> economically and politically capable of peaceful prosperity and
> democratic living—has been subordinated to the power
> strategies of the four major victorious powers. . . .
> Consequently, the progress toward prevention of another
> European war so far has been sadly disappointing.

Nonetheless, the writer had not given up hope that peace,
prosperity, and stability could be achieved. In a similar
series of articles the *New Republic* was anxious that
"unless Russia and the Western democracies can agree on
a German settlement, tensions will increase unbearably."
The journal went on to resolve, in "plain English," that the
result of unbearable tension was war. Despite concern, its
editors concluded that the air had been cleared, and the
forthcoming meeting at Paris presented the best chance for
peace.[33]

Observations from Moscow gave little indication that the
Soviets intended to be any more cooperative than before. In
late June, Ambassador Smith had reported an interview
between CBS newsman Richard Hottelet and former Soviet
Foreign Minister Maxim Litvinov, who had been very
critical of his own leaders and their policies. He judged that
"the [foreign affairs] outlook was bad" and that "differences
between East and West have gone too far to be reconciled."
He had told Hottelet that even if the Western allies conceded
to Soviet desires regarding Trieste, the Italian colonies, and
Germany, they only would be faced with another "series of
demands." According to Litvinov, the Kremlin had no
intention of bettering relations. Nor was there any
indication of change in policy when Molotov returned to
Moscow from Paris. The Soviet press continued to assail the
United States and Great Britain for their warlike gestures
and imperialistic activities. Indeed, the vision of Molotov
confronting a majority of smaller nations, each desiring to
modify the treaties and assert its importance, only made the
prospect of a successful peace conference seem more
remote.[34]

Aware of the difficulty of the task awaiting Byrnes, the
Washington Post asked citizens to go to the airport to show
support for the secretary of state as he left for the peace
conference. Over three thousand people, including
Truman, Supreme Court justices, and cabinet members,

gathered at Washington's National Airport on July 27 to encourage Byrnes on his eleventh trip across the Atlantic. He was accompanied again by Senators Connally and Vandenberg; this time, however, they went not to stiffen his spine but to demonstrate the fullest support of Congress. As the secretary boarded the president's plane, the *Sacred Cow*, Truman wished him luck in achieving a just peace. *Time* commented that "he would need luck. . . . Once more the U.S. and Russia were meeting at the council table, and once again it would be a meeting between political enemies, not friends." Listed as American diplomatic weapons were "its military potential, the atomic bomb, the moral force of its people."[35]

Notes

1. Gormly, *Collapse of the Grand Alliance*, 163–64; Bill Jones, *The Russian Complex: The British Labour Party and the Soviet Union* (Manchester, England, 1977), 128–37; *Newsweek* 28 (June 10, 1946): 43–46.

2. Rothwell, *Britain and the Cold War*, 251–61; minute, May 24, 1946, F.O. 371, N6734/140/38, PRO.

3. Rothwell, *Britain and the Cold War*, 251–61; Gormly, *Collapse of the Grand Alliance*, 167–69; *Newsweek* 27 (June 17, 1946): 40–44.

4. *Newsweek* 27 (June 20, 1946): 46–47; ibid. (June 17, 1946): 40; ibid. (June 24, 1946): 38.

5. *Newsweek* 27 (June 24, 1946): 38; Ward, *Threat of Peace*, 104–5.

6. *Newsweek* 27 (May 20, 1946): 40–41; ibid. 28 (July 8, 1946): 34; ibid. (July 15, 1946): 40; Rabel, *Between East and West*, 90–91; Bogdan C. Novak, *Trieste, 1941–1954: The Ethnic, Political, and Ideological Struggle* (Chicago, 1970), 252–57; *FRUS: Foreign Ministers, 1946* 2:506–7.

7. *Time* 48 (July 15, 1946): 29; *Newsweek* 28 (July 8, 1946): 34–35; *FRUS: Foreign Ministers, 1946* 2:508–9, 544–45; *FRUS: Eastern Europe, 1946* 6:758–59, 768–71; Ward, *Threat of Peace*, 105.

8. Ward, *Threat of Peace*, 105–9; *FRUS: Foreign Ministers, 1946* 2:558–63.

9. *FRUS: Foreign Ministers, 1946* 2:570–76, 579–83; Ward, *Threat of Peace*, 105–9.

10. *FRUS: Foreign Ministers, 1946* 2:598–601.

11. Ibid., 614–16, 641–46; Ward, *Threat of Peace*, 108–11.

12. *FRUS: Foreign Ministers, 1946* 2:617–26, 631–39, 648–62; Ward, *Threat of Peace*, 110–11.

13. *FRUS: Foreign Ministers, 1946* 2:668–80, 683–95; Ward, *Threat of Peace*, 111–12.

14. *FRUS: Foreign Ministers, 1946* 2:703–11; Ward, *Threat of Peace,* 112–14.

15. *FRUS: Foreign Ministers, 1946* 2:703–11.

16. Ibid., 715–25.

17. Ibid., 731–38.

18. Ibid., 738–42.

19. Ibid., 742–51; Ward, *Threat of Peace,* 111–13.

20. *FRUS: Foreign Ministers, 1946* 2:749–51.

21. Ibid., 753–70, 774–75; Ward, *Threat of Peace,* 114–15.

22. One commission ultimately was established for each of the treaties: one for Italian economic issues; one for Italian military and legal issues; one for economic issues involving Romania, Bulgaria, Hungary, and Finland; and, finally, one that was general and plenary (*FRUS: Foreign Ministers, 1946* 2:781–99).

23. Ward, *Threat of Peace,* 116–17; Charles E. Bohlen, *Witness to History, 1929–1969* (New York, 1973), 255.

24. *FRUS: Foreign Ministers, 1946* 2:801–15, 817–27, 828–42; Ward, *Threat of Peace,* 115–18.

25. *FRUS: Foreign Ministers, 1946* 2:842–50.

26. Ibid., 860–77.

27. *Time* 48 (July 22, 1946): 25; Rothwell, *Britain and the Cold War,* 320–24; Byrnes, *Speaking Frankly,* 180–81.

28. Byrnes, *Speaking Frankly,* 180–81; Anne Deighton, "The 'Frozen Front': The Labour Government, the Division of Germany and the Origins of the Cold War, 1945–7," *International Affairs* 63 (Summer 1987): 451–56.

29. Ward, *Threat of Peace,* 120–21; Gimbel, *American Occupation,* 71–82.

30. *Time* 48 (July 22, 1946): 38–39; *FRUS: Foreign Ministers, 1946* 2:881–98, 907–16.

31. Herken, *Winning Weapon,* 225–26; *Newsweek* 28 (August 26, 1946): 22.

32. *Time* 48 (July 22, 1946): 25; *FRUS: Foreign Ministers, 1946* 2:928–37.

33. *San Antonio Express News,* July 15, 1946; ibid., August 1, 1946; *Newsweek* 28 (July 22, 1946): 38; *Time* 48 (July 22, 1946): 25; Saville Davis, "Costly Harmony at Paris," *New Republic* 115 (July 15, 1946): 38–39; "The Air Clears at Paris," ibid.

34. *FRUS: Eastern Europe, 1946* 6:763–65, 767–71.

35. *Time* 48 (August 5, 1946): 5; Ward, *Threat of Peace,* 124–26.

VII

The Paris Peace Conference, August 6– October 13, 1946

Leaving the capital with the good wishes of a nation, Byrnes knew that a just peace might be impossible to achieve and that the stability once thought to be the result of a carefully crafted peace might have to be obtained through other means. Celebrating Air Power Day, in recognition of the tests at Bikini Atoll, many Americans were pronouncing that military strength, not diplomacy, was the surest source of security. Others believed that events in Germany, China, Eastern Europe, and the eastern Mediterranean soon would overshadow those in Paris. Still, Byrnes flew across the Atlantic with a fleeting hope that, as war bred war, "so peace can be made to breed peace."[1]

The Conference Opens

As the delegations converged on Paris the city readied itself to host nearly 1,500 officials representing twenty-one nations. Although most of the chic had retreated to various Mediterranean resorts, hotels were filled to capacity, the best being reserved for the major powers. The Big Three delegates returned to their five-star accommodations, while conferees from other governments vied for less prestigious and less expensive locations. In the quest for suitable rooms, the twenty-two Australian representatives provided a moment of amusement by protesting that they were too democratic for the Ritz. They finally settled for the less luxurious Palais d'Orsay, which they shared with the proletarian Bulgarians. Some suggested that the real reason behind the Australians' choice had more to do with francs than ideology.

On the afternoon of July 29, amid pomp and circumstance, the conference began as the delegates entered the Senate Chamber of the Luxembourg Palace. Representatives of minor nations and experts entered first, with those of the four powers coming last and all sitting in a horseshoe. Byrnes and the U.S. delegation arrived with great dignity and were placed on the extreme right. Molotov and his entourage strode into the room with a "consciousness of power" and sat on the left. The arrangement, an accident of the alphabet, graphically depicted the dynamics of the conference: the Americans on one side, the Soviets on the other, and the rest being pulled from both directions. With flashbulbs exploding, Georges Bidault welcomed the assembled representatives. Their task, he said, was a monumental one:

> It is to us that the long-suffering, sorely-tried peoples of the world, the weak in their anxiety and the simple honest folk turn—to ask us to-day to reject forever the evil forebodings lavished upon us by the prophets of ill and to set up in common accord, and in the service of justice and liberty, a world delivered from this scourge, which, unlike others, becomes more formidable as time passes—I mean the plague of war.[2]

Following Bidault's speech and his election as president of the meeting, the delegates formed a committee to determine rules directing the treaty commissions and the full conference. The Commission on Procedure would meet in the morning, and that afternoon the conference would begin work in plenary session. Those who had predicted hard and bitter negotiations were proved correct. It was soon apparent that at least two views about the nature of the conference and its procedure existed. Led by the Australians and strongly supported by the New Zealanders and Belgians, one group advocated letting the nations not represented on the Council of Foreign Ministers play a major role in shaping the peace treaties and voting on recommendations. An opposing group, headed by the indomitable Molotov and upheld by Poland, Yugoslavia, and Czechoslovakia, adhered to the principles that the ultimate right to prepare the treaties belonged to the Council of Foreign Ministers and that any suggestions from the conference should be determined by a two-thirds vote. The disagreement first arose among members of the Commission on Procedure, when the Australian and Dutch delegates objected to the two-thirds requirement. They proposed that a simple majority decide. Molotov immediately accused the Australians of trying to create blocs and, with an air of finality, concluded that his opponents "must reject all attempts to set off twelve or thirteen votes against seven or eight."

During the second plenary session, Molotov continued his effort to limit the influence of the conference. He announced that it was "sufficient to become familiar with the . . . draft treaties in order to see that the democratic countries which prepared them performed in this case a work which is in the main in keeping with the interests of countries, big and small, which are anxious to strengthen world peace and security of nations." Not only were the decisions made by the four powers in everyone's best interest, but also those disagreeing were threats to peace. The agreements of the council, Molotov warned, were being "assailed by all sorts of reactionary elements who are stuffed with absurd anti-Soviet prejudices" and sought to frustrate the cooperation of the big powers.[3]

Unaffected by the speech, Dr. Hubert V. Evatt, chief of the Australian delegation, questioned the council's decisions. "The right of making the Peace should belong to all those nations who have been partners in achieving the common victory," he stated. There was no aspect of the various treaties that could not be opened to discussion and reconsideration. It was, he remarked, "the obligation as well as the right of the nations which have not shared in the preparation of these drafts to analyze them in the light of sound general principles and make such constructive criticisms and specific recommendations as are called for." He requested the creation of "special fact-finding commissions" to report to the conference on issues affecting the treaties.[4]

While the plenary sessions continued with lengthy speeches, the Commission on Procedure grabbed the headlines. The debate over voting grew more heated as the British and the Americans backed the simple majority. On

August 2, Byrnes announced that the United States "would not be bound by the agreements as to procedure" adopted by the council and that the conference should determine its own rules. Molotov, supporting the two-thirds vote, accused the secretary of inconsistency and deserting the council. With the commission polarized, the British offered a compromise, arguing that there should be two forms of recommendation from the conference: one for those receiving two thirds of the vote, another for those with a simple majority. China and the United States quickly moved to support the proposition. New Zealand, Brazil, the Netherlands, and Australia continued to favor a simple majority in all cases. William Jordan, a New Zealand delegate, declared it was absurd that 35 percent could overrule 65 percent. He received loud applause.

Later that day the Norwegians and Canadians moved in favor of the British compromise, while Molotov, in some of his strongest language, opposed consideration of any form other than the two-thirds majority. He was staunchly backed by what many termed the "Red Dwarves": Poland, Yugoslavia, Czechoslovakia, the Ukraine, and Belorussia. Byrnes responded by reading the record from the council decisions, which clearly expressed the right of the United States not to support the voting procedures. He then dared the minister to print his statement in the Soviet press. Playing to a larger audience in his reply, the secretary firmly believed that he was generating Western public opinion against Soviet behavior. Molotov accepted the challenge and promised to see that Byrnes's comments were printed.

The exchange between Molotov and Byrnes made international headlines but won no converts on the voting issue. The Netherlands, New Zealand, Australia, India, South Africa, Brazil, Belgium, and Greece continued to support a simple majority. The Soviet Union and the Red Dwarves steadfastly clung to the two-thirds rule. The New Zealand proposal of a simple majority was soon defeated, 11 to 9. After several more votes and extensive maneuvering the British compromise was passed, 15 to 6.

Molotov made another attempt to invalidate the commission's decision. He submitted that any change in procedure needed a two-thirds majority to be valid. Byrnes rushed to confront the Soviet minister, pointing out that he

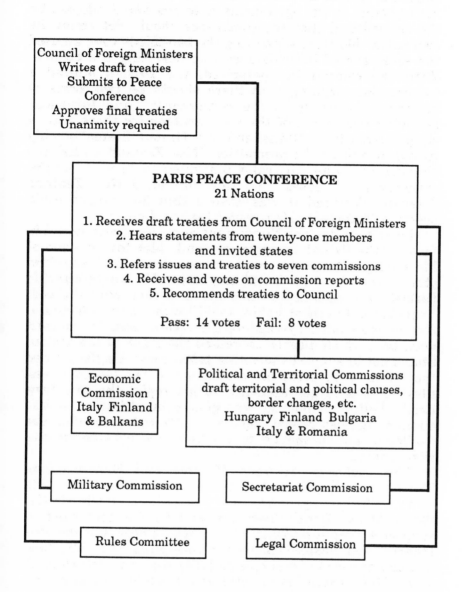

The process of treaty making as determined by September 1946.

was now violating the rules established by the council and was himself inconsistent while denouncing the United States for the same fault. "Now only Mr. Molotov would do that," Byrnes added. With a sense of triumph, he watched the commission vote against the Soviets in what would become an increasingly common ratio: 15 to 6.[5]

Stone Bottom Molotov was not yet finished. On August 8, as the Commission on Procedure reported its decisions to the full conference, he entered late and announced that he had an observation to make. During the next fifty minutes, he reasserted the Soviet demand for the two-thirds rule. "It will lead to no good to set a majority against a minority," Molotov intoned; the commission had made an "egregious error" and created an "erroneous proposal." He specifically attacked Britain and the United States for their about-face since the council meeting and their disregard for the decisions of the four powers. However, the minister saved his harshest comments for Evatt, accusing the Australian of wanting to use the simple majority to obtain anti-Soviet decisions. To prove his point, Molotov referred to a local newspaper story that boasted that the West "had scored" a victory over the Soviet Union through the commission's decision. According to Molotov, "as a golden rule all conferences should attain unanimity."

In the debates and votes that followed, it was clear that the Paris Peace Conference would not conform to the golden rule. British delegate Albert V. Alexander, Evatt, and Byrnes heaped scorn on Molotov's position and the claim that they had created an anti-Soviet bloc. "Whence comes this talk of blocs?" the secretary asked. "What loose and wicked talk this is! . . . Repetition of an inaccurate statement will not make it accurate." Furthermore, he announced that they were "not going to gang up against any nation. But I would be less than frank, if I did not say that those who have insisted most loudly on unanimity here have not shown quite the same desire to achieve unanimity."

As expected the Red Dwarves quickly supported Molotov and condemned the commission's decision. It was "extremely dangerous" and represented "an unjustifiable claim to exercise a dictatorship," protested the Ukrainian delegate Dimitri Manuilsky. After a vain attempt by the French to find language that both sides could agree upon, the president of the conference called for the vote on the

Soviet proposal to table the commission's recommendation. The Russians lost again by 15 to 6. Turning to the commission's report on procedure, the conference considered it section by section. When asked if the Soviet Union wanted the assembly polled on the passage dealing with voting procedure, Molotov cynically responded that it was unnecessary since their votes already had been cast. Paul-Henri Spaak of Belgium, however, requested a roll call, and the commission's recommendation was accepted by 15 to 6. With all the sections examined, President Bidault asked for a vote on the final document. "Organization and Procedure of the Peace Conference" was accepted by 15 to 4, with Czechoslovakia and Poland abstaining.[6]

In the recess, Byrnes celebrated what he considered a major victory, one that permitted the voices of the smaller powers, of world opinion, to resound over the protests of the Soviet Union. In London, when Molotov had deadlocked the conference over French and Chinese participation in drafting the peace treaties, Byrnes had told his aide Walter Brown, "We offered them five and they would not take it, now we will give them 50." The promise had been fulfilled.

The battle over voting was only a prelude. During the weeks that followed, acrimonious confrontations among the delegates became nearly daily occurrences. From August 10 to 15 the conference listened to the former enemies protest parts of the draft treaties and ask for modifications. Alcide de Gasperi of Italy led the way and, like the representatives of Romania, Bulgaria, Finland, and Hungary who followed, complained that the territorial and reparations clauses were too harsh and needed to be changed. Whether calm and reasoned or emotional and brash, their speeches drew hostile replies from the assembled delegations. On numerous occasions the responses even generated more tension than the original protest. Molotov, not unexpectedly, managed to attack bitterly both Italy and the United States in his reply to de Gasperi, although he later told the premier not to take his denunciation seriously; it "was just polemics." However, Byrnes was in no mood to ignore belligerence. The language of diplomacy was becoming tense, sweeping aside any "fiction that the European Allies were in harmony."

The verbal war reached a climax on August 15, when Byrnes strongly asserted that he could no longer ignore the many "misrepresentations levelled against the United States." Making no apology for American positions, the secretary objected to the Soviet allegation that some of the Great Powers had enriched themselves as a result of the war. He hoped that the accusers had not meant his country, "which came so unhesitantly to the support of the Soviet Union when in peril." Byrnes emphasized that the United States had provided its ally over $11 billion. Andrey Vyshinsky, in an almost light manner, responded that he did not believe that the secretary's oration would "contribute to the success" of the conference and he would not "enter into any polemics with him." The following day, however, *Pravda* charged Byrnes with acting like a "provincial prince": high-handed, undignified, and undemocratic.[7]

Following the acid exchange of August 15, the conference broke into its commissions to begin actual consideration of the treaties. The confrontations did not cease. Immediately the Soviets angered all but their Dwarves by demanding that, in the discussions of the Romanian, Bulgarian, Hungarian, and Finnish documents, France should not be allowed to vote. Jordan of New Zealand, for one, was tired of the Soviet delegates' bad manners and obstructionism and called their view "blasted old rot."

Clearly, quiet and businesslike negotiations had been replaced by vocal and public diplomacy. Byrnes and Molotov seemed to be taking turns painting brilliant verbal pictures for their listeners, casting each other as an obstacle to an enduring peace. One newspaper characterized the discussions at Paris as a "new school of slugging diplomacy," a style that was having the desired effect on home audiences. In both the United States and the Soviet Union, opinion was becoming increasingly nationalistic and hostile.[8]

Byrnes intended his performance to convince those who still regarded the West as too harsh that the Soviet Union was the true threat to peace. Repeatedly, he presented himself as the champion of small nations and majority rule, fighting against the Kremlin and its puppets who opposed democratic decisions. Highlighting Molotov's actions, speeches, and control over the East European states, the secretary wanted to drive home the image of a regime standing in the way of stability. By mid-August his efforts appeared successful. The senior editor of *Time* decided that the magazine's international news focus should be on the Soviet Union and that his reporters should intensify their efforts to acquire information from the State Department, scholars, and "anti-Soviet publicists." David Lawrence wrote in his national column that at Paris moral diplomacy was gaining ground against those representing "the totalitarian areas of Europe" and praised the American delegation. Some observers were suggesting that more than moral diplomacy would be necessary to maintain stability. "U.S. to Fight Soviet Expansion," shouted a headline in the *San Antonio Express News*. What caused this and similar announcements across the nation on August 17 was the report of Russia's demand that Turkey permit its bases in the Dardanelles.[9]

Problems in the Eastern Mediterranean

The Soviet request to Turkey had actually been made more than one week earlier, on August 7. At that time, the Russian chargé d'affaires in Washington had informed the State Department that the Kremlin wanted substantial changes to the Montreux Convention. Written in 1936 and signed by Bulgaria, France, Britain, Greece, Japan, Romania, Turkey, the Soviet Union, and Yugoslavia, the agreement had returned control of the straits to Turkey, which in return promised to respect freedom of transit from the Aegean to the Black Sea. Turkey also was allowed to deny passage to any nations at war and to warships if its government felt threatened. The Soviets had long sought to have the convention either changed or scrapped. They desired free passage of their warships and to share the responsibility of defending the straits. The latter arrangement would include establishing Red Army forces in Turkey, which, naturally, rejected any change.

In April 1945, as the Red Army pushed across southeastern Europe, the Soviet Union demanded that Turkey revise the Montreux Convention and permit Russian military bases in the straits. Unable to persuade the United States to join them, the British loudly protested the Soviets' demands on Turkey and asked that the issue be discussed by the Big Three at Potsdam. London was concerned that the request represented an effort to control and dominate Turkey, but State Department assessments were less alarming. Britain and the Soviet Union each were trying to ensure that the strategically placed nation would be within its sphere of influence. The position that Truman carried to Potsdam placed primary interest on keeping the matter from becoming a major international dispute and maintaining right of passage for merchant ships. As for the Montreux Convention, the president agreed that some modifications were in order. Prime Minister Churchill also arrived in Potsdam ready to consider some amendments. During their discussions with the Soviets the Western leaders affirmed their support for the revision of the convention and for freedom of navigation through the straits. However, they questioned the needs and rights that the Russians presented to justify a base along this passageway. Unable to agree, Stalin refused to permit even the mention of the area in the final communiqué. The issue remained just beneath the surface of big-power diplomacy, with the Soviets pressuring the smaller country until the beginning of August 1946, when their demands regarding the straits were again presented.

Among State Department officials there was growing alarm about Soviet intentions in the eastern Mediterranean. The American ambassador to Turkey saw Moscow's demands as a threat to Turkish sovereignty. Loy Henderson, chief of the Near Eastern and African Division, agreed. Between August 7 and 15 he and other top-level officials evaluated the Russian note. They also took notice of reports describing three hundred thousand Red Army troops massed on Turkey's borders. On August 12, Henderson asserted that the threatened country was of "vital interest" to the United States, and, if it fell, the Soviets would have a clear "advance to Persian Gulf and Suez." The "fat is in the fire again," he concluded. On August 15, Assistant Secretary of State Dean Acheson outlined the "facts" to President Truman. The Kremlin wanted to "control Turkey" and, if successful, would move to "control . . . Greece and the whole of the Near and Middle East." He declared that "the only thing which will deter the Russians" was "the conviction that the United States is prepared if necessary, to meet aggression with force of arms." Truman accepted the estimate and believed that he "might as well find out whether the Russians were bent on world conquest now, as in five or ten years."

The United States was not bluffing in its determination to protect Turkey and the straits from Soviet aggression and control. To underline the American commitment the U.S. Navy dispatched a flotilla of destroyers from the Twelfth Fleet to the Mediterranean and on August 23 ordered the carrier *Franklin D. Roosevelt* to dock at Athens. When the Soviet press attacked the U.S. move as "gangster diplomacy," Admiral William ("Bull") Halsey responded: "It's nobody's damn business where we go. We will go anywhere we please." Most Americans agreed with him.[10]

If Soviet demands on Turkey generated alarm, news about Yugoslav fighters forcing down an American transport plane on August 9 and then shooting another C-47 on the 19th made the public extremely angry. The Truman administration kept information of the earlier incident from the people until the 17th. By that time, the United States had apologized for the inadvertent overflight of Yugoslavia and protested its incursions into the American zone at Trieste. Tensions then reached an explosive level on August 20, when the Yugoslav government informed Washington that it had downed the second plane. Five Americans had died as the aircraft, already burning, crashed into a mountain. Rather than apologize, Marshal Josip Broz Tito insisted that the United States "issue strict orders" to prevent flying over his territory so that such "unfortunate accidents might be avoided" in the future. "U.S. Near War in Yugoslavia, Another Plane Shot Down" was typical of newspaper headlines across the country.

In Washington, Paris, Belgrade, and Moscow, diplomats responded to the growing crisis. The State Department drafted a harshly worded protest to Tito. In Paris, Byrnes met with the Yugoslav delegate, Edvard Kardelj, and in strong terms decried both incidents, announcing that the United States "could not tolerate the shooting down of American planes or the detention of American citizens." Many believed that, unless Tito met U.S. demands, the conference was over. Byrnes also issued instructions that flights from Vienna to Italy be resumed on August 23 with fighter escorts, which were to "take all necessary measures to protect our planes." He told the State Department to do everything it could "to stop further shipments of supplies of any sort by UNRRA [United Nations Recovery and Relief Administration] for Yugoslavia." Because 73 percent of UNRRA's funds came from the United States, the secretary, like many Americans, was angry that Yugoslavia was still receiving such aid. The department regrettably informed him that the funds could not be cut off.[11]

Byrnes believed that no country "guilty of . . . outrageous and unfriendly conduct" toward the United States should get aid. He therefore judged that Czechoslovakia also should be denied consideration of further assistance. When Vyshinsky had replied to the secretary's tongue-lashing on August 15, Byrnes had noticed that the Czech delegation had "heartily applauded." Immediately, he decided to take action. "I am convinced," he informed Acheson, "that the time has come when we should endeavor by all fair means to assist our friends" and not those "engaged in a campaign of vilification of the United States and distortion of our motives and policies." Meeting privately with Jan G. Masaryk, the Czechoslovak foreign minister, Byrnes exclaimed that "there would be an end to relief appropriations or credits to a government whose officials could applaud a denunciation of the United States as a government seeking to dominate the world by 'hand-outs.' "[12]

While Byrnes lectured Masaryk, he also watched, no doubt with some amusement, as Molotov apparently lectured Kardelj. The Soviet minister then left for Moscow to confer with Stalin. One rumor circulated that Molotov, having failed to win the vote on the procedural issue, was being called home in disgrace to be replaced. Meanwhile, Vyshinsky remained behind to continue the dissection of the draft treaties.[13]

As Molotov departed, tensions remained high in the eastern Mediterranean. American relations with Yugoslavia were still strained. Tito orally had regretted the deaths of U.S. airmen and had ordered his forces not to shoot down any planes violating Yugoslav airspace. But a spoken apology was not enough for Washington; it wanted his regrets in writing. Moreover, the marshal still was accusing the United States of violating his territory. Adding to the pressure, rumors were flying that twenty Yugoslav divisions were massed on Trieste's boundary. American reporters noted that the city was being called "Bataan" by U.S. troops stationed there.

The diplomacy of firmness continued into September. The United States demanded a written response from Tito and, after keeping a Yugoslav official waiting for thirty minutes, informed him that there had not been over one hundred American violations of Yugoslav airspace. The country's policies and information were declared wrong, and, under the present conditions, it "would not get a dime or pair of shoes from" the United States. The danger lessened by the second week in September, after Tito presented a written apology. Nonetheless, there were many Americans who strongly believed that behind his actions was the guiding hand of Stalin and that the Soviet Union was attempting to expand its influence in the eastern Mediterranean.[14]

German Policy and the Stuttgart Speech

While the American public worried and grew angry about events in Turkey and Yugoslavia, U.S. officials and many observers of international affairs recognized that the eastern Mediterranean was of secondary importance. The question that truly might determine the political orientation of Europe concerned Germany, where Byrnes now wished to assert U.S. policy. Accompanied by Senators Arthur Vandenberg and Tom Connally, he flew to Berlin to board a train for Stuttgart. There, on September 6, the secretary addressed a gathering of officials representing Germany and other countries. His purpose was to clarify American policy toward Germany and wrest the diplomatic advantage away from the Russians. First, he emphasized Washington's determination to prevent the Sovietization of Germany. Instead, the United States would promote self-government, economic revival, and territorial unification. Although primarily aimed at a German audience, the pronouncement of the commitment was meant also for Soviet and French ears. In expanding on U.S. goals, Byrnes stressed the necessity of economic unity and praised the efforts to join the British and American zones. "If complete unification cannot be secured," he stated, "we shall do everything in our power to secure the maximum possible unification."

Arriving in Germany for the Stuttgart speech, September 1946. Left to right: Senator Tom Connally, James F. Byrnes, Senator Arthur H. Vandenberg, and General Lucius Clay. (Robert M. Cooper Library, Clemson University)

American and British officials, angered by Soviet and French opposition to a unified Germany, were afraid the Kremlin's propaganda was wooing many Germans into supporting local and Russian Communist party ideals. They pointed to Soviet-generated stories about Western discord and apathy and the general uncertainty of Anglo-American policy as being especially effective. Officials also reported that there was a widespread belief among the Germans that the Western troops might soon depart, leaving only Soviet forces.

At Stuttgart, Byrnes counteracted those rumors and tried to restore German faith in U.S. policy. As he told Secretary of the Treasury John W. Snyder, he rejected the idea "that while the Soviets would remain, the Americans would leave." Inside the city's opera house, he called for German political and economic revival and unification. He assured his listeners that the United States had a long-term commitment to their country and Europe, stating that "security forces will probably have to remain in Germany for a long period. I want no misunderstanding. We will not shirk our duty. We are not withdrawing. We are staying here. As long as there is an occupational army in Germany, American armed forces will be part of that occupational army."[15]

The speech received a poor press in France, Poland, and the Soviet Union, but in Britain and the United States it was heralded as "wonderful" and "a message of hope." Some regarded it as not only a major statement of policy but also a recognition of the division between East and West. Joseph Alsop, commenting for the *New York Herald Tribune*, was blunt. After reminding his readers of Lenin's dictum "Who controls Germany controls Europe," he pictured Byrnes directly responding to Molotov's opening gambit of July 10. "The United States," he pronounced, "has now begun a struggle for Germany against the Soviet Union."[16]

While not everyone was as hostile toward the Soviets as Alsop, public opinion in Britain and the United States was turning against them. Russian and Communist actions at Paris and around the world worked to convince observers that the Kremlin and its allies were threats to peace. Across the United States, newspapers carried numerous articles describing "Red" and "Communist" activities and highlighting the fears of those who opposed Soviet expansionism. Congressmen touring the Pacific believed that Russian policies were creating "the imminent danger of another Pearl Harbor in Korea, Trieste, or Alaska." Archbishop Robert E. Lucey proclaimed that the "atheistic, Communistic, and imperialistic" Soviet Union was "stalemating the peace" at Paris and called upon Western statesmen to write a just peace.[17]

Henry A. Wallace and U.S. Foreign Policy

Observing American public opinion throughout the spring and summer, Lord Inverchapel, British ambassador to the United States, reported to the Foreign Office that the anti-

Soviet campaign in the U.S. press had created a near
hysteria about possible war with the Russians. He also
noted a major shake-up in the Truman administration: the
resignation of Secretary of Commerce Henry A. Wallace,
former vice president and the highest and most prominent
critic of American policy toward Moscow and Soviet
expansionism.[18]

Since the beginning of 1946, Wallace had witnessed and
recounted in his diary the growing anti-Soviet views within
the administration and the nation. In July, as Byrnes faced
Molotov in Paris, Wallace still thought that he might make
a difference, convincing Truman and others that the tough
U.S. policy toward the Russians might lead both countries
into a war that neither wanted. On July 23 the secretary of
commerce wrote a twelve-page, single-spaced letter to the
president explaining his views and fears. He emphasized
that American "distrust of the Russians" was being
generated by the press and was pushing "public opinion . . .
against Russia." Wallace believed that Soviet fears were
justified and understandable and that, in the name of peace,
the United States "should be prepared, even at the expense
of risking epithets of appeasement, to agree to reasonable
Russian guarantees of security."

Truman made no official reply to the letter but, during a
cabinet meeting the following day, agreed that they needed
to "be patient with Russia." Wallace, who put little faith in
the president's mental abilities, noted that, in his next
breath, Truman supported Byrnes's brusque actions in
Paris. In his diary he wrote: "I suspect there has never
been a President who could move in two different directions
with less time intervening than Truman. He feels
completely sincere and earnest at all times and is not
disturbed in the slightest by the different directions in which
his mind can go almost simultaneously. I say this realizing
that he always agreed with me on everything."[19] Perhaps
because he knew that the president seemingly assented to
whatever he suggested, the secretary of commerce agreed to
speak on foreign policy at a fund-raiser for the National
Citizens' Political Action Committee in New York at
Madison Square Garden. Since the committee was opposed
to much of the administration's domestic and foreign
policies, it was assumed that Wallace's speech, "A Way to
Peace," would be critical toward the tough approach with

the Soviets. What was not expected was that his remarks would receive presidential support.[20]

Hours before the scheduled speech, Wallace had released draft copies to reporters, who quickly noticed that he seemed to refute many of the tactics being practiced by Byrnes. According to the commerce secretary, the United States was "reckoning with a force which cannot be handled successfully by a 'Get Tough with Russia' policy. 'Getting tough' never brought anything real and lasting—whether for schoolyard bullies or businessmen or world powers. The tougher we get, the tougher the Russians will get."[21] Wallace also stated that Washington "should recognize that we have no more business in the political affairs of Eastern Europe than Russia has in the political affairs of Latin America, Western Europe, and the United States." Clearly, he was advocating a course that was not being followed in August 1946. Yet Wallace had reviewed his speech with Truman, who read the document, discussed it, and gave it his stamp of approval. When, during a press conference, reporters asked Truman if it was true that he had read the speech and agreed with its contents, he replied: "That is correct."

The address only served to intensify the ongoing debate over whose views should represent American foreign policy. The State Department quickly avowed no knowledge of or support for Wallace's opinions. Pressure immediately mounted for Truman to clarify his position. From Paris came news that Byrnes, Connally, and Vandenberg were "boiling mad." The secretary of state was uncharacteristically quiet, but Vandenberg sarcastically stated that he could only "cooperate with one Secretary of State at a time."[22]

In Washington the president lamely denied that he had endorsed the contents, telling a press conference: "It was my intention to express the thought that I approved the right of the Secretary of Commerce to deliver that speech. I did not intend to indicate that I approved the speech." He left without permitting any questions. *Time* called his excuse a "clumsy lie." Truman's apologists quickly moved to justify his inept explanation, reporting that the president only had thumbed through the speech.[23]

Whether he only glanced at the remarks or took over one hour discussing them, as Wallace's diary contends, the

controversy refused to die down. Returning to Washington
on September 16, Wallace stood behind his words, even in
the face of Truman's recent disavowal. He promised to
speak on the subject again. The following day, rumors
arose of Wallace's July 23 letter to the president, and
reporters hounded the White House, demanding to see it.
Finally, Charles G. Ross, Truman's press secretary,
released the letter without the chief executive's knowledge.
When Truman heard of the action, he was nearly hysterical
and instructed Ross to stop publication. It was too late. The
document was out, and the press and public were in an
uproar. It not only challenged Byrnes's diplomacy and
objected to U.S. atomic and military aims but also, because
Truman had read and not opposed it, raised questions about
who directed foreign policy. One headline broadcast that
Wallace urged Washington to "give in to Russia." Again,
pressure mounted on Truman to solidify foreign affairs and
control his staff. The president agreed to see Wallace the
next day, September 18.

Learning of the meeting, Byrnes, who had remained
silent so far, wired Truman a message beforehand in which
he threatened to resign immediately if Wallace was not
stopped in his attacks on U.S. policy. He asserted that such
pronouncements had impaired the ability of the Paris
delegation to negotiate. Truman also heard from Admiral
William Leahy, Secretary of the Navy James Forrestal,
Secretary of War Robert Patterson, and atomic energy
adviser Bernard M. Baruch, all of whom were critical of
Wallace and wanted his removal. Baruch warned that he
too would otherwise resign.

As the administration's leading liberal, Wallace had a
sizable and politically important following. Truman
realized that letters arriving in the White House supported
the errant secretary nearly 5 to 1. Caught in a political and
diplomatic squeeze, the president met with Wallace for over
two and one-half hours, and, despite his growing dislike for
the secretary, the discussion was friendly and to the point.
Wallace asserted that thousands of Americans were afraid
that the administration's tough policy would lead to war.
According to Wallace's diary, the president had listened
and even seemed apologetic when asking him to stop
making critical statements. Truman explained that
"Jimmie Byrnes had been giving him hell . . . threatening to

leave Paris," and that he must request Wallace to refrain from making any more speeches touching on foreign policy. Upon leaving, the secretary met a throng of reporters and told them that he had not been asked to resign and that he would make no public statements until the Paris Peace Conference was over.[24]

The compromise was not enough for many, including Byrnes, who spoke to Truman via Teletype and explained that temporarily silencing Wallace would do nothing to support Byrnes's own diplomacy. The work of the American delegation was "at a standstill," he informed Truman; Wallace's criticisms had destroyed U.S. policy "in a day" and could only encourage Molotov. If the Soviet minister "believed on October 23 there would be a re-examination of the question of permitting Wallace to again attack your policy he would derive great comfort." Without directly telling the president to fire Wallace, Byrnes firmly pushed him in that direction. Truman, in turn, congratulated Byrnes on an excellent job and told him that the delegation had his total backing and that the situation would be clarified the next morning, September 20. Wallace was then removed from the cabinet, with the president stressing his support for the current diplomacy at Paris. Satisfied, the secretary of state and his delegation turned their attention once more to the proceedings of the treaty commissions.

Wallace's dismissal met with general public approval; most Americans also seemed satisfied with Byrnes's diplomacy. A Gallup poll asked citizens if their feelings toward Russia were more or less friendly than one year earlier. The majority, 62 percent, said they were less friendly, while 28 percent believed that their attitudes were about the same. Only 2 percent of those questioned thought more highly of the Soviets.[25]

Throughout 1946, public opinion in the Soviet Union had undergone a similar change. Just as Byrnes had used diplomacy to shape world views, so, too, did the Russian leaders. Throughout the Paris meetings of the four powers and the peace conference, Molotov and his staff had pictured the United States, followed by its puppet, Great Britain, as creating a bloc against the Soviet Union and thereby threatening peace. Tass repeatedly stressed that security rested upon the willingness of the West to work with

Moscow and assailed Byrnes and Bevin as anti-Soviet
reactionaries. Such attacks increasingly focused on the role
of the United States. Britain, once the main target of abuse
by Soviet media, had become since mid-1946 a mere pawn, a
second-string player. Russian commentators told national
and global audiences that the Anglo-Saxon bloc intended
world domination and that the Americans were attempting
to impose a "forced peace" on the world, much like that of
imperial Rome and Hitler's Germany.

"Day in day out during past months," reported Elbridge
Durbrow, the American chargé d'affaires to the Soviet
Union, the "tom-toms of Soviet propaganda have beat out
themes that American and British reactionaries are
seeking to foment a new war against USSR." Western
observers also noted a major domestic attempt to purify the
thinking of the Russian people and to purge those
considered too close to the West. On September 9 the Soviet
Writers Union ousted its "weak members" and passed a
resolution to "expose the nature of capitalist encirclement."
Some days earlier, Maxim Litvinov, regarded by many as a
pro-West statesman, was relieved of his duties. Rumors in
Washington, Paris, and London held that even Molotov
might be replaced because he had failed at Paris. Frank
Roberts, the British chargé d'affaires in Moscow, reported a
50 percent "turnover in Soviet and Party personnel" and that
the city was gripped by a "war scare."

Durbrow warned Washington that, while assessing
Soviet public opinion was difficult, there "was no doubt that
propaganda line has conjured up widespread fear of new
world war." As in the United States, the Soviets were being
convinced by word and deed that the relationship between
the two powers was no longer one of friendship and
alliance.[26]

The Final Days of the Conference

In Paris, work went on. Molotov had returned from
Moscow, and contentious debates continued with little
result. Wanting to speed up the process and promote
solutions, Bidault suggested that the Council of Foreign
Ministers meet concurrently with the peace conference. As
if international tension had risen high enough, Soviet and

American spokesmen worked to cool the atmosphere. On September 24, Stalin gave an uncharacteristic interview to Alexander Werth of the London *Sunday Times.* The generalissimo denied that there was any danger of war or capitalist encirclement. "It was necessary," he said, "to make strict distinction between furor about 'new war,' which is being raised at the present time, and real danger of 'new war' which does not exist."

In evaluating Stalin's comments, British and American observers were cautious and discounted any significant change in his policy. Durbrow explained to the State Department that the apparently soothing words might have been the consequence of the tougher U.S. policy:

> During the past several months USSR has been talking and acting tough to Western democracies. These tactics have failed to intimidate USA and Britain. Rather they have resulted in increased firmness in American and British policy. Final demonstration of resolute American policy was showdown on Wallace. Stalin may now estimate that he had best change his truculent tune. He may feel that his bluff had been called and from now on he would do well to follow a somewhat more circumspect policy.

Lending validity to this evaluation, Molotov suddenly began to show signs of being more cooperative. By the end of September, both he and Byrnes seemed anxious to complete the writing of the treaties and to move on to finalizing and approving them.[27]

In informal meetings of the council, the four powers moved to unknot the differences and thus permit the close of the peace conference. During their fifth session, on September 24, the ministers determined that the treaty commissions should finish work on October 5 and the conference should end ten days later. On October 3, they agreed on voting procedures for the treaties and to limit debate on related provisions to thirty minutes for each delegation.[28]

From October 7 to 15 the delegates of the twenty-one nations appeared to reside at the Luxembourg Palace. Some sessions went nearly until dawn. One meeting took seventeen hours, with only a ten-minute recess at 4:00 A.M. Occasionally, delegates lost interest or fell asleep, to be jarred awake by a poll. Caught off guard by a roll call, the Yugoslav delegate, Alex Bebler, was forced to switch his

"Something Everybody Has Felt Like Doing" (*San Antonio Express News,* August 1946)

vote twice on a single issue. When called upon, the startled man indicated a yea, only to find Molotov frowning at him. He immediately reversed himself, but Stone Bottom still scowled. Finally, Bebler abstained and thereby received a smile from the foreign minister.[29]

Through it all, in an avalanche of yeas, nays, and abstentions, 94 amendments were considered, and the draft peace treaties were approved—a total of 233 articles and 33 annexes. For the first two days the conference voted on the Italian treaty. The results generally pleased Byrnes and Bevin. Understandably, Molotov was less happy. Reparations were kept to an acceptable level, and the Free Territory of Trieste was established with a governmental structure acceptable to the West. Representing the minority view, the Soviets objected to the disposition and internationalization of the city.

The votes on the Italian document began a pattern that soon became predictable. Articles agreed upon by the council nearly always received four-power support, with the Soviet Union upholding its view that the Big Three and France had an obligation to back council decisions. Thus, Molotov voted for the internationalization of Trieste even though he had spoken against it. Amendments offered by the commissions, however, were another matter. Here the minister was under no such restriction and usually opposed majority proposals such as those that would establish a strong governorship for Trieste and deny reparations to Albania. Since the results in the plenary sessions nearly always matched those of the commissions, Molotov usually lost 8 to 5.[30]

In the remaining days of the conference, the plenary sessions dealt with the Romanian, Bulgarian, Hungarian, and Finnish treaties. Molotov and his supporters could only watch and protest as Byrnes and Bevin successfully added the internationalization of the Danube and Open Door clauses to the Balkan treaties. The Red Dwarves and the Soviets complained that the latter provided an opportunity for "private capitalists" armed with dollars to "become the veritable owners of whole states." But the measures were approved.[31]

At 5:30 in the afternoon on October 15, 1946, the Paris Peace Conference ended, not in a sense of triumph but in exhaustion. Another step had been taken toward finalizing the satellite treaties and ensuring the stability of Europe. The effort had been tedious and the arguments frequent. Bevin summarized many delegates' views when he commented: "Rebuilding the world is far more difficult than waging war, for there is no compulsion to agree." Fewer and fewer political observers believed that security and peace rested in the completion of the documents for the satellites and Austria, Germany, and Japan. Many relied more on a balance of power among the Big Three and less on international harmony or the United Nations. Within the Foreign Office, the State Department, and the Kremlin, despite outward protestations, the compulsion to cooperate had disappeared and was being replaced with the need to protect and, if possible, extend spheres of influence.[32]

Notes

1. August 1, 1946, was officially called Air Power Day and was celebrated across the United States. *San Antonio Express News*, August 1 and 2, 1946; *Time* 48 (July 22, 1946): 25; ibid. (August 5, 1946): 5, 22.

2. *Newsweek* 28 (July 29, 1946): 30–31; Ward, *Threat of Peace*, 127–28; *FRUS: Paris Peace Conference: Proceedings, 1946* (Washington, DC, 1970), 3:48–52.

3. *FRUS: Peace Conference, 1946* 3:48–52.

4. Ibid., 48–55; Ward, *Threat of Peace*, 129–30; *Time* 48 (August 12, 1946): 22.

5. *FRUS: Peace Conference, 1946* 3:65–66, 68–81, 104–5, 123–31; *Newsweek* 28 (August 19, 1946): 36–40; Ward, *Threat of Peace*, 129–33.

6. *Time* 48 (August 19, 1946): 26–28; *FRUS: Peace Conference, 1946* 3:131–62. The *San Antonio Express News* informed its readers on August 10 that "Byrnes spurs victory over Red vote plan."

7. *San Antonio Express News*, August 16, 1946; *Time* 48 (August 26, 1946): 22; Ward, *Threat of Peace*, 135–36; *FRUS: Peace Conference, 1946* 3:175–85, 186–87, 191–98, 221-36; *Newsweek* 28 (August 26, 1946): 33–36.

8. *Newsweek* 28 (August 14, 1946): 32; *San Antonio Express News*, August 14, 1946.

9. Gormly, *Collapse of the Grand Alliance*, 156–58; Gaddis, *Long Peace*, 39–40; Liebovich, *Origins of the Cold War*, 129–30; *San Antonio Express News*, August 15 and 17, 1946.

10. Jonathan Knight, "American Statecraft and the 1946 Black Sea Straits Controversy," *Political Science Quarterly* 90 (Fall 1975): 451–75; *FRUS: The Near East and Africa, 1946* (Washington, DC, 1969), 7:824–50; *Time* 48 (September 9, 1946): 21; Kuniholm, *Near East*, 18, 53–55, 218–20, 260–67, 355–64.

11. *FRUS: Eastern Europe, 1946* 6:920–28; Ward, *Threat of Peace*, 137; *Time* 48 (September 2, 1946): 21–22; ibid. (September 9, 1946): 29; Byrnes, *Speaking Frankly*, 144–46; *San Antonio Express News*, August 20 and 22, 1946.

12. Ward, *Threat of Peace*, 136; Byrnes, *Speaking Frankly*, 143–44; Pollard, *Economic Security*, 47–48; *FRUS: Eastern Europe, 1946* 6:216.

13. *Time* 48 (September 9, 1946): 29. Vyshinsky proved to be as caustic as Molotov, insulting the Italians on September 4. After having said that "everyone knows Italians are better at running away than at fighting," he was challenged to at least two duels (*Time* 48 [September 16, 1946]: 31).

14. *Time* 48 (September 2, 1946): 21–22; *FRUS: Eastern Europe, 1946* 6:927–47, 949–56.

15. U.S. Department of State *Bulletin* 15 (September 15, 1946): 496–501.

16. Gimbel, *American Occupation*, 84–87; Gimbel, "Potsdam Agreement," 242–63; Ward, *Threat of Peace*, 139–40; *Newsweek* 28 (September 16, 1946): 40–41; *Time* 48 (September 9, 1946): 29–30; Pollard, *Economic Security*, 94–105.

17. *San Antonio Express News*, September 1 and 23, 1946. See also the *Los Angeles Times* and *Christian Science Monitor*, August–September 1946.

18. *Time* 48 (September 9, 1946): 21; Gormly, *Collapse of the Grand Alliance*, 157–58; Lord Inverchapel to Foreign Office, September 2, 1946, F.O. 371, AN2259/1/46, PRO.

19. Walton, *Henry Wallace*, 95–96.

20. Ibid., 79–97.

21. Ibid., 103.

22. Ibid., 97–108; Ward, *Threat of Peace*, 141–43; *Time* 48 (September 23, 1946): 21–22, 28; Byrnes, *Speaking Frankly*, 239–43.

23. *Time* 48 (September 23, 1946): 21–22. Vandenberg obviously believed that the president's explanation was not true. He told Pierson Dixon that Truman had actually "written in the margin of Wallace's speech, 'This will make Jimmy sore' " (Dixon, *Double Diploma*, 227).

24. Walton, *Henry Wallace*, 108–17; *Time* 48 (September 30, 1946): 21–23; *Newsweek* 28 (September 30, 1946): 19–21; *San Antonio Express News*, September 18, 1946.

25. Ward, *Threat of Peace*, 142–44: *Time* 48 (September 30, 1946): 21–23; *Newsweek* 28 (September 30, 1946): 19–21; Walton, *Henry Wallace*, 111–17; *San Antonio Express News*, September 18, 1946.

26. *FRUS: Eastern Europe, 1946* 6:778–71, 782–84; Gormly, *Collapse of the Grand Alliance*, 159–63.

27. *FRUS: Eastern Europe, 1946* 6:778–81, 782–84; Ward, *Threat of Peace*, 144–48; *Time* 48 (October 21, 1946): 29; ibid. (November 4, 1946): 31.

28. *FRUS: Peace Conference, 1946* 3:654–59.

29. *Time* 48 (October 21, 1946): 29.

30. *FRUS: Peace Conference, 1946* 3:693–758; *Time* 48 (October 14, 1946): 30.

31. *Time* 48 (October 14, 1946): 30; *FRUS: Peace Conference, 1946* 3:758–859.

32. *FRUS: Peace Conference, 1946* 3:859–61; *Time* 48 (October 14, 1946): 30; ibid. (October 21, 1946): 29.

VIII

Quest for Stability,
Quest for Security

The Paris Peace Conference was not the final step in either
the writing or the approving of the treaties, nor did the
responsibility belong to the United Nations. The process
ended where it had begun, with the Big Three, plus France,
in their capacity as the Council of Foreign Ministers.
Wanting to conclude the treaties before the end of the year,
the council decided to hold its next session in New York
while the United Nations met. As delegates converged on
the city, it was clear where power truly rested. The four
council members, representing their governments'
interests, would determine whether the world organization
was to have any real authority. The influence of the major
powers was underlined as President Truman spoke to the
opening session of the United Nations General Assembly.
He stressed that the problems facing the Big Three were not
insurmountable and that they should work together to
ensure peace. He also asked that the larger body avoid the
divisions of the council and "set an example of mutual give
and take" for the four powers to copy.

Despite the president's optimism, those examining
possible international systems concluded that the range of
choices had narrowed considerably since Potsdam. Few, if
any, now believed that the big powers were willing to
relinquish control to a world organization. Most assumed
that any emerging system would be directed by the major
powers, each supported by its sphere of influence. The
central remaining questions involved the number of these
powers (two or three?) and the degree of aggression between
them. W. Averell Harriman saw the world divided into two
very hostile blocs. He asserted that the Soviets had

"declared psychological warfare on the United States" and that, as a "war of ideology," it was a "fight to the death."

Although suspicious of Moscow's intentions the majority of Americans were not ready to agree with Harriman. Instead, they hoped, much like Truman, that a cooperative relationship between the Soviet Union and the United States still might be reestablished. Those decrying Soviet foreign policy and those hoping for better relations looked to the next session of the Council of Foreign Ministers as an opportunity to prove their perceptions correct.[1]

The New York Meeting of the Foreign Ministers

As the Paris Peace Conference was ending, State Department officials frantically scurried around New York seeking suitable accommodations and the personnel necessary to hold the November 1946 meeting of the Council of Foreign Ministers. It was not easy. The city, already hosting the General Assembly, was filled almost to capacity. Finally, after Secretary of State Byrnes intervened, the manager of the Waldorf-Astoria Hotel agreed to rent the sixth and seventh floors for individual offices and suites on the thirty-seventh story to house the council sessions. In addition, there were interpreters and security guards to be hired as well as communications and other services to be provided. A twenty-four-hour buffet was opened at a cost of $250 per day. All had to be functioning before November 4 for the scheduled first gathering of the council.

In dribs and drabs the delegates arrived. Molotov and Andrey Vyshinsky traveled on the luxurious *Queen Elizabeth*. Calling it his "first vacation since the Revolution," the minister stayed in a $1,350 suite, strolled the decks, attended formal dinners, and even took a turn steering. Arriving on October 22, he and his deputy appeared unusually cheerful, indeed acting more like tourists than obstinate negotiators. Molotov signed autographs and joked with reporters, while Vyshinsky attended Mass at Saint Patrick's Cathedral.

As the council session opened, Molotov made it evident that he was still the premier hard-line bargainer. He demanded that a Yugoslav representative be allowed to address the council on the proposed Italian treaty. Neither Byrnes nor Ernest Bevin thought it necessary, having heard Yugoslavia's position many times before. Of more concern was the possibility that the Soviets might withdraw their support from previously approved articles of the treaty, especially those dealing with the Yugoslav border and Trieste. Ill and exhausted from his time in Paris, the English minister was blunt: "Do I take it that our original decision . . . still stands?" Although Molotov gave an evasive reply, Bevin, Byrnes, and Maurice Couve de Murville, who had replaced Georges Bidault, agreed to the request. However, they demanded that an Italian also be invited to speak on the treaty.

Molotov intended to oppose many, if not all, of the recommendations made at Paris. In a series of pronouncements, he rejected article after article of the Italian treaty. At one time he found "no reason for the acceptance"; at another, he said that the article "was at variance" with the original document. By the end of the first session the only motion he had accepted was to adjourn to the bar for cocktails.[2]

During the next few days this pattern was repeated over and over. Tempers flared. Byrnes adopted a "praying mantis attitude" and proposed that Yugoslavia receive no reparations unless it signed the Italian treaty. Visibly angry, Molotov accused the American of being dictatorial and violating previous agreements. Byrnes coldly responded that the "accusation was unwarranted" but he had grown accustomed to it. Among the ministers, accord was rare and came only on unimportant issues. By the end of the second day, three articles had been accepted, seven deferred.

Not even social functions were spared from diplomatic maneuvering. During a Soviet reception, Molotov asked Bevin if he thought that the recent Republican political victories would alter American policies. Bevin shot back an emphatic "no" and said that "warfare across the conference table" would have no effect either. The comment had little impact. The next afternoon, four articles were deferred and three adopted. When the other treaties were considered they fared no better. The Romanian treaty saw only one article adopted, as did the Finnish. For Bulgaria, all articles were deferred except for one that was withdrawn. For Hungary, all were deferred.[3]

On November 12, no closer to finalizing the documents than he was before the peace conference, Molotov finally disclosed what many present considered his price for reaching any agreements. The Soviet minister had "a box full" of amendments regarding Trieste for the council to consider. Again, he got his own way. For the next three days his colleagues listened and responded to a barrage of recommendations. Like grinding stones the ministers debated, rejected, offered alternatives, and even found some solutions. Eventually the Trieste discussions focused on the relationship between the appointed governor and the legislature, the control of the police force, and the date for withdrawal of British and American troops. Molotov wanted the popularly elected legislature to govern the police and to have a dominant role in the government. Bevin and Byrnes preferred putting administrative power in the governor's hands. After one week of heated debate the Soviet minister retreated a small step. He suggested a sharing of power, with the governor commanding the police in time of emergency. Less than thrilled with the concession, Bevin and Byrnes asked for a definition of "shared control" and "emergency." The debate ground on.[4]

The pace of events was becoming nightmarish as the ministers divided their time among social activities, United Nations and council sessions, and a variety of other political and diplomatic functions. Pierson Dixon wrote on November 14:

> The pressure is becoming appalling. . . . We are getting entangled on the U.N.O. side (veto, Spain, disarmament etc.), which is a heavy burden on top of the Council of Foreign Ministers, with Trieste at its supreme crisis and all the general F.O. work, especially Egypt and Palestine, with which we continue to deal. . . . We are saved by our meals out, wonderful food, and the excitement of a walk along 5th Avenue.

Already ill, Bevin suffered a minor heart attack on November 20 while out walking. Nonetheless, he was back at work the next morning, giving "a powerful extempore speech" to the General Assembly and attending another unproductive council session from 4:00 to 7:45.[5]

By Saturday, November 23, Byrnes had concluded that the council might as well end its sessions unless some agreements were quickly found. Sarcastically, he suggested to his colleagues that, at the rate they were going, they would not finish the Trieste question before Christmas. The Italian treaty, he went on, no doubt would keep them busy until 1950. Fearing that Byrnes might actually terminate negotiations, Molotov sought a private meeting. The secretary said that it was best "to admit frankly that they could not agree and announce their disagreement to the world"; the "world would not come to an end because of their disagreement."

Responding to Byrnes's readiness to end the conference, Molotov affirmed that he wanted to finalize the treaties and, in turn, asked if they might not find "a little something" to encourage the Yugoslavs to accept the Italian document. As the ministers talked, they moved closer to finding solutions and decided to continue the negotiations. Slowly, during the following sessions, they reduced the points of friction. By Thanksgiving evening, November 28, they had reached agreement on a wide range of questions, including Trieste. The only key issue still unresolved was reparations.

Believing that he had made concessions on the Yugoslav-Italian border, Molotov expected his colleagues to do likewise on reparations. Specifically, he wanted to increase the amount paid to Yugoslavia and to add Albania to the list of recipients. The rest of the council thought otherwise. Bevin was adamant that Greece should receive the same amount of reparations as Yugoslavia. As for Albania, Byrnes considered zero the appropriate amount. Days of confusing, and sometimes humorous, haggling followed. At one point, Molotov wanted $145 million for Yugoslavia and Greece, while Bevin demanded $155 million. When neither would give in, Couve de Murville dared to "suggest the middle figure of $150 million." At first the two disputants appeared to ignore their French colleague. Undaunted, he repeated his suggestion. Finally, Bevin and Molotov reluctantly accepted his compromise but then immediately began fighting over how much of it should be paid by Italy and how much by Bulgaria. Byrnes, meanwhile, remained constant: Albania should receive nothing.[6]

By December 5 the council had patched together five peace treaties. Byrnes and Bevin were pleased, for they had obtained more than either had thought possible. Despite Molotov's initial obstructionism, forty-seven of the fifty-three recommendations made by a simple majority of the peace conference in Paris had been approved. Five days later the ministers agreed to instruct their deputies to sign the finished treaties.

Most observers credited the shift in Soviet behavior to Byrnes's firm stand. However, few believed that Molotov's reasonableness and the treaty agreements signaled any real change in Moscow's policy. Thus, the applause and congratulations that accompanied the council ministers as they left New York was guarded. Praise was less than enthusiastic, and the treaty process was not considered to play an important part in the quest for peace and stability.

The same weeks that saw the completion of the peace treaties also began the final phase in the shaping of a postwar international system. Increasingly the powers were replacing conference diplomacy, which emphasized Big Three cooperation, compromise, and unity, with a sphere-of-influence/balance-of-power outlook. Rather than resting security requirements on an international system, the Soviet Union and the United States were relying on an independent approach guaranteed by their own strength and negotiation. An editorial in the *Los Angeles Times* asked the nation to face up to the Russians and announced that the best to be expected was "an armed peace for the next few years." As 1947 began, *Time* named James Francis Byrnes "Man of the Year." A few weeks later, while honoring the South Carolinian for his accomplishments, the news magazine stated that the day of diplomats like him had passed. He was a fixer, a politician, a negotiator; the new global challenges facing the United States required a man of bigger and tougher stature.

George C. Marshall and Changes in Policy

Even as *Time* was applauding Byrnes, Truman was hastening to name his successor, General George C. Marshall, who as chief of staff of the armed forces had organized the victories over Germany and Japan. The president's choice was in China, attempting without success to bring Communists and Nationalists into a government, when on January 3 he was requested to return to Washington "for consultation on China and other matters." Having been asked previously if he would serve as secretary of state, Marshall knew what "other matters" involved. When he was sworn in on January 20 the new secretary stressed that he had no political ambitions and sought only to implement the policies of the U.S. government. *Time* strongly approved of the appointment. The general was "clearly a bigger man than his predecessor," the magazine declared. *Newsweek* observed that, while Byrnes's policy "had been one of firm, if sometimes oblique, negotiations with the Kremlin," Marshall would "be tough, direct, and completely in the open." The writer concluded that "if the Soviet Union could not understand offers of cooperation, perhaps it could grasp Marshallian toughness."[7]

The new secretary assumed his responsibilities as the country was shifting the basis of its policy toward the Soviet Union. The image of a unified world influenced by the major powers was being replaced by one of division both global and among the Big Three. Words describing American policy had changed. No longer were "patient" and "firm" used; instead, the key word now was "tough."

Adviser Charles Bohlen, who frequently articulated options for the State Department, observed:

> The United States is confronted with a condition ... which is at direct variance with the assumptions upon which, during the period directly after the war, major United States policies were predicated. Instead of unity among the great powers ... there is complete disunity between the Soviet Union and the satellites on one side and the rest of the world on the other. There are, in short, two worlds instead of one.[8]

Supported by the Joint Chiefs of Staff and the State Department, he argued that Washington needed to act "politically, economically, financially, and in the last analysis, militarily" to protect the rest of the world from Soviet expansionism. An anonymous official confidently reported to the press that a war was "going on everywhere—in Greece, in France, in Korea and in many other places" and the United States was "losing ground." It was "impossible to negotiate" with the Soviets, the informant firmly insisted, and the nation must "either yield to them or to tell them 'No.'" *Newsweek* labeled Marshall's new policies as "containment—containment of Russia."[9]

The Foreign Office had reached similar conclusions. Despite Soviet concessions at Paris and New York, its policymakers believed that Britain "should quite unostentatiously reorganise our world as quickly and as actively as we can without the Russians." When Prime Minister Attlee suggested that London should work harder to "come to an agreement with Stalin," Bevin forcefully disagreed. The Kremlin was "committed to the belief that there is a natural conflict between the capitalist and the communist worlds," he instructed his superior. "If we speak to Stalin as you propose . . . we shall get as much of Stalin's goodwill as we got of Hitler's after Munich." Bevin's views prevailed. Britain would not seek a compromise and would work instead to put its own house in order, even building its own atomic bomb. "We've got to have the bloody Union Jack flying on top of it," the foreign minister insisted.

Bevin and the Foreign Office also agreed that it was necessary to continue encouraging the Americans to take a more direct role in Europe, the Middle East, and anywhere else Soviet expansionism threatened their interests. The British were pleased with Byrnes's determination to confront Molotov at Paris and welcomed the U.S. decision to merge their occupation zones and provide financial aid only to those nations supporting Western policies. Furthermore, they were enthusiastic about the American show of force in the eastern Mediterranean following the Soviet demands on Turkey and the Yugoslav downing of a U.S. plane. The question facing the Foreign Office was whether the concern and military display were temporary or part of a permanent commitment. Many Americans had the same question.[10]

As the Paris Peace Conference had neared its end, columnist Walter Lippmann became more and more concerned about Soviet behavior. He wrote that the United States should promote peace by establishing its naval and air power in the eastern Mediterranean, in or near Turkey. What he did not know was that Bevin and Byrnes, between their confrontations with Molotov, privately had discussed the possibilities of American aid for Greece, Turkey, and

Iran. By December, Washington was moving to fill the vacuum in the region left by receding British influence. Iranian Prime Minister Ahmad Qavam, convinced of American support, ordered his troops into rebellious Azerbaijan, restoring governmental authority. U.S. satisfaction with the move, however, was balanced with renewed concern for the eastern Mediterranean.

Throughout the first two months of 1947, reports from Greece and Turkey stressed that growing economic chaos there increased instability and created opportunities for the extension of Soviet influence. Within the State Department the Near Eastern and African Division informed Secretary Marshall on February 20 that the situation in Greece was critical and its pro-Western government was near collapse. The consensus in the department was that the United States would have to increase its commitment in order to maintain regional stability. At the same time, Bevin and Chancellor of the Exchequer Hugh Dalton "agreed . . . that we should put up a strong telegram to the United States asking them what they were going to do and on the other hand telling the Greeks that we could not continue [to support them] for the sole purpose of bringing matters to a head."[11]

On February 21 the British reported that they were unable to maintain their financial commitments to Greece and Turkey. Already considering increasing its aid to the Athens government, the United States was prepared to act. Five days later the State and War departments recommended a general assistance program to both countries that would replace Britain in the eastern Mediterranean, thereby providing stability and security. Truman concurred. Within the administration, there was a new degree of certainty regarding America's world role. The president told his cabinet that the $250 million requested for Greece and Turkey was "only the beginning" and that it would take "the greatest selling job ever facing a President" to get congressional and public support for the new commitments.

Over the next two weeks the public was treated to a growing number of official statements about the importance of the eastern Mediterranean to world peace. On February 27, Marshall and Assistant Secretary of State Dean Acheson met with selected congressional leaders, including Arthur Vandenberg and Tom Connally, to

"Self-Portrait of the Weary Atlas" (*San Antonio Express News*, March 1947)

convince them that a real crisis existed in Greece and that a diplomatic and financial commitment was needed to prevent the region from falling under Soviet influence. Marshall spoke first, followed by the more alarming Acheson. Both stressed the strategic importance of the region and voiced fears that the Russians would use "victories" in Greece and Turkey to extend their doctrine throughout the area. Marshall and Acheson's rhetoric worked; the congressional delegation left, persuaded that the United States must intervene to stop the spread of communism and Soviet power. Senator Vandenberg even recommended that Truman should "scare the hell out of the country" to ensure wide support.[12]

By the beginning of March 1947, the press definitely reflected the attitude projected by the State Department. One editorial commented that if Greece went "Communist the iron curtain would extend into the Mediterranean [and] . . . the Soviet Union's sphere of influence would face no serious obstacle to spreading over the oil-rich Middle East." Senator Herbert R. O'Conor announced that the issue was "a test of strength between Russia and the United States." In the official statements and in the media the actual events in Greece and Turkey were being forgotten and pushed into the background, while the ideological struggle between democracy and communism was being emphasized. Many State Department officials, including George Kennan, lamented the simplification of reality. But Acheson understood that, to legitimate the adoption of new foreign policy, symbols and not facts were needed. He argued that the average American, "with a fair education, a family, and a job," had ten minutes at most to consider world politics. If Washington was to inform that citizen, its message had to be obvious. Acheson claimed that, if the government "made our points clearer than truth, we did not differ from most other educators and could hardly do otherwise." All was in place for Truman to make to Congress and the world a pronouncement that would direct American foreign policy on a "new course." In introducing Truman, Vandenberg asked the "Senator from Florida to suspend order that we may keep our date with destiny."[13]

Largely written by Acheson and presidential adviser Clark Clifford, Truman's March 12 address requested $400 million in aid for Greece and Turkey. It envisioned a world divided into two halves: the free and unfree. In announcing what would be called the Truman Doctrine, the president stressed that the United States should support those "resisting attempted subjugation by armed minorities or by outside pressure." He closed by declaring that

> the seeds of totalitarian regimes are nurtured by misery and want. They spread and grow in the evil soil of poverty and strife. They reach their full growth when the hope of a people for a better life has died.
> We must keep that hope alive.
> The free peoples of the world look to us for support in maintaining their freedoms.
> If we falter in our leadership, we may endanger the peace of the world—and we shall surely endanger the welfare of our own Nation.[14]

Toward a Bipolar World

While Truman did not mention the Soviets by name, almost all his listeners recognized the USSR as the promoter of totalitarianism and instability. His call for the United States to work unilaterally, if necessary, to protect world peace by containing the growth of Soviet power and influence was widely accepted and applauded. Senator Edwin Johnson thought that it sounded like a declaration of war, while Representative Charles A. Eaton said that the United States must choose "between slavery and freedom as the foundation of the new world civilization." Symbols rather than facts, emotion rather than reality, were being praised. Some saw reality and voiced concern. Critics feared that any effort to negotiate with the Soviets was gone and that Truman had placed the country on a path toward war. Others, ignoring the administration's assertion that the aid was for only Greece and Turkey, interpreted the commitment as open-ended and predicted that it would eventually bankrupt and exhaust the nation. Senator Walter George did not see how Truman's speech could be "characterized as a mere plea for assistance to Greece and Turkey." If it were only for economic aid, he pointed out, it could be easily restricted, but the president had put the "nation squarely on the line against certain ideologies" that could not be limited.

George was correct. The United States had embraced a new strategy to maintain peace and stability, the containment policy. Within the cabinet there was no question that the choice of a new American role was the right one. Admiral William Leahy noted that cabinet members realized that the new policy meant the "projection of the United States into the political problems of Europe" and that it was "a direct and positive change in the traditional policy of the United States." From a multinational setting there had suddenly emerged a bipolar world. Global spheres of influence were being established on the premise that peace required a balance of power between Washington and Moscow. The U.S. goal was to use its economic and military strength to block further Soviet expansion. The United States would seek to maintain or restore political stability and economic vitality in selected nations and regions. Truman explained the new strategy to Eleanor Roosevelt: "If the Greek-Turkish land bridge between the continents is one point at which our democratic forces can stop the advance of Communism that has flowed steadily through the Baltic countries, Poland, Yugoslavia, Rumania, Bulgaria, to some extent Hungary, then this is the place to do it, regardless of whether or not the terrain is good."[15] Of the possible world systems projected in the spring of 1945, the only one that still seemed viable two years later was that of hostile spheres of influence led by the two superpowers.

Having selected and announced the system of containment, the Truman administration began to implement it throughout the rest of 1947. The United States sought to use tools that would accomplish its goal at the lowest cost. Propaganda and diplomacy were the cheapest instruments, but alone they could not be expected to prevent the spread of Soviet power. Certainly, economic assistance was necessary for many parts of the world, and, if that failed, military commitments would be required.

As U.S. officials assessed the needs of Europe in 1947, they concluded that economic help should be the primary means to ensure a non-Communist Western Europe. The country already had lent nearly $9 billion to Europe, but more was required to ward off possible economic collapse. Communism, it was assumed, thrived on such chaos. Following a drought in 1946, Europeans were suffering through an extremely harsh winter. Large numbers lived on less than 1,200 calories per day and faced shortages not only in food but also in nearly every other commodity. They confronted soaring inflation—over 80 percent in France. Industrial and agricultural production, after a surprising increase in 1946, had fallen and was still below prewar levels. The United States could supply many goods, but, with a cash shortage, Europeans had no money to purchase these items. Most American politicians and business leaders feared that their country might slip into a recession unless a European market for U.S. exports were reestablished. Within the administration the central question was not whether to offer economic aid but how to make it available and whether to include the Soviet Union and the East European satellite states.

The Policy Planning Staff, which Secretary Marshall had created in April to develop the aid concept, decided to ask Europeans to generate a program for the use of American assistance and to invite the Soviets to the initial discussions. Including Moscow seemed inconsistent with the goals of the recently announced Truman Doctrine, and it looked unlikely that Congress would approve any aid package that would funnel U.S. dollars to the Russians. Nevertheless, Kennan, who headed the Policy Planning Staff, argued successfully that Eastern Europe and the Soviet Union should not be excluded. It was "a hell of a big gamble," Bohlen admitted, but neither man believed that the Kremlin would participate in any plan that called for the economic integration of Europe. If the Soviets rejected the program, Kennan noted, the United States would not be responsible for the "division of Europe."[16]

The Marshall Plan, formally presented by the secretary of state during his Harvard commencement speech on June 5, 1947, asked the Europeans to draft a unified recovery plan that "would place Europe on its feet economically" and promised U.S. support. While the precise nature of the economic assistance was yet undecided, the administration was seeking to use it to create political stability for Western Europe, a strategically vital region.[17]

Bevin leapt at the invitation and accepted the American offer on June 13. He and French Foreign Minister Bidault called a meeting of all interested parties for June 26. The Soviets were invited but told that the discussions were to be exclusively economic in nature—no politics. He informed Bidault that, if the Russians "were willing to come in on the basis that there was a job to be done of a purely economic character, with the object of getting America to help to irrigate world trade," then they would be welcomed. Privately, Bevin hoped that they would reject the offer. While addressing the Political Society at Eton, he was asked if he believed the Soviets would accept the invitation. The minister chuckled and replied: "Tsar Alexander still hasn't answered Castlereagh's question."[18]

Much to the surprise and alarm of most observers, when the European delegates assembled in Paris to discuss the Marshall Plan, Molotov and nearly one hundred Soviet advisers arrived. Had the gamble failed? It was soon clear that it had not. After consulting with Moscow, he rejected the idea of a joint European plan as violating national sovereignty and suggested that they should merely present the United States with a list of needs. Bevin and Bidault opposed his idea, saying that Molotov desired nothing more than a "blank check" from America. In the evening, Bevin informed the U.S. ambassador to France, Jefferson Caffery, that negotiations had broken down and that he was pleased. It was a result the minister had "anticipated and even wished for," and he was "glad that the cards had been laid on the table and that the responsibility will be laid at Moscow's door."[19]

The responsibility Bevin referred to was that of dividing Europe. When Molotov left Paris, he demanded that the East European nations also depart, making an apparently clean break between East and West. The United States used the Soviet rejection of the Marshall Plan as an effective propaganda tool; it helped Washington seize the diplomatic initiative and ensure that other nations looked toward the Western superpower for leadership. Assessing the impact of his government's actions on the Soviets, the American chargé d'affaires in Moscow, Elbridge Durbrow, reported that with the Truman Doctrine and Marshall Plan the United States had "clearly captured [the] political warfare offensive."[20]

While the United States institutionalized its new international system based on political, economic, and, if necessary, military containment, the Soviet Union also was recognizing the existence of a bipolar world. Throughout

January and February 1947 the Kremlin had sent mixed signals to the West. Officials, including Stalin, continued to voice trust in the ability of the big powers to work out their problems, and Britain was asked to renegotiate its Anglo-Soviet treaty of friendship. Some regarded these actions as a continuation of the conciliatory behavior shown at New York. But, at the same time, critics of the Soviet Union pointed out that the Russian media continued to denounce British and American leaders and policies as reactionary and threatening to the state's security. This position was greatly strengthened in the summer of 1947, after the announcement of the Truman Doctrine and Marshall Plan, when Soviet hostility toward the West dramatically increased.

Stalin stopped his efforts to restore life to the Grand Alliance. Increasingly, Western leaders such as Attlee, Bevin, Truman, and Marshall were attacked in the Soviet media, which stressed not only Western hostility but also the ability of the Soviet people and the Communist state to withstand such aggression. One Russian official wrote:

> The imperialists will not let go. They wish to encircle the Soviet Union with a . . . circle of military aggression. . . . We shall . . . shake off the fetters now being prepared for us by imperialistic gangsters and warmongers. . . . No hand, not even one armed with the atomic bomb, will succeed. . . . Those who today are sowing the murderous winds of another war will reap the storm of revolution.[21]

Reflecting the harsher Soviet attitude was the announcement in October of the formation of the Cominform, a propaganda agency. In an official address, Andrey Zhdanov, much as Truman had done, divided the globe politically, economically, socially, militarily, and ideologically: the Western antidemocratic imperialist camp against the Soviet-led democratic anti-imperialist camp. Analyzing speeches given at the Cominform meeting, Ambassador Walter Bedell Smith concluded that they constituted "a declaration of political and economic war against the U.S." The Foreign Office believed that the formation of the agency proved that the Soviet Union was not interested in "the idea of cooperation" and compromise. Bevin and the British government had recognized the division of the world into spheres of influence.[22]

By the winter of 1947, each of the three major powers had moved from the Grand Alliance, an international system based on cooperation, to the belief that there was little chance of harmony until one side gave up its ideology. The quest for stability was now firmly linked to national security, in both the East and the West. Diplomacy had given way to deterrence; the Cold War as an international system had become a reality.

Notes

1. Larson, *Origins of Containment*, 298–300. A Foreign Office evaluation of American public opinion made in the winter of 1946 discovered that, while an "overwhelming majority" supported a "firmer policy" toward the Soviet Union, another "substantial majority" blamed the United States equally for the hostility between the two powers. (John Balfour to Foreign Office, October 31, 1946, F.O. 371, N15252/971/38, PRO).

2. *FRUS: Foreign Ministers, 1946* 2:969–88; Ward, *Threat of Peace*, 153–55; *Time* 48 (October 28, 1946): 31; ibid. (November 4, 1946): 31.

3. *FRUS: Foreign Ministers, 1946* 2:988–90, 993–1111; Ward, *Threat of Peace*, 157–59; Bullock, *Bevin*, 325–26.

4. Ward, *Threat of Peace*, 159–62; *FRUS: Foreign Ministers, 1946* 2:1111–60.

5. Dixon, *Double Diploma*, 240–41.

6. *FRUS: Foreign Ministers, 1946* 2:1256–69, 1285–96; Ward, *Threat of Peace*, 160–66; Byrnes, *Speaking Frankly*, 152–53.

7. Forrest C. Pogue, *George C. Marshall: Statesman, 1945–1959* (New York, 1987), 131–51; Ward, *Threat of Peace*, 170–71; *Time* 48 (December 23, 1946): 23; ibid. 49 (January 6, 1947): 23–27; ibid. (March 10, 1947): 24–26; *Newsweek* 28 (December 23, 1946): 37–38; ibid. 29 (March 17, 1947): 23.

8. Gaddis, *Long Peace*, 56–57.

9. *Time* 49 (March 24, 1947): 18–20; *Newsweek* 29 (March 24, 1947): 23–25; Gaddis, *Long Peace*, 56–57; Larson, *Origins of Containment*, 301–7.

10. Bullock, *Bevin*, 348–53; Smith, "Climate of Opinion," 636–38, 644–47; Gormly, *Collapse of the Grand Alliance*, 157–60, 165–73.

11. Bullock, *Bevin*, 368–70.

12. Ibid.; Gormly, *Collapse of the Grand Alliance*, 157; Pollard, *Economic Security*, 107–32; Larson, *Origins of Containment*, 307–9; Dean Acheson, *Present at the Creation: My Years in the State Department* (New York, 1969), 291–95.

13. Acheson, *Present at the Creation*, 375; Larson, *Origins of Containment*, 309–11; Liebovich, *Origins of the Cold War*, 134–35;

Newsweek 29 (March 24, 1947): 23. Senator Spessard Holland was speaking to the Senate on limiting the president to two terms.

14. *Public Papers of the Presidents: Harry S. Truman, 1945–1953,* vol. 3, *1947* (Washington, DC, 1963), 176–80; *Newsweek* 29 (March 17, 1947): 22; ibid. (March 24, 1947): 23–27; *Time* 49 (March 10, 1947): 24–25; ibid. (March 24, 1947): 18–19, 25; Larson, *Origins of Containment,* 308–16; Joseph M. Jones, *The Fifteen Weeks: February 21–June 5, 1947* (New York, 1964), 150–65.

15. Larson, *Origins of Containment,* 312–16; U.S. Congress, Senate Committee on Foreign Relations, *Legislative Origins of the Truman Doctrine: Hearings Held in Executive Session,* 80th Cong., 1st sess. (Washington, DC, 1973).

16. Pollard, *Economic Security,* 132–38; Michael J. Hogan, "The Search for a 'Creative Peace': The United States, European Unity, and the Origins of the Marshall Plan," *Diplomatic History* 6 (1982): 267–85.

17. One State Department official commented that the Marshall Plan was like "a flying saucer—nobody knows what it looks like, how big it is, in what direction it is moving, or whether it really exists" (*FRUS: The British Commonwealth; Europe, 1947* [Washington, DC, 1972], 3:239–41).

18. Bullock, *Bevin,* 400–409.

19. *FRUS: British Commonwealth, 1947* 3:308–9; Bullock, *Bevin,* 419–22; Pollard, *Economic Security,* 136–39.

20. *FRUS: British Commonwealth, 1947* 3:308–19; Liebovich, *Origins of the Cold War,* 134–35; U.S. Congress, Senate Committee on Foreign Relations, *Legislative Origins of the Truman Doctrine*; Gormly, *Collapse of the Grand Alliance,* 165.

21. Gormly, *Collapse of the Grand Alliance,* 166.

22. Ibid., 154–73; Paolo Spriano, *Stalin and the European Communists* (London, 1985), 270–85; B. Thomas Trout, "Rhetoric Revisited: Political Legitimation and the Cold War," *International Studies Quarterly* 19 (September 1975): 251–84; Larson, *Origins of Containment,* 312–24; Smith, "Climate of Opinion," 643–46.

Epilogue

When Truman, Stalin, and Churchill met in Potsdam, it seemed logical that their wartime alliance would extend into the postwar period. No one knew in the summer of 1945 exactly what form their relationship would take, but, in the joyous days after the surrender of Germany, few wanted to forecast anything but a stable peace resting on the cooperation of the Big Three. To those visualizing harmony the conditions seemed more than favorable. In the United States, people were anxious to finish the fight with Japan and to begin life in what was called America's century. They realized that tensions among nations, even the Big Three, would exist, but generally Americans believed that, between the fledgling United Nations and the cooperation of the major powers, an enduring peace was close at hand. Editors of the *Los Angeles Times* wrote that, because the United States had no interest except international concord, the country would play a vital role in solving problems and safeguarding a stable world system. Walter Lippmann took a similar approach, suggesting that the most important postwar function of the United States might be adjusting the differences between the Soviet Union and the United Kingdom. At the official level, Secretary of State Edward R. Stettinius stated that "the vital national interests of the United States and each of our Allies are bound up in maintaining and cementing the peace of our wartime partnership . . . the extent of our agreement is far wider and more fundamental than the extent of our differences." Across the nation, most citizens, including Truman and his administration, were extremely confident that a lasting settlement was obtainable and that the U.S. vision of peace should be the central element in fostering a harmonious and prosperous postwar world.[1]

Americans were not alone in their expectations. Among the British and the Soviets there was widespread optimism that cooperation was the road to postwar stability and economic development. To encourage a better Big Three relationship, several Labour leaders suggested that the socialist element in the United Kingdom could act as a "Third Force" and mediate between Communist Russia and capitalist America. Several on the British left went further and advocated London's staying aloof from Washington while being friendlier with Moscow. More common was the suggestion that Britain and the United States take special care to understand the Russians and to encourage their genuine participation in postwar affairs. Even the British press played its part by not printing stories that showed the Russians in a bad light. Within the Soviet Union, similar positions were being taken. The state-controlled press repeatedly presented favorable images of Britain, the United States, Roosevelt, and Churchill, implying that those predicting conflict between capitalism and communism represented only a minority made up of reactionary, warmongering Fascists.[2]

The vision of a stable, harmonious peace quickly faded in the spotlight of international politics that was turned on Potsdam. Slowly but steadily the relationship between the Anglo-American powers and the Soviet Union deteriorated until, by the winter of 1947, the unity of the Grand Alliance lay shattered. By that time a new postwar system was discernable, a system that rested not so much on discussion and negotiation as upon a balance of power between two rival blocs. The West called the system containment, while the Soviets described it as two camps and defended their efforts as protecting socialism against imperialist, capitalist encirclement.

The road to containment had passed through two stages—cooperation and then acceptable rivalry—before arriving at immutable hostility. The first phase lasted throughout the Potsdam Conference and extended in a weakened form through the foreign ministers' meetings in Moscow in December 1945. During this period, serious disagreements emerged over Eastern Europe, atomic energy, and Iran as each power began to confirm its suspicion that their differences were stronger than their similarities. The conflict was evident at Potsdam but was covered over with secrecy, vague language, and delay.

At London, negotiations simply failed as the Big Three dealt with the realities of power in Italy and in central and Eastern Europe. To many observers, it seemed as if the possibility for harmony had vanished, but none of the three powers was yet ready to deny the chance of a cooperative postwar relationship. The Soviet press published stories downplaying the London differences, Attlee and part of the Labour party pushed for reconciliation, and Truman approved Harriman's visit to Stalin. There then followed Byrnes's December dash to Moscow to reestablish a working relationship with the Soviet Union. Britain had little choice but to work also to find points of agreement and continue the process of formalizing a settlement through the peace treaties for Hitler's European allies. The Moscow accords provided the last real opportunity for the Big Three to rekindle the Grand Alliance and project it into a postwar system.

The failure of the Big Three to implement the Moscow agreements marked the beginning of the second stage in the development of the containment policy. It was a phase that provided, for a brief period, a chance of cooperative global rivalry short of a cold war. Bevin felt that, while the West and the Soviet Union would not be friends, they could live with each other in peace. A British working paper suggested that a "Three Monroe Doctrine" system might be possible, but the idea was rejected by the United States and failed to arrest the movement toward the hostile two-camp arrangement that finally resulted.[3] Increasingly, as the Paris Peace Conference swung into gear and as other disputes erupted around the globe, both the Anglo-American governments and Moscow came to believe that, for domestic and international reasons, cooperative rivalry with imprecise boundaries and relationships could not work and that a more static division of the world needed to be established as a basis for stability. On the diplomatic level, patience was replaced with firmness. By the completion of the treaties, with the documents for Finland, Italy, Romania, and Bulgaria ratified, no true peace was in sight. The Cold War had broken out, and the world was seen by Washington and Moscow as divided into two hostile blocs.

Assessing responsibility for the Cold War international
system is at best difficult and probably impossible without
access to primary Russian documents. If such an approach
was to be avoided, both the United States and the Soviet
Union would have needed to take stronger actions to
indicate mutual acceptance and trust. Secretary of War
Henry Stimson, departing office as the London meeting
began, wrote to Truman that "the only way you can make a
man trustworthy is to trust him; the surest way to make
him untrustworthy is to distrust him and show that
distrust."[4]

The foundation of confidence was built during the war by
President Franklin D. Roosevelt, who had hoped that long-
term interest in stability and peace would overcome initial,
short-term differences. But during and after Potsdam that
trust and acceptance were hard to find. Neither Stalin nor
Truman, Molotov nor Byrnes tried to cultivate those
qualities for any length of time. The opposite seemed true,
especially after the Moscow Conference, as the Soviet Union
and the United States continually launched statements and
policies that appeared to threaten not only international
stability but also the basis for each nation's security.

lack of trust

Those who place the major responsibility for the Cold
War on the Soviet Union argue that Stalin, as dictator and
leader of a totalitarian system, easily could have moderated
the nation's interests to meet U.S. objections and ensure
peace. According to this view, if the generalissimo was not
an expansionist wanting to overrun central and Western
Europe, he should have articulated the defensive and
limited nature of his goals to the Truman administration
and the American public. Instead, the Russians would not
accept the U.S. vision for a stable and prosperous world or
trust that Washington accepted the legitimacy of the Soviet
Union and recognized its need for some degree of influence
over regions along its borders. Moscow needed "a hostile
international environment" to maintain control and the
integrity of the Soviet state. Thus, Stalin was either an
expansionist or unwilling to communicate his aims, and
the United States, supported by Britain, had no other option
than to react aggressively.[5]

In reaching this interpretation, advocates maintain
that, to show their peaceful intentions in Eastern Europe,
the Soviets could have slowed or halted the process of

communization, given more political power to traditional opposition parties, and instituted free elections. Instead, Moscow decried capitalist encirclement, began an internal drive to strengthen the state politically and economically, hurriedly consolidated military gains around the globe, used subversion and indirect military penetration in Iran, Sinkiang Uighur, and Greece, and rejected U.S. efforts to unify and rebuild Germany and Europe. To Americans already suspicious of communism and Soviet intentions, these actions, added to Molotov's behavior during the Paris meetings, appeared to be ample proof that Moscow was not willing to work for international stability and, in fact, would take all opportunities to expand the USSR's political influence. In an anonymous article in *Foreign Affairs* in 1947, George Kennan explained, with crushing simplicity, the need for the containment system: Soviet foreign policy moved "along a prescribed path, like a persistent toy automobile, wound up and headed in a given direction, stopping only when it meets some unanswerable source."[6] His words mirrored the official U.S. position, which would become reality for following administrations: "In the period from 1944 to 1947, Soviet policy was single-minded, if not always successful, in its pursuit of the aims laid down by Stalin: to exploit the Allies' victory to bring the world nearer to Soviet Communism."[7]

Other analysts place a large amount of the blame on the United States and its unwillingness to accept expressed Soviet needs and to articulate to the Russians and Stalin that Washington trusted them and recognized the legitimacy of their system and state. Some explain U.S. behavior as an outgrowth of the American Open Door ideology, which sought to ensure for the nation's businesses access to world markets. Still others credit U.S. actions to a general arrogance of power that translated the country's tremendous economic and military strength and accomplishments into a moral, ideological superiority. According to this theory, many Soviets feared that the West still hoped to destroy their state. To convince them that America intended to be a friend and thereby avoid the Cold War, the United States should have shelved its presumptuousness and global goals and demonstrated an affirmation of the Soviet Union's right to rule and enjoy the fruits of its victory. To ease fears and mistrust, Washington

needed to recognize Russia's new borders, its diplomatic
equality, and its spheres of influence in Eastern Europe.
Instead, the U.S. government continued to follow the path
suggested by Ambassador Harriman, who stated that the
administration should supply assistance to the Soviets only
if they "played the international game with us in
accordance with our standards."[8]

In the eyes of the critics of U.S. policy, Stalin arrived at
Potsdam with two primary tests of his allies' good
intentions. First, he wanted assurances that he and his
country would be treated as equals and that all international
questions requiring the attention of either the United States
or Great Britain would also receive the consideration of the
Soviet Union. Second, he made it obvious that he wanted
Western approval of a Soviet sphere of influence over
Eastern Europe. Fulfillment of these criteria would have
muted American arrogance and given a signal that the
United States accepted the legitimacy of the Soviet system.

At best, Stalin received mixed responses and conflicting
signals at Potsdam. He no doubt viewed Truman and
Churchill's secrecy about the nature of the atomic bomb as a
blow to Soviet equality. But he could view the decisions on
Poland and Germany and the formation of the Council of
Foreign Ministers as indications that Britain and the
United States would continue to negotiate with him as a
partner and would consider his positions. From the Soviet
perspective, Potsdam provided no reason to deny the
prospects of a stable peace based on the cooperation of the
Big Three. Just as certainly, however, it convinced the
Soviet leaders that at future meetings they would have to
negotiate arduously to protect their interests against horse
traders such as Byrnes and hardened union negotiators
such as Bevin.

After Potsdam, there ensued a series of American and
British actions that, from the viewpoint of Moscow, not only
undermined previous understandings but also threatened
the foundations of the Soviet Union. Continued Anglo-
American support for non-Communist elements within
Romania and Bulgaria and efforts to open the region to
Western economic penetration were regarded as hostile
attempts to deny the Soviets influence over an area vital to
their national security. Byrnes's work to patch up failing
U.S.-Soviet relations in the last months of 1945 could only

have generated further distrust when, in 1946, he and the United States reversed the cooperative spirit of the Moscow Conference. Not only did Bernard Baruch's plan eliminate any possibility of sharing atomic information, but also Byrnes mounted a propaganda attack that denied the legality of Soviet policy and emphasized that the Russians were the chief obstacle to concluding the treaties and establishing peace. Statements by Washington that condemned Molotov for relying on a bloc of Red Dwarves at Paris but ignored a larger Anglo-American bloc and that also challenged the Soviet Union's need for a hand in directing Eastern Europe but applauded exclusive U.S. control in Japan and Anglo-American influence in Italy could not be just arrogant; they had to be hostile. When, in 1947, the Truman administration announced its doctrine and the Marshall Plan, it appeared to the Soviets that the United States was demanding modification of their internal system as the price for Soviet cooperation and for the formation of an international system.

Given the situation, the belief that U.S. actions divided the world into two camps and necessitated a rapid Sovietization of Eastern Europe seems as logical as the view that Russian expansionism forced the United States to institute its containment policy. To evaluate and assess either theory fully and to determine if the Cold War international system could have been avoided requires an examination of Soviet records, but, even without such information, and using existing American and British documents, one can conclude that U.S. policymakers made few efforts after the Potsdam Conference to reassure Moscow that mutual cooperation was possible and that Washington had no intention of seeking the destruction of the Soviet state.

Furthermore, American intelligence evaluations of the Soviet Union consistently pointed out that the war had exhausted the country and that it would be no threat to the United States or the West. A State Department evaluation in December 1945 concluded that, for at least five years, "the United States need not be acutely concerned about the current intentions of the Soviet Union [and has] considerable latitude in determining its policy toward the U.S.S.R." The memorandum postulated that, if Washington took a combative attitude toward Moscow, the

Soviets would respond with "aggressive, expansionistic
anti-capitalistic" policies. Two months later, Bohlen and
Gerold Robinson took a similar position, projecting the
same consequences.⁹ These documents show that
American leaders knew that alternative policies were
feasible and that for a period of time, perhaps as long as five
years, the United States could cooperate and even
compromise with the Soviet Union without unduly
endangering the country or international peace. Truman's
administration had the choice of downplaying U.S.-Soviet
differences and American rhetoric, ignoring Moscow's
undiplomatic behavior, but after January 1946 the United
States took another course.

Britain and France found that Americans, aware of
their economic, military, and moral power, all too often
were arrogant. Both nations expressed distaste for the
tactics and policies that one exasperated British official
labeled as pure U.S. "jungle diplomacy." Yet, despite their
complaints about Washington's approach, the British
trusted the United States and believed that they could direct
American policy to their own benefit. The Russians,
recalling few positive diplomatic experiences with the
United States and the West in general, hardly could have
been expected to be as trusting as the British. American
demands for non-Communist governments in Eastern
Europe and attacks on the Soviet system only supported the
belief that the United States wished to see the destruction of
the Soviet Union.¹⁰ Again, however, without access to
Russian sources, it is impossible to determine whether,
with the United States taking a different, more conciliatory
approach toward the Soviet Union, the Cold War could have
been avoided. Such a road was not taken, and a pervasive
international system quickly emerged that would shape
world history at least until the 1990s.

In the decades that followed the institutionalization of
the Cold War in 1947, the system has gone through several
stages as new American and Soviet leaders have made
adjustments to it. Throughout all the modifications,
however, the basic foundations of the system rested
untouched until the winter of 1989–90. With the loosening of
Communist control in Eastern Europe and the institution of
democratic reforms, including the creation of a multiparty
system within the Soviet Union, the premises on which the

Cold War was based—fear and suspicion of the West and of Soviet communism—may erode, permitting trust, collaboration, and even conciliation, the road not taken in 1946. As the 1990s begin, the Cold War may be going through its final stage and eventually may be replaced by another system.

Notes

1. Gormly, *Collapse of the Grand Alliance*, x. Edward R. Stettinius, Jr., "The Economic Basis for Lasting Peace," U.S. Department of State *Bulletin* 12 (April 8, 1945): 594; *Los Angeles Times*, September 12, 1945.

2. Jones, *Russian Complex*, 58–120; memorandum, February 1946, F.O. 371, N3859/605/38, PRO; Jonathan Schneer, "Hope Deferred or Shattered: The British Labour Left and the Third Force Movement, 1945–1949," *Journal of Modern History* 56 (June 1984): 197–226; Gormly, *Collapse of the Grand Alliance*, x–xi.

3. Memorandum, April 18, 1945, F.O. 371, U2885/2885/36; memorandum, December 17, 1945, F.O. 371, U10134/6550/70; memorandum, August 6, 1945, F.O. 371, Z9639/13/7, all in PRO.

4. Henry L. Stimson and McGeorge Bundy, *On Active Service in Peace and War* (New York, 1948), 649–50.

5. *FRUS: Eastern Europe, 1946* 6:721–23; Gaddis, "Evolution of U.S. Policy Goals," 331–40.

6. George F. Kennan [X, pseud.], "Sources of Soviet Conduct," *Foreign Affairs* 25 (July 1947): 566–82.

7. Memorandum, "Review of Soviet Policy: World War II – Present," May 8, 1967, Department of Defense, National Security File: USSR, vol. 15, Lyndon Baines Johnson Library, Austin, Texas.

8. William H. Chafe, *The Unfinished Journey: America since World War II* (New York, 1986), 50. For an analysis of American attitudes toward the Soviet Union and Soviet communism see Eduard M. Mark, "October or Thermidor? Interpretations of Stalinism and the Perception of Soviet Foreign Policy in the United States, 1927–1947," *American Historical Review* 94 (October 1989): 937–62.

9. Memorandum, "The Capabilities and Intentions of the Soviet Union as Affected by American Policy," RG 59, DS 711.61/12–1045. For the Charles Bohlen and Gerold Robinson report see this volume, Chapter IV, p. 114.

10. Memorandum, August 26, 1945, F.O. 371, Z9943/514/17; John Balfour to Foreign Office, December 21, 1945, F.O. 371, AN3835/35/45, both in PRO; Gaddis, "Evolution of U.S. Policy Goals," 305–24.

Bibliography

In addition to all the works cited in the preceding chapters the following list contains other sources that have helped form my view of the period, including some whose arguments, while of undeniable significance, run counter to those presented above. For fuller bibliographies on the origins of the Cold War the student should consult Richard D. Burns, ed., *Guide to American Foreign Relations since 1700* (Santa Barbara, 1982); and J. L. Black, *Origins, Evolution, and Nature of the Cold War: An Annotated Bibliographic Guide* (Santa Barbara, 1986).

Archival Collections

Churchill College Library, Cambridge University, Cambridge, England
    Lord Halifax Papers
Robert M. Cooper Library, Clemson University, Clemson, South Carolina
    Walter Brown Papers
    James F. Byrnes Papers
Lyndon Baines Johnson Library, Austin, Texas
    National Security File
London School of Economics and Political Science
    Hugh Dalton Papers
National Archives, Washington, DC
    Modern Military Branch
        Record Group 107: Office of the Secretary of War
        Record Group 165: War Department General and Special Staffs
        Manhattan Project Files, 1942–1945
        Secretary of the Navy Files, 1945–46
    State Department Branch
        Record Group 59: General, 1945–1947
            Lot M 88: Council of Foreign Ministers

Record Group 353: Interdepartmental and
Intradepartmental Committees
H. Freeman Matthews File, 1945–1947
Public Record Office, Kew, London
Cabinet Papers, 1945–46
Chief of Staff Records, 1945
Foreign Office 371: General Correspondence, 1945–
1947

Published Government Documents

Ministry of Foreign Affairs of the USSR, *Correspondence between the Chairman of the Council of Ministers of the U.S.S.R. and the Presidents of the U.S.A. and the Prime Ministers of Great Britain during the Great Patriotic War of 1941–1945.* 2 vols. New York, 1965.
Truman, Harry S. *Public Papers of the Presidents: Harry S. Truman, 1945–1953.* 8 vols. Washington, DC, 1961–66.
U.S. Congress. Senate Committee on Foreign Relations. *Legislative Origins of the Truman Doctrine: Hearings Held in Executive Session.* 80th Cong., 1st sess. Washington, DC, 1973.
U.S. Department of State. *Bulletin.* Vols. 12–15. Washington, DC, 1945–46.
———. *Papers Relating to the Foreign Relations of the United States: Diplomatic Papers, The Conference of Berlin (The Potsdam Conference), 1945.* 2 vols. Washington, DC, 1960.
———. ———: *Diplomatic Papers, The Conferences at Malta and Yalta, 1945.* Washington, DC, 1955.
———. ———: *Diplomatic Papers, 1945.* Vol. 2. *General: Political and Economic Matters.* 1967.
———. ———: *Diplomatic Papers, 1945.* Vol. 4. *Europe.* 1968.
———. ———: *Diplomatic Papers, 1945.* Vol. 5. *Europe.* 1967.
———. ———: *Diplomatic Papers, 1945.* Vol. 6. *The British Commonwealth; The Far East.* 1969.
———. ———: *1946.* Vol. 1. *General; The United Nations.* 1972.
———. ———: *1946.* Vol. 2. *Council of Foreign Ministers.* 1970.
———. ———: *1946.* Vol. 3. *Paris Peace Conference: Proceedings.* 1970.
———. ———: *1946.* Vol. 5. *The British Commonwealth; Western and Central Europe.* 1969.
———. ———: *1946.* Vol. 6. *Eastern Europe; The Soviet Union.* 1969.
———. ———: *1946.* Vol. 7. *The Near East and Africa.* 1969.
———. ———: *1946.* Vol. 8. *The Far East.* 1971.

————. ————: *1947*. Vol. 3. *The British Commonwealth; Europe.* 1972.

Books and Articles

Acheson, Dean. *Present at the Creation: My Years in the State Department.* New York, 1969.
Adamthwaite, Anthony. "Britain and the World, 1945–9." *International Affairs* 61 (1985): 223–35.
Agar, Herbert. "Our Last Great Chance." *Survey Graphic* 34 (May 1945): 153–57.
Alperovitz, Gar. *Atomic Diplomacy: Hiroshima and Potsdam.* New York, 1965.
Anderson, Terry. *Ambiguous Partnership: Britain and America, 1942–1948.* New York, 1981.
Baker, Elisabeth. *Britain in a Divided Europe, 1945–1970.* London, 1971.
————. *Churchill and Eden at War.* London, 1978.
Baldwin, Frank, ed. *Without Parallel: The American-Korean Relationship since 1945.* New York, 1974.
Banks, Michael. "Where We Are Now." *Review of International Studies* 11 (1985): 220–37.
Bennett, John Wheeler, and Anthony Nicholls. *The Semblance of Peace.* New York, 1972.
Berezhkov, V. *History in the Making.* Moscow, 1980.
Bernstein, Barton J. "The Perils and Politics of Surrender: Ending the War with Japan and Avoiding the Third Atomic Bomb." *Pacific Historical Review* 48 (1977): 1–27.
Best, Richard A., Jr. *"Cooperation with Like-Minded Peoples": British Influences on American Security Policy, 1945–1949.* New York, 1987.
Bohlen, Charles E. *Witness to History, 1929–1969.* New York, 1973.
Boll, Michael M. *Cold War in the Balkans: American Foreign Policy and the Emergence of Communist Bulgaria, 1943–1947.* Lexington, KY, 1984.
Boyle, Peter G. "The British Foreign Office and American Foreign Policy, 1947–1948." *Journal of American Studies* 16 (1982): 373–90.
————. "The British Foreign Office View of Soviet-American Relations, 1945–46." *Diplomatic History* 3 (1979): 307–20.
Buhite, Russell D. *Decisions at Yalta: An Appraisal of Summit Diplomacy.* Wilmington, DE, 1986.
Bullock, Alan. *Ernest Bevin: Foreign Secretary, 1945–1951.* New York, 1983.
Burton, J. W. *World Society.* New York, 1972.

Butow, Robert J. C. *Japan's Decision to Surrender.* Stanford, 1954.

Byrnes, James F. *Speaking Frankly.* New York, 1947.

Cadogan, Alexander. *The Diaries of Sir Alexander Cadogan, 1938–1945.* Edited by David Dilks. New York, 1972.

Campbell, John C. "Negotiating with the Soviets." *Foreign Affairs* 24 (1956): 305–19.

Chafe, William H. *The Unfinished Journey: America since World War II.* New York, 1986.

Churchill, Winston S. *The Second World War.* Vol. 6, *Triumph and Tragedy.* Boston, 1953.

Clay, Lucius D. *Decision in Germany.* Westport, CT, 1970.

Clemens, Diane S. *Yalta.* New York, 1970.

Craig, Gordon A., and Alexander L. George. *Force and Statecraft: Diplomatic Problems of Our Time.* New York, 1983.

Cumings, Bruce. *The Origins of the Korean War: Liberation and the Emergence of Separate Regimes.* Princeton, 1981.

Dallek, Robert. *The American Style of Foreign Policy: Cultural Politics and Foreign Affairs.* New York, 1983.

Daniels, Robert V., ed. *A Documentary History of Communism.* Vol. 2, *Communism and the World.* Hanover, NH, 1987.

Davis, Lynn Ethridge. *The Cold War Begins: Soviet-American Conflict over Eastern Europe.* Princeton, 1974.

Deighton, Anne. "The 'Frozen Front': The Labour Government, the Division of Germany, and the Origins of the Cold War, 1945–7." *International Affairs* 63 (Summer 1987): 451–56.

DeSantis, Hugh. *The Diplomacy of Silence: The American Foreign Service, the Soviet Union, and the Cold War, 1933–1947.* Chicago, 1980.

de Zayas, Alfred M. *Nemesis at Potsdam: The Anglo-Americans and the Expulsion of the Germans.* London, 1977.

Dixon, Pierson. *Double Diploma: The Life of Sir Pierson Dixon, Don and Diplomat.* London, 1968.

Donovan, Robert J. *Conflict and Crisis: The Presidency of Harry S. Truman, 1945–1948.* New York, 1977.

Dougherty, J. E., and R. L. Pfalatzgraft, Jr. *Contending Theories of International Relations: A Comprehensive Survey.* New York, 1981.

Edmonds, Robin. *Setting the Mould: The United States and Britain, 1945–1950.* New York, 1986.

Ethridge, Mark, and C. E. Black. "Negotiating on the Balkans, 1945–1947." In *The Kremlin and World Politics,* edited by Philip Mosely. New York, 1960.

Eubank, Keith. *The Summit Conferences, 1919–1960*. Norman, OK, 1966.

Feis, Herbert. *The Atomic Bomb and the End of World War II*. Princeton, 1966.

———. *Between War and Peace: The Potsdam Conference*. Princeton, 1960.

———. *Contest over Japan: The Soviet Bid for Power in the Far East*. New York, 1968.

Forrestal, James V. *The Forrestal Diaries*. Edited by Walter Millis and E. S. Duffield. New York, 1951.

Gaddis, John Lewis. "The Evolution of U.S. Policy Goals toward the USSR in the Postwar Era." In *Gorbachev's Russia and American Foreign Policy*, edited by Seweryn Bialer and Michael Mandelbaum. Boulder, 1988.

———. *The Long Peace: Inquiries into the History of the Cold War*. New York, 1987.

———. *Strategies of Containment: A Critical Appraisal of Postwar American National Security Policy*. New York, 1982.

———. *The United States and the Origins of the Cold War, 1941–1947*. New York, 1972.

Gardner, Lloyd C. *Architects of Illusion: Men and Ideas in American Foreign Policy, 1941–1949*. Chicago, 1970.

Gason, Robert A. "American Foreign Policy and the Limits of Power: Eastern Europe, 1946–1950." *Journal of Contemporary History* 21 (July 1986): 347–66.

Gaulle, Charles de. *The Complete War Memoirs of Charles de Gaulle*. New York, 1967.

Gimbel, John. *The American Occupation of Germany, 1945–1949*. Stanford, 1968.

———. "On the Implementation of the Potsdam Agreement: An Essay on U.S. Postwar German Policy." *Political Science Quarterly* 87 (June 1972): 242–69.

Gormly, James L. *The Collapse of the Grand Alliance, 1945–1948*. Baton Rouge, LA, 1987.

———. "The Washington Declaration and the 'Poor Relation': Anglo-American Atomic Diplomacy, 1945–46." *Diplomatic History* 8 (1984): 125–43.

Harbutt, Fraser J. *The Iron Curtain: Churchill, America, and the Origins of the Cold War*. New York, 1987.

Harriman, W. Averell, and Elie Abel. *Special Envoy to Churchill and Stalin, 1941–1946*. New York, 1975.

Harris, Kenneth. *Attlee*. London, 1982.

Hathaway, Robert M. *Ambiguous Partnership: Britain and America, 1944–1947*. New York, 1981.

Herken, Gregg. *The Winning Weapon: The Atomic Bomb in the Cold War, 1945–1950*. New York, 1980.

Hess, Gary B. "The Iranian Crisis of 1945–1946 and the Cold War." *Political Science Quarterly* 76 (1974): 117–46.

Hogan, Michael J. "The Search for a 'Creative Peace': The United States, European Unity, and the Origins of the Marshall Plan." *Diplomatic History* 6 (1982): 267–85.

Hoyt, Edwin P. *Closing the Circle*. New York, 1982.

Jones, Bill. *The Russian Complex: The British Labour Party and the Soviet Union*. Manchester, England, 1977.

Jones, Joseph M. *The Fifteen Weeks: February 21–June 5, 1947*. New York, 1964.

Kennan, George F. [X, pseud.]. "Sources of Soviet Conduct." *Foreign Affairs* 25 (July 1947): 566–82.

Kennedy, Paul. *The Rise and Fall of the Great Powers: Economic Change and Military Conflict from 1500 to 2000*. New York, 1987.

Kimball, Warren F., ed. *Churchill and Roosevelt: The Complete Correspondence*. Vol. 3, *Alliance Declining*. Princeton, 1984.

Knight, Jonathan. "American Statecraft and the 1946 Black Sea Straits Controversy." *Political Science Quarterly* 90 (Fall 1975): 451–75.

———. "Russia's Search for Peace: The London Conference of Foreign Ministers, 1945." *Journal of Contemporary History* 13 (1978): 137–63.

Kolko, Gabriel. *The Politics of War*. New York, 1969.

Kolko, Gabriel, and Joyce Kolko. *The Limits of Power: The World and United States Foreign Policy, 1945–1954*. New York, 1968.

Kovig, Bennett. *The Myth of Liberation: East-Central Europe in U.S. Diplomacy and Politics since 1941*. Baltimore, 1973.

Kuklick, Bruce. "The Division of Germany and American Policy on Reparations." *Western Political Quarterly* 23 (June 1970): 276–93.

Kuniholm, Bruce R. *The Origins of the Cold War in the Near East: Great Power Conflict and Diplomacy in Iran, Turkey, and Greece*. Princeton, 1980.

LaFeber, Walter. *America, Russia, and the Cold War, 1945–1966*. New York, 1980.

Larson, Deborah Welch. *Origins of Containment: A Psychological Explanation*. Princeton, 1985.

Leffler, Melvyn P. "The American Conception of National Security and the Beginnings of the Cold War, 1945–48." *American Historical Review* 89 (1984): 346–81.

Lewis, William Roger. *The British Empire in the Middle East, 1945–1951: Arab Nationalism, the United States, and Postwar Imperialism*. Oxford, 1984.

Liebovich, Louis. *The Press and the Origins of the Cold War, 1944–1947.* New York, 1988.

McCagg, William O., Jr. *Stalin Embattled, 1943–1948.* Detroit, 1981.

McFarland, Stephen L. "A Peripheral View of the Origins of the Cold War: The Crises in Iran, 1941–47." *Diplomatic History* 4 (1980): 333–51.

McNeil, William H. *America, Britain, and Russia: Their Cooperation and Conflict, 1941–1946.* New York, 1953.

Maier, Charles S. "The Two Postwar Eras and the Conditions for Stability in Twentieth Century Western Europe." *American Historical Review* 86 (April 1981): 327–52.

Mark, Eduard M. "American Policy toward Eastern Europe and the Origins of the Cold War, 1941–1946." *Journal of American History* 68 (September 1981): 313–36.

———. "Charles E. Bohlen and the Acceptable Limits of Soviet Hegemony in Eastern Europe: A Memorandum of 18 October 1945." *Diplomatic History* 3 (1979): 201–13.

———. "October or Thermidor? Interpretations of Stalinism and the Perception of Soviet Foreign Policy in the United States, 1927–1947." *American Historical Review* 94 (October 1989): 937–62.

Mastny, Vojtech. *Russia's Road to the Cold War: Diplomacy, Warfare, and the Politics of Communism, 1941–1945.* New York, 1979.

Matray, James I. *The Reluctant Crusade: American Foreign Policy in Korea, 1941–50.* Honolulu, 1985.

Mee, Charles L., Jr. *Meeting at Potsdam.* New York, 1975.

Messer, Robert L. *The End of an Alliance: James F. Byrnes, Roosevelt, Truman, and the Origins of the Cold War.* Chapel Hill, NC, 1982.

———. "Paths Not Taken: The United States Department of State and Alternatives to Containment, 1945–1946." *Diplomatic History* 1 (1977): 297–319.

Moran, Lord Charles. *Churchill: Taken from the Diaries of Lord Moran: The Struggle for Survival, 1940–1945.* Boston, 1966.

Morgenthau, Hans J. *Politics among Nations: The Struggle for Power and Peace.* 5th rev. ed. New York, 1985.

Novak, Bogdan C. *Trieste, 1941–1954: The Ethnic, Political, and Ideological Struggle.* Chicago, 1970.

Nye, Joseph S., Jr. "Arms Control after the Cold War." *Foreign Affairs* 68 (Winter 1989–90): 44–64.

Paterson, Thomas G. *On Every Front: The Making of the Cold War.* New York, 1979.

———. *Soviet-American Confrontation: Postwar Reconstruction and the Origins of the Cold War.* Baltimore, 1973.

Pelz, Stephen. "Decision on Korean Policy." In *Child of Conflict: The Korean-American Relationship, 1943–1953*, edited by Bruce Cumings. Seattle, 1983.

Penrose, E. F. *The Revolution in International Relations: A Study in the Changing Nature and Balance of Power.* London, 1965.

Pfau, Richard. "Containment in Iran, 1946: The Shift to an Active Policy." *Diplomatic History* 1 (1977): 359–72.

Pogue, Forrest C. *George C. Marshall: Statesman, 1945–1959.* New York, 1987.

Pollard, Robert A. *Economic Security and the Origins of the Cold War, 1945–1950.* New York, 1985.

Ponomaryov, B., A. Gromyko, and V. Khvostov, eds. *History of Soviet Foreign Policy.* Moscow, 1974.

Quinlan, Paul D. *Clash over Romania: British and American Policies toward Romania, 1938–1945.* Los Angeles, 1977.

Rabel, Roberto G. *Between East and West: Trieste, the United States, and the Cold War, 1941–1954.* Durham, NC, 1988.

Rose, Lisle A. *After Yalta: America and the Origins of the Cold War.* New York, 1973.

Rothwell, Victor. *Britain and the Cold War, 1941–1947.* London, 1982.

Ryan, Henry B. "A New Look at Churchill's 'Iron Curtain' Speech." *Historical Journal* 22 (1979): 895–920.

———. *The Vision of Anglo-America: The US-UK Alliance and the Emerging Cold War, 1943–1946.* Cambridge, England, 1987.

Schneer, Jonathan. "Hope Deferred or Shattere d: The British Labour Left and the Third Force Movement, 1945–1949." *Journal of Modern History* 56 (June 1984): 197–226.

Sherwin, Martin J. *A World Destroyed: The Atomic Bomb and the Grand Alliance.* New York, 1975.

Sherwood, Robert E. *Roosevelt and Hopkins: An Intimate History.* New York, 1948.

Sigal, Leon V. *Fighting to a Finish: The Politics of War Termination in the United States and Japan.* Ithaca, 1988.

Sipols, Vilnis. *The Road to Great Victory.* Moscow, 1985.

Smith, Raymond. "A Climate of Opinion: British Officials and the Development of British-Soviet Policy, 1945–7." *International Affairs* 64 (1988): 631–47.

Smith, Raymond, and John Zametica. "The Cold Warrior: Clement Attlee Reconsidered, 1945–7." *International Affairs* 61 (1985): 237–42.

Spriano, Paolo. *Stalin and the European Communists.* London, 1985.

Stettinius, Edward R., Jr. "The Economic Basis for Lasting Peace." U.S. Department of State *Bulletin* 12 (April 8, 1945): 593–94.
Stimson, Henry L., and McGeorge Bundy. *On Active Service in Peace and War.* New York, 1948.
Stueck, William W., Jr. *The Road to Confrontation: American Policy toward China and Korea, 1947–1950.* Chapel Hill, NC, 1981.
Taubman, William. *Stalin's American Policy: From Entente to Détente to Cold War.* New York, 1982.
Tehran, Yalta, and Potsdam Conferences. Moscow, 1969.
Thomas, Hugh. *Armed Truce: The Beginning of the Cold War, 1945–1946.* New York, 1987.
Thompson, Kenneth W. *Understanding World Politics.* Notre Dame, 1975.
———. *Winston Churchill's World View: Statesmanship and Power.* Baton Rouge, LA, 1983.
"To the Stalin Mausoleum." By "Z." *Daedalus* 119 (Winter 1990): 295–344.
Trout, B. Thomas. "Rhetoric Revisited: Political Legitimation and the Cold War." *International Studies Quarterly* 19 (September 1975): 251–84.
Truman, Harry S. *Memoirs.* Vol. 1, *Year of Decisions.* Garden City, NY, 1955.
———. *Off the Record: The Private Papers of Harry S. Truman.* Edited by Robert H. Ferrell. New York, 1980.
Truman, Margaret. *Harry S. Truman.* New York, 1973.
Ulam, Adam B. *Expansion and Coexistence: The History of Soviet Foreign Policy, 1917–1967.* New York, 1968.
Vandenberg, Arthur H. *The Private Papers of Senator Vandenberg.* Edited by Arthur H. Vandenberg, Jr. Boston, 1952.
Walker, Samuel J. "The Decision to Use the Bomb: A Historiographical Update." *Diplomatic History* 14 (1990): 97–114.
Wallace, Henry A. *The Price of Vision: The Diary of Henry A. Wallace, 1942–1946.* Edited by John M. Blum. Boston, 1973.
Walton, Richard J. *Henry Wallace, Harry Truman, and the Cold War.* New York, 1976.
Ward, Jeremy K. "Winston Churchill and the 'Iron Curtain' Speech." *History Teacher* 1 (1968): 5–13.
Ward, Patricia D. *The Threat of Peace: James F. Byrnes and the Council of Foreign Ministers, 1945–1946.* Kent, OH, 1979.
Warner, Geoffrey. "The Division of Germany, 1946–1948." *International Affairs* 51 (January 1975): 60–70.

Williams, William Appleman. *The Tragedy of American Diplomacy.* Rev. ed. New York, 1962.
Woodward, Sir Llewellyn. *British Foreign Policy in the Second World War.* 3 vols. London, 1970–71.
Yergin, Daniel. *Shattered Peace: The Origins of the Cold War and the National Security State.* Boston, 1977.
Zhukov, Georgy K. *The Memoirs of Marshal Zhukov.* New York, 1971.

Periodicals

Chicago Tribune
Christian Science Monitor
Courier-Journal (Louisville)
Life
Los Angeles Times
Nation
New Republic
Newsweek
New Times (Moscow)
New York Times
Observer-Reporter (Washington, PA)
Pittsburgh Press
Public Opinion Quarterly
San Antonio Express News
Time
Times (London)

Index

Acheson, Dean, 113, 182, 207
Agar, Herbert, 3
Ala, Hussain, 122
Alexander, Albert V., 178
Alsop, Joseph, 187
Argentina, 16, 17, 19
Atlantic Charter, 10, 11, 139
Atomic bomb: 24, 35–36, 60;
  Alamogordo test, 35; decision to
  use, 23; at Hiroshima, 62; and
  Interim Committee, 23; at
  Nagasaki, 62; and Soviets, 59–60
Atomic diplomacy, 65, 79, 168
Attlee, Clement, 32, 33, 52–53, 61, 90,
  206
Azerbaijan, 120, 121, 207. *See also* Iran

Barnes, Maynard, 111
Baruch, Bernard M., 190, 223
Bebler, Alex, 193, 195
Bevin, Ernest, 33, 53–54, 63, 77, 153,
  196, 202; and atomic bomb, 206; on
  British power, 89; and Bulgaria, 85;
  and Byrnes, 85; on Byrnes, 131, 206;
  and Germany, 57, 143–44, 147, 166–
  67; and Iran, 96, 98–99, 100, 112–
  13; and Italian colonies, 134–35,
  141, 156–57; and Italian reparations, 136–37, 203; and Italy, 134;
  at London Foreign Ministers
  Conference, 78–86; and Marshall
  Plan, 212–13; and Molotov, 83, 86,
  100, 164; at Moscow Foreign
  Ministers Conference, 91, 94–101;
  at New York Foreign Ministers
  Conference, 200–204; at Paris
  Foreign Ministers Conference, 131,
134–48, 156–67, 169; at Paris Peace
Conference, 174–81, 192–96; and
peace conference, 140, 161–62; and
peace treaties, 201–4; on procedural
dispute (London), 85, (Paris), 164,
175–79; and Romania, 85; and
Soviet Union, 112, 135–36, 153–54,
206, 213, 219; with Stalin, 98; and
Trieste, 137, 160, 202; on United
Nations, 3; on U.S. policy, 147, 206
Bidault, Georges, 201; and French
  policy, 133; and Marshall
  Plan, 212–13; at London Foreign
  Ministers Conference, 78; at Paris
  Foreign Ministers Conference, 134,
  140, 142–43, 147, 155, 156, 159,
  160, 167, 168; at Paris
  Peace Conference, 174, 179, 192
Bierut, Boleslaw, 50
Bohlen, Charles E., 5, 114, 116, 124, 164,
  205, 212, 224
Bratianu, Constantin, 85
Bretton Woods Conference, 3
British Somaliland, 135
Brown, Walter, 81
Bulgaria, 45–48, 72, 80–82, 99, 111–12,
  159; and Bevin, 85; and Byrnes, 81,
  82, 85, 89, 112; and Soviet Union,
  85; and United States, 45–46
Byrnes, James F., 22–24, 75, 148, 173,
  204; appointment as secretary of
  state, 22; and atomic bomb, 24, 60;
  and atomic diplomacy, 65, 79; and
  Bulgaria, 81, 82, 85, 89, 112; and
  Churchill's Fulton speech, 118;
  and Council of Foreign Ministers,
  37–38, 131; on Czechoslovakia,
  184; and Germany, 41–45, 145–48,
  165–68, 185–87; and Iran, 100, 120–
  24; and Italian colonies, 134, 135,

237